This excellent new collection of essays is a welcome addition to the recent trend of exploring science-and-religion issues in different cultural contexts. With contributions from six continents, it provides novel and eye-opening insights into the interactions between the sciences and Christian communities in diverse settings, offering fresh perspectives on a number of traditional topics in the field. Highly recommended!

**Peter Harrison, DLitt, PhD**
Professor Emeritus of History and Philosophy, University of Queensland, Australia
Professorial Research Fellow, University of Notre Dame, Australia

It is refreshing and essential to read this book on the interface between science and Christian faith! Each chapter engages a local context in its particularity in ways that speak to our diverse global realities. It sacrifices neither the integrity of Christian faith or science and invites a continuous dialogue and integration that is essential to human dignity, harmony with creation, and our relationship with God. May it encourage more conversation and action!

**Archbishop Linda Nicholls**
Primate, Anglican Church of Canada
Member of the Anglican Communion Science Commission

This fascinating collection of essays is eloquent testimony to the growing maturity of science-theology engagement. It seriously considers the contextual (cultural, political, and historical) nature of both disciplines while also recognizing fundamental similarities across significant differences. I commend it to students and practitioners alike.

**Vinoth Ramachandra, PhD**
Former Secretary for Dialogue and Social Engagement,
International Fellowship of Evangelical Students

If one is to fully comprehend the diversity of science and Christianity relations throughout the world, Brownnutt and Fox's volume is a must-read. The significant effort that the editors put into covering all major geographical areas around the globe is unprecedented, and the appendixes on organisations and publications will become an invaluable resource for future engagement. What is certainly commendable is the depth, originality, and clarity with which the authors engage with the different local social and religious backgrounds in their explorations of diverse relations between science and Christianity.

**Ignacio Silva, DPhil**
Professor of Theology and Sciences, Austral University, Argentina
Professor of Philosophy of Religion, Pontifical Catholic University of Argentina

# Global Perspectives on Science and Christianity

GLOBAL LIBRARY

# Global Perspectives on Science and Christianity

Edited by
Mike Brownnutt
and
Keith R. Fox

GLOBAL LIBRARY

© 2024 Mike Brownnutt and Keith R. Fox

Published 2024 by Langham Global Library
*An imprint of Langham Publishing*
www.langhampublishing.org

Langham Publishing and its imprints are a ministry of Langham Partnership

Langham Partnership
PO Box 296, Carlisle, Cumbria, CA3 9WZ, UK
www.langham.org

ISBNs:
978-1-83973-988-0 Print
978-1-78641-043-6 ePub
978-1-78641-044-3 PDF

Mike Brownnutt and Keith R. Fox hereby assert their moral right to be identified as the Author of the General Editor's part in the Work in accordance with sections 77 and 78 of the Copyright, Designs and Patents Act 1988.

All rights reserved. No part of this publication may be reproduced, stored in a retrieval system or transmitted, in any form or by any means, electronic, mechanical, photocopying, recording or otherwise, without the prior written permission of the publisher or the Copyright Licensing Agency.

Requests to reuse content from Langham Publishing are processed through PLSclear. Please visit www.plsclear.com to complete your request.

All Scripture quotations, unless otherwise indicated, are from The Holy Bible, English Standard Version® (ESV®), copyright © 2001 by Crossway, a publishing ministry of Good News Publishers. Used by permission. All rights reserved.

Scripture quotations marked (NKJV) are taken from New King James Version (NKJV). Copyright © 1982 by Thomas Nelson, Inc. Used by permission. All rights reserved.

**British Library Cataloguing-in-Publication Data**
A catalogue record for this book is available from the British Library

ISBN: 978-1-83973-988-0

Cover & Book Design: projectluz.com

Langham Partnership actively supports theological dialogue and an author's right to publish but does not necessarily endorse the views and opinions set forth here or in works referenced within this publication, nor can we guarantee technical and grammatical correctness. Langham Partnership does not accept any responsibility or liability to persons or property as a consequence of the reading, use or interpretation of its published content.

# Contents

Foreword: Science and Religion: The "Glocal" Turn ................. ix
David N. Livingstone

1   Global Perspectives: Less Like Big Macs, More Like Rice ............ 1
Mike Brownnutt, University of Hong Kong

2   The History and Future of Christians in Science .................. 15
Andrew Halestrap, University of Bristol, UK
Keith R. Fox, University of Southampton, UK
Paul Ewart, University of Oxford, UK

3   The Blurred Boundaries between "Science" and "Religion" in
Asian Thought ..................................................... 37
Mike Brownnutt, University of Hong Kong, Hong Kong (SAR)

4   The Quest for Presence: Social and Theological Aspects of
Science-Faith Dialogue in Brazil .................................. 61
Guilherme de Carvalho, Brazilian Association of Christians in
    Science, Brazil

5   Darwin's Dragons: 150 Years of Greek Orthodox Apologetics and
the Challenge of Darwinism ....................................... 91
Kostas Tampakis, National Hellenic Research Foundation, Greece
Efthymios Nicolaidis, National Hellenic Research Foundation, Greece

6   Of Science, Religion, and Culture: An African Reflection ......... 111
Bernard Boyo, Daystar University, Kenya
Samuel M. Karenga, Mount Kenya University, Kenya
Peter G. Kirira, Mount Kenya University, Kenya

7   Doing Science and Theology in a Secular, Siloed, Multicultural
New Zealand Society ............................................ 131
Nicola Hoggard Creegan, New Zealand Christians in Science/Ngā
    Karaitiana Kimi Matū, Aotearoa New Zealand

8   Canadian Perspectives on Christianity and Creation Care ........ 151
Henry Brouwer, Redeemer University, Canada
Edward Berkelaar, Redeemer University, Canada
John Wood, The King's University, Canada

David Clements, Trinity Western University, Canada

9   Christian Engagement with Artificial Intelligence across the
    Continents................................................... 175
       Ah Chung Tsoi, University of Macau, Macau (SAR)
       Martin Ester, Simon Fraser University, Canada

10  Engaging the Church and Wider Christian Community in
    Science-Faith Dialogue ...................................... 201
       Ruth M. Bancewicz, The Faraday Institute for Science and Religion, UK

Conclusion: Local Perspectives of Global Significance............ 223
   Mike Brownnutt, University of Hong Kong, Hong Kong (SAR)

Authors......................................................... 229

Appendix 1: Organizations and Institutions...................... 237

Appendix 2: Journals ........................................... 255

Subject and Author Index ....................................... 263

# Foreword

## Science and Religion: The "Glocal" Turn

David N. Livingstone

As a neologism, "glocal" – an ugly synthesis of "global" and "local"—is perhaps not the most elegant of terms. To some it smacks of faddish philosophizing, of in-vogue theorizing, maybe of what Charles Taylor once called the "fog from Paris". To casually dismiss it, however, would be a profound mistake. For it speaks to a critical insight that snakes its way through the essays that constitute this volume and indeed through the forms of life that constitute modernity. The term has its origins in business economics where it was used to identify the simultaneous presence of universalizing *and* particularizing processes in the tailoring of business products to the needs and desires of local markets. Since then it has colonized numerous other territories – sociology, human geography, education, tourism, agriculture and so on. Frequently it manifests itself in the mantra "Think globally, act locally" – a rallying call perhaps most conspicuous among environmentalists urging local community action in order to combat global ecological breakdown. The concept can be pressed even further. To writers like Bruno Latour, the global is actually local at every point. A rail network cannot be experienced "globally" because it is made up of a myriad of local points – stations, signals, platforms and the like. The global, to Latour, is simply a collection of all the locals.

The essays which follow disclose in numerous ways what I am calling the "glocal turn." Three in particular stand out, to me at least, from thinking alongside the authors below about the relationship between science and Christianity. First, reading these various chapters impressed on me the sense that there is an imperative to "localise the global," to register how what we think of as global science and religion ground themselves differently in a host of local settings. Second, pondering on the narratives the authors relate about science and Christianity in different global settings, underscores the need to transcend conventional, and often Western, boundaries, both between and within, what we too casually label "science" and "religion." And third, keeping the global and local in dialogue, reminded me that in different venues, different stress points are visible in oppositional encounters between religious outlooks and scientific convictions, as are those arenas in which practitioners of science and people of faith may engage in productive dialogue and mutual enrichment. I call these "combat zones" and "sites of exchange" respectively, and identifying the different forms they assume in different times and spaces moves the conversation beyond the popular stereotype and caricature to which we have become too accustomed. Accordingly, a few thoughts on each of these three impulses, I hope, may help highlight some of the ways in which the science-religion nexus might be re-orientated and thereby enriched.

## Localising the Global

As these essays remind us, science and Christianity are global phenomena. Both have spread around the world in remarkable ways. At the same time, they have distinctly local manifestations. To put it another way, both are, essentially, "glocal." Right from the start this means that issues of science and religion cannot be understood or resolved on a one-size-fits-all basis. This is simply because scientific theories and theological declarations are always encountered in particular spaces. Books "do not stay where they are written" as one contributor writes. Indeed, they move from location to location, from site to site, from time to time. The literary critic, Edward Said, pointedly captured the significance of this mobility in an arresting essay titled *Traveling Theory*. Here he reminded his readers that audiences routinely encounter texts in circumstances that are markedly different from the situation in which the author wrote. The movement of any theory into a new place, he observed, "necessarily involves processes of representation and institutionalization different from those at the point of origin." And this, as he put in 1982, "complicates any account of the transplantation, transference, circulation, and commerce of theories and ideas."[1] Precisely the same is true of the movement of science and theology around the globe.

As this volume makes clear, in different settings scientific theories and practices have been encountered differently depending on the local political culture, the complexion of ecclesiastical authority, the prior history of science-

---

1. Edward Said, "Traveling Theory," reprinted as chapter 10 of *The World, the Text and the Critic* (London: Vintage, 1991), 226.

religion interchange, the trajectory of higher education, and the like. This means that the story of science and religion took different shapes in the context of frictions between the Greek Orthodox Church and the values of the modern Greek state; in New Zealand's secular political culture; and in fraught tensions between the Catholic mind and the successive waves of European materialism, often of French derivation, that Brazil experienced. Those particularities mattered in those places, but they mattered in ways that make little sense in understanding, say, Asian and African ways of thinking about science and faith. Imposing Western categories on these latter venues fails to take seriously the need to localise the global. Indeed, awakening to the challenges of decolonizing our own cherished convictions about the nature of "science" and "religion" requires a re-envisioning of "the Western tradition" itself as another form of local culture. When we begin to achieve this new sense of self awareness and, as one contributor notes, when we encounter thought-forms that seem strange and bizarre to us, we have begun the journey towards seeing ourselves as others see us.

Besides these considerations, the impetus to localise might seem misguided in the light of the global reach of digital devices and the modern technologies of communication. But as the discussion of the cultures of generative Artificial Intelligence (AI) across continents shows, there remain profound differences in the ways in which this new technology is encountered across the face of the earth. Europe, we learn, remains heavily invested in the development of AI, but casts a cautiously critical eye on this new technology as governments harbor concerns about its more sinister possibilities. Their position is the need for developing legislative regulation of AI is strong. In China, by contrast, AI has been enthusiastically mobilised in the service of a social-credit system that calculates citizens' honesty, integrity, and so on, as a means of maintaining surveillance over the population. Given the different complexion of political ideology, religious sentiment, and state governance in these different settings, it is surely obvious that thinking about the questions that the science and practice of AI pose to philosophy and theology is markedly different in different venues. Among these the moral, legal, and spiritual challenges of military robotics, workplace automation, clinical diagnostics, and driverless vehicles, readily spring to mind. These have to be addressed "glocally" by dwelling on the local articulations of global forces.

## Transcending Boundaries

The presumption that science and religion occupy different spheres has long been a staple of Western thinking on the subject. At least since the European Enlightenment, there has been a strong inclination to relegate religion to the domain of private subjectivity and to operate with the assumption that science, by contrast, embodies the virtues of objectivity and internal logic devoid of extra-scientific "contaminants." This Western construct cannot be sustained. And the reflections in the following chapters on the engagement of science and religion worldwide confirm the imperative to transcend the comfortable and conventional boundaries with which both professionals and publicists have long operated.

The need to de-colonize the Western understanding of science and religion as non-overlapping realms comes through in numerous ways in the chapters that follow. In Asian cultures, for instance, the boundary between "science" and "religion" can be blurred to say the least. Using the example of acupuncture, one contributor discerns a fusion of both "scientific" and "religious" impulses at the heart of this medical therapy. To ask whether acupuncture is scientific or religious is simply misguided. It is similar with other bipolarities that have long played a foundational role in the construction of the West's mental apparatus: faith and reason, theory and practice, fact and belief, knowledge and opinion, and their near neighbors.

African healing practices display something of the same fusion. Holistic medicine here, which frequently blends traditional practices with Western medical diagnostics, resists the mapping of any simple gulf between science and religion. What undermines reductive aspirations is the emphasis on human wholeness that many African conceptions of personhood embody. This means that medical explanations are often hybrid, multi-dimensional, and pragmatic, blending modern bio-medical therapies with folk cures, and resisting the segregation of mind and body, the spiritual and the secular, the individual and the communal, in the treatment of disease.

Category-busting cases like these cannot be shoe-horned into the West's comfortable cartography of science and religion occupying different cognitive realms. Indeed, they resonate with crucial episodes in the history of Western science itself which defy any such simple classification. The celebrated German astronomer Johannes Kepler, for instance, cast his own horoscope every day thereby transgressing what we now consider a critical separation of astronomy and astrology. Again, the pioneering seventeenth-century student of natural philosophy, William Derham, presented his scientific findings in such works as *Physio-theology* and *Astro-theology*. Pondering on whether he was doing science or theology would be to misconstrue his task. And in the *General Scholium*, appended to his famous treatise *Principia Mathematica*, Isaac Newton invoked divine intervention to retain the stability of the solar system. None of this, of course, is to claim truth for the assertions made by these natural philosophers; rather it is to resist the temptation to categorize these works in ways that conform to later sensibilities rather than to the ambitions of the authors themselves.

This list could doubtless be extended. Among a group of young Filipino scientists, for example, we hear that the point of tension between scientific practice and Christian principle lies not in questions concerning natural law and miracles, and the like, but in the ways in which the management of research teams often violates the principles of natural justice. Again, in Brazil, we learn of the importance of developing what is here called "transversalist communities" which cross rigid boundaries between science, economics, ethics, and politics to undermine the "predatory attitudes" that thwart constructive conversations across the science-religion interface.

In other times and places mapping a clear line between science and non-science seems more rhetorical than realistic. Where was the border between ethnic prejudice and racial anthropology in the old American South? Was there any crisp line of demarcation between eugenics and genetics in Britain in the early years of the twentieth century? Can a clear boundary be drawn between the politics of nuclear weapons and particle physics in the United States during World War II? To even ask these questions is to imply how they should be answered.

Surely further exemplification is not necessary. Instead, it's appropriate to remind ourselves of an article published forty years ago by Larry Laudan on the project to forensically demarcate what he refers to as "the scientific estate" from other spheres of inquiry. In concluding his work, *The Demise of the Demarcation Problem*, Laudan observed: "If we would stand up and be counted on the side of reason, we ought to drop terms like 'pseudo-science' and 'unscientific' from our vocabulary; they are just hollow phrases which do only emotive work for us."[2] That still needs to be heard.

---

2. Larry Laudan, "The Demise of the Demarcation Problem", in R. S. Cohen and L. Laudan (eds), *Physics, Philosophy and Psychoanalysis* (Dordrecht: D. Reidel, 1983), 111–127: 111, 125.

## Fields of Battle / Sites of Exchange

Finally, attending to the "glocalities" of science and religion encourages the thought that in different contexts, different issues trigger conflict between scientific conceptions and religious beliefs, while others have the potential to foster dialogue and conciliation. There are, to put it another way, different fields of battle and different sites of exchange – what I have elsewhere called "flash points" and "trading zones"[3] – in how local relationships between science and religion are transacted. These narratives challenge simplistic portrayals of the science-religion encounter as either pugilistic or irenic.

Perhaps not surprisingly the question of evolution and creation has persistently surfaced as a battlefield in a number of locations across the world. But the pattern of engagement has taken a variety of forms in local contexts. In Great Britain, the Research Scientists Christian Fellowship – a precursor to Christians in Science – nurtured an openness to evolutionary theory among evangelical elites, not least by incorporating within its ranks eminent figures in the scientific community, though its strategy to defuse that particular conflict was not universally welcomed. In New Zealand, we learn, the absence of such "mediating" institutions and the exclusion of theology from the universities, mean that American-style creationism has been able to secure a firm foothold among evangelical churchgoers. Here, evangelical communities routinely presume an inevitable antagonism to science and have lost any memory of earlier rapprochements between Darwinism and Christianity. In Greece, Darwinism has also been a flash point. Critically important here was the perception of Darwin's theory as an ally of materialism and Marxism which the Greek Orthodox Church found unsettling. This ideological confrontation engendered the inclination to indiscriminately associate Darwinism with ills of all kinds. In Brazil, opposition to Darwinian biology, particularly among Pentecostals of one stripe or another, has fostered a suspicion of scientific endeavour and of academic elites more generally.

Evolution and creation, however, have not been battle lines everywhere. In other venues, different trouble-spots dominate the horizon. In African locations, vaccinations for polio, COVID-19, tetanus, and so on have proven to be a combat zone between some Christian groups and medical expertise. Polio immunization, we discover, was resisted among religious leaders in Northern Nigeria in 2003 over fears that the vaccine was "deliberately laced with anti-

---

3. David N. Livingstone, "Which Science? Whose Religion?", in John Hedley Brooke and Ronald L. Numbers (eds), *Science and Religion Around the World* (New York: Oxford University Press, 2011), 278–296.

fertility agents." Again, in 2014, the Catholic church in Kenya boycotted delivery of the tetanus vaccine to women of reproductive age. In other times and in other places, different pressure points have been evident. In the early modern period, for example, the close connection between the tradition of natural magic and the new natural philosophy was troubling to some religious believers, Jews in particular, on account of Talmudic prohibitions of occult practices and the arts of augury. New theories of matter during the period of the so-called Scientific Revolution were seen as a challenge to certain conceptions of the Eucharist. And while Copernicanism was troublesome to the Catholic hierarchy in Galileo's day, Arabic renditions of the heliocentric system caused no comparable uproar among Ottoman scholars. That list could certainly be extended at great length.

Focusing too exclusively on the diverse lines of battle that have been drawn between science and religion, however, obscures those sites of exchange where dialogue has been less fraught and sometimes fruitful. Africa provides a case in point. We have just noted the opposition between some church leaders and elements in modern medical practice. Concurrently, however, a more promising interplay between western clinical medicine and folk healing practices has widened the conception of illness and restoration, while the traditional use of medicinal plants and herbal drugs has been incorporated into treatments of various sorts. For many such medical practitioners the spiritual and the secular, soul and body, science and faith, are inextricably intertwined.

In a very different venue, Canada, resource conservation and environmental stewardship have emerged as arenas that are witnessing a fertile integration of science and religion. Under the rubric "caring for creation," a variety of initiatives drawing inspiration from environmental science *and* theological contemplation are taking place. Concerns about the future of the entire globe have animated a range of local projects that are establishing sites of exchange between earth science and religious faith. As illustration of the particularities of these ventures, we are introduced in this collection to a number of individuals whose remarkable environmental achievements have been inspired by theological reflections of one sort or another. While other tales could well be told of Christian resistance to the greening of theology and even of outright opposition to environmental action, these stories show how zones of battle can be transformed into sites of exchange – how swords may be turned into ploughshares.

* * *

In its aim to bring the local and the global into dialogue, *Global Perspectives on Science and Christianity* makes a welcome intervention into how we ought to think about science, Christianity, and "science and Christianity." In dwelling on what I have dubbed "the glocal turn," I have focused on only a few of the themes that struck me as I read through the text; I have been enriched by them. Readers will be rewarded in multiple ways by the riches that are in store below.

# 1

# Global Perspectives: Less Like Big Macs, More Like Rice

Mike Brownnutt, University of Hong Kong

## Abstract

Science is an international enterprise, and Christianity is a world religion. It stands to reason that the engagement of Christianity with science should be a global topic. However, the term "global" can be used in different ways, and it is important to identify which usage is appropriate in relation to science and religion.

When an international business franchise has a global product, that product is the same the world over. Such uniformity means that, once you know what a Big Mac tastes like in California, you know what a Big Mac tastes like anywhere. Paradoxically, this version of globalization allows us to ignore the globe. By contrast, a global staple such as rice finds novel and interesting expressions in each setting. Every expression addresses common human needs, yet every expression is uniquely embedded in the local context. This version of globality awakens us to the richness that global engagement can provide.

The engagement of science and Christianity globally is less like a Big Mac, and more like rice. We must recognize that different places are indeed different. They have different concerns and different insights. Any hope that the views of one place can stand as an exhaustive proxy for all others is forlorn. At the same time, we must recognize that different places are similar. There are points of contact and commonality, meaning that engagement between diverse perspectives is both possible and enriching.

## Seeing Things Differently

I found myself involved in a discussion about vaccines, vaccine hesitancy, and the church. This can be a thorny issue where science, facts, and hope mix with emotion, hearsay, and fear. One participant, Alvin, hoped to point out the absurdity of vaccine conspiracy theories, attempting to allay fears and open the door to accepting sound science: "The church should be promoting vaccines. Why would the government work with industry to kill its own people?" Bunmi, from a different country than Alvin, responded with a grim reality: "Because that is how government and industry work in my country! If the church will not speak out for the oppressed, who will?"

There is no one-size-fits-all answer regarding the appropriate engagement between science and Christianity that holds for all settings. Within their own respective contexts, Alvin and Bunmi's positions were both reasonable. But as soon as we step beyond our own backyard, we must reckon with a great diversity of reasonable positions.

Life cannot be neatly divided out into separate parts: one bit that is religious, one that is scientific, others that are political, commercial, educational, or cultural. All culture is religious; all science is commercial; all education is political; all parts flow into and out of all other parts. It would be nice to say that vaccines arose from scientific research, and science pursues truth, and Christianity should support such noble truth-seeking endeavors. But vaccines also arose from politics, and politics involves power and trust. And vaccines also arose from commerce, and commerce involves markets and greed. Discussions of science and religion do not exist above the fray of these other geographically varying considerations; rather, they are necessarily embedded within them. We must take such embedding seriously.

If you trust your government, and your markets are well regulated, you can more or less bracket them out, and point to something that looks like "pure" science. And – what a surprise! – you can engage with this science independent of politics. Vaccines save lives, Christians like saving lives. The cry goes up: People need to understand the science; these vaccines are good for us.

But what if your government is not trustworthy? Or your commerce is poorly regulated? Vaccines can become an instrument of the state, wielded against the poor. Christians seek justice for the poor. The cry goes up: People need to understand the politics; these vaccines are bad for us.

A book written in one place or the other, if it stayed in that place, would be fine. Each set of people would be equipped to provide appropriate Christian engagement with their respective situations. But we live in a globalized world, and books do not stay where they are written. Books written in North America become required reading on courses taught in Africa. And a post on social media from Africa can go viral in North America within a day.

A stance based on a healthy mistrust of the system in one place can become a crackpot conspiracy in another, with disastrous consequences for individuals and society. A stance based on a healthy trust in the system in one place can become a naïve death wish in another, with disastrous consequences for individuals and society. So, what can we do?

The genie is out of the bottle. We live in a globalized world, and that situation is here to stay. We cannot return to an age where news traveled no faster than a horse could ride, and books were reproduced no faster than a scribe could write; nor would we want to. But to live well in a globalized world, there are two things we must recognize: Different places are different. And different places are similar.

## Different Places Are Different

McDonald's is a poster child of globalization. There could be few more archetypical global chains. But McDonald's paradigm of "global" is simply a universal copying of one instance of "local." Big Macs in Hong Kong, Nairobi, and Athens all taste the same, because they all taste like the hamburgers in San Bernardino, California. And if they don't taste the same, there is something wrong, and a guy gets sent out from the USA to fix it.

No one needs to go to São Paulo to find out what a Big Mac there tastes like. You just go into your nearest McDonald's and eat a Big Mac there, because a Big Mac in São Paulo will taste just the same. McDonald's version of globalization allows us to ignore the globe. Unfortunately, we are so used to McDonald's, that we sometimes think of science and Christianity in the same way.

Science is a "global" practice, with universal laws: Newtonian mechanics is the same in the UK and in New Zealand. And Christianity is a "global" religion: one body of believers, with one faith, and one Lord. But it all goes wrong when we adopt McDonald's version of globalization, and universally copy one instance of the local. When we do that, there becomes no point in asking how science and religion relate to each other in New Zealand, because we already know how they relate to each other in the UK. In the McDonald's version of science and religion, if the view in New Zealand is the same as the view in the UK, we can ignore it (because it has nothing to add). And if the view in New Zealand is different from the view in the UK, we can either ignore it (because it is wrong) or we can send a guy out to fix it.

But this is not how science or Christianity works![1] We need a much richer view of globalization. And the first step is to recognize that different places are different.

I grew up in Europe, and was involved in conversations about science and religion there. I thought about all sorts of questions. I had an opinion on the meaning of the word "day" in Genesis 1. I was comfortable with being a scientist and believing in miracles. I had even published some thoughts on things that could (or could not) be said concerning quantum mechanics and free will. But, as I had discussions beyond Europe, and as was illustrated by Alvin and Bunmi's conversation above, it became clear that different places are *different*. They have different questions, different concerns, different assumptions. They have different ways of reasoning, and different criteria for accepting something as an answer.

I was in a discussion with one of my students at the University of Hong Kong, and there was a particular question she was interested in: "Could an artificial intelligence become a *qi* master? And if not, why not? And if so, how? And what would happen if it did? And how can we build AI to take these opportunities and dangers into account?"

Sometimes I think there is a scale: from questions I do not know the answer to, through questions that I have never thought of asking, to questions that I am not sure can be asked. The questions my student posed all fell at various places along that scale. (And, for readers who think that the involvement of *qi* makes this a question about science and Confucianism, rather than science and Christianity, remember that much Chinese thought sees no reason to exclude *qi* from a Christian cosmology. As I say, people can view things differently.)

Moreover, the new questions I encountered in Hong Kong just kept coming.

- "If we established a monastery on the moon, how would the monks' changed relationship to the earth influence their theology?"
- "What is a biblical Christian approach to parking lots?"
- "How can Christians address the existential threat to society posed by Candy Crush Saga?"
- "Do rocks go to heaven?"

---

1. For consideration of the global diversity of science, see David N. Livingstone, *Putting Science in Its Place: Geographies of Scientific Knowledge* (Chicago: University of Chicago Press, 2003). For consideration of the global diversity of Christianity, see Gene L. Green, Stephen T. Pardue, and K. K. Yeo, eds., *Majority World Theology: Christian Doctrine in Global Context* (Downers Grove: IVP Academic, 2020).

Pressing concerns, all. And although they may not be questions that old white guys in the UK get bent out of shape over, that does not stop them from being interesting – and even important – questions. We cannot suppose that books or lectures or videos on topics that scratch the itch for one region will get anywhere near the issues with which another region wrestles.

Moreover, the new questions that arise can vary significantly even over short distances, as I discovered on taking a short plane ride to visit a friend in the Philippines.

Carlos goes onto campus every day, and faces down the problem of keeping an experiment running stably, knowing that the electricity grid can cut out without warning. How can he publish papers to compete with universities that take a stable grid for granted? And how can he attract anyone to work in his group, when the brightest and the best go to countries that can keep the lights on? And how can he engage in science that helps to pull his country up by its bootstraps, when the problems his country needs to solve are not the cutting-edge ones that get on the front cover of *Nature*?

In a system set up so that the rich get richer and the winners keep winning, Carlos is painfully aware that science is inseparable from justice or, all too often, from injustice. And he knows that Christianity has a deep concern for justice. So the only puzzle for him is why so many books about science and Christianity talk about origins, while so few talk about justice. Certainly, for many scientists, justice and science is not an existentially pressing or career-shaping theme. And I do not suggest that everyone needs to start talking about how Christianity can enrich science by informing the discourse on the relationship between science and justice. But it would be nice if *someone* started talking about it.

There are several benefits to taking local issues seriously and engaging with them. The first, and most obvious, is that it addresses the issues that people actually face. Consider a group of Filipinos who fully accept that science is compatible with miracles, which they see regularly, but who struggle to grasp how science can be compatible with justice, which they see all too rarely. There is no sense in foisting on them answers to concerns that they do not have, when we can foster among them a fruitful discussion about the concerns they do have.

Beyond addressing the questions people actually have, taking local perspectives seriously validates those questions, and it validates Christian engagement with them. If the discourse takes place on Western terms, Filipinos learn that religion is not relevant to the issues they face; they learn that their own culture is not relevant to the issues they face; and they learn that the issues they face are not as important as the issues that other people face.

Taking local perspectives seriously underscores the fact that religion does have something relevant to bring to bear, and that their own cultures and experiences are important.

Beyond validating the questions, taking local perspectives seriously elevates people, and it elevates their insights. While they may not know or care about someone else's struggles, people can be experts about their own situation. If you want hard-won insight into reconciling a loving God with a typhoon that levels islands, ask a Filipino. They do not need to wait for outsiders to deign to show an interest; they are already there in the thick of it. And being in the thick of it, they bring their own distinctive insights, their own understanding of what is actually the problem being faced, and what actually constitutes a solution.

Finally, taking local issues seriously enriches the global discourse. To understand why this is so, we must turn to the other key insight of global perspectives: that different places are similar.

## Different Places Are Similar

If different places were simply different, the consideration of local perspectives might lead to nothing but a collection of assorted curiosities. We become like some Victorian anthropologist, gathering trinkets from exotic places to display in cabinets. There is no point of contact with our own situation. Nothing to stop things which are different from becoming simply alien. There is no relevance, nothing to learn, just an accumulation of unrelated, unconnected, local perspectives.

And, at first glance, this might seem the necessary fate of something like Alvin and Bunmi's vaccine discussion. Their views are different. Practically polar opposites. What can one learn from the other? And how could any lessons from one place have any application elsewhere? How could the local insights transcend the local to enrich a global perspective?

While Alvin and Bunmi's respective views seem distinct on the surface, the dynamics going on underneath are actually very similar. Best of all, the odd, apparently alien framing provokes us from our complacent comfort to see our own situation with fresh eyes.

The situation in Alvin's country had been so carefully molded by modernist ideals that he found it hard to see how different the modern caricature is from reality. He could get so much done by bracketing out politics and commerce that he could forget that this bracketing was always only ever an approximation, a simplification, a fudge. And in situations where the deviation from that simplification got too big to ignore, he was able to write it off with special pleading: Sure, Big Tobacco corrupted the smoking discussion, but that was just a few corrupt individuals. Sure, Big Oil corrupted the climate discussion, but science self-corrected eventually. Sure, the military-industrial complex shapes research priorities, but the actual factual results at which scientists ultimately arrive are objective and independent. Or so we tell ourselves.

And because of all this bracketing, fudging, and special pleading, he allowed himself to forget that science always and necessarily involves human beings, and trust, and trust issues; petty rivalries and power plays; hopes, dreams, fears, ideals, virtues, and vices. This is something that Bunmi, as a Christian living under a corrupt government, was never able to forget. Alvin and Bunmi's situations were different, inasmuch as one lived and worked under a corrupt regime and the other did not. But their situations were similar, inasmuch as the science being done in each of their countries was indeed messy. And Bunmi's insight awakened Alvin to better see his own situation.

In the end, the key application that Alvin found for this was not related to vaccines, but to his own discipline of atmospheric physics. The scientific facts are clear. The Christian call to act is theologically solid. But he found some people were unconvinced, and remained unconvinced, even in the face of more scientific data and more theological exposition. Inspired by Bunmi's insight, he realized he was ultimately facing a trust issue: If a person doesn't trust scientists, then the unanimity of scientific opinion is not a reason to accept climate change, but to reject it. And if a person is sure that the church is corrupted and in thrall to the scientists, then the fact that *Laudato Si'* and the Paris Climate Accords[2] are pulling in broadly the same direction does nothing but entrench that person in his or her skepticism.

Bunmi's local view (that her country's institutions could not be trusted) highlighted a global truth, that understanding the role played by trust (or the lack thereof) in issues relating science and religion can be pivotal. Alvin was initially shocked by differences between Bunmi's local view and his own. But that shock dislodged him from his complacency and opened his eyes to a global claim he had overlooked. This in turn allowed him to reassess his thinking on some of his own local concerns.

Once the initial spark was set, the new questions just kept coming: What (if anything) makes industrial research into wind power more trustworthy than

---

2. Pope Francis, "Encyclical Letter *Laudato Si'* of the Holy Father Francis on Care for Our Common Home" (Vatican City, 2015), https://www.vatican.va/content/francesco/en/encyclicals/documents/papa-francesco_20150524_enciclica-laudato-si.html; United Nations Framework Convention on Climate Change, "Paris Agreement," 21st Conference of the Parties (United Nations, 2015), https://unfccc.int/sites/default/files/english_paris_agreement.pdf.

industry research into oil drilling? What role does character formation play in science education? Do the arguments for a separation of church and state have parallel arguments regarding a separation of science and state? On and on. New, globally significant questions, which arise when one takes seriously the local concerns of a vaccine-hesitant African.

## Big Macs and Rice

Having claimed that Big Macs have warped our understanding of what it means to be properly global, let me propose a better global foodstuff for our metaphor: rice.

Rice is a properly global foodstuff. Like the Big Mac, it can be found everywhere. But, unlike the Big Mac, its ubiquity is not predicated on a universal copying of one instance of "local." While places the world over have rice, each place makes it their own. Rice in Brazil is not grown, or cooked, or eaten in the same way as rice in Hong Kong. A Hong Konger may get on a plane to São Paulo to see what rice is like there, and learn something when tasting it, because it is not the same as the rice back home. Moreover, when the Hong Konger finds it to be different, he or she should not feel the need to show Brazilians how to "do it properly." Rather, the Hong Konger can be enriched and take delight in a different approach to familiar activities.

As well as there being differences between rice in each place, there are similarities, points of contact. Rice in each place addresses common human needs: needs regarding sustenance, as we ingest its calories; needs regarding relationship, as we gather round a shared table; needs regarding labor and commerce, as we grow, buy, and sell it.

The commonalities provide a bridge, preventing the "different" from becoming simply "alien." The Hong Konger can be inspired by methods of washing the rice and the use of garlic, and take such ideas home to his or her own cooking. And yet in the differences there is a constant agitation, preventing the global from becoming uniform. The Hong Konger's rice will forever remain embedded in specific aspects of history, geography, culture, commerce, and politics; and this local embedding provides a distinctiveness which none of the lessons learned from Brazil will erase.

## A Book of Global Perspectives

The story starts with a UK-based group called Christians in Science. This group has a long history of serving scientists in the UK who are Christians, and has been able to tailor its activities to the UK situation. To extend such work beyond the UK, the Templeton World Charity Foundation (TWCF) funded a set of regionally specific projects under the theme "Internationalizing Christians in Science." These were intended to encourage culturally sensitive and constructive interactions among those who are interested in the relationship between science and the Christian faith. Through this theme and similar calls, TWCF provided funding to a group of similar, though independent, organizations around the world:

- Brazilian Association of Christians in Science (Brazil);
- Canadian Scientific and Christian Affiliation (Canada);
- Science and Orthodoxy around the World (Greece);
- Faith and Science Collaborative Research Forum (Hong Kong SAR);
- Christian and Scientific Association of Kenya (Kenya);
- New Zealand Christians in Science (New Zealand); and
- Christians in Science (UK).

Taken together, these seven projects provide in-depth cultural insights into the engagement of science and Christianity in seven different countries, on six different continents. The intention of this book is to draw together and present some of the insights from what these groups have found.

In selecting topics, we wanted to dig deeper than simply asking, for example, "What's the Brazilian view of origins?" For instance, we first wanted to know, "What's the Brazilian view of what's interesting?" So I phoned up the various groups and asked them each to provide a list of science-and-Christianity topics that they found interesting. The only conditions we set were that the topics should bring insight that was distinctive to their region, and that such insight should be of interest beyond their region. I received a whole inbox-full of topics.

The topics ranged far and wide, from ones I had thought about before (e.g. transhumanism) to ones I had never thought of (e.g. how being an island nation influences your view of science and religion). Some were relatively general (e.g. the nature of personhood), while others were wonderfully specific (e.g. have you ever noticed how the shortcomings of Feynman diagrams illuminate our understanding of the Trinity?). Some topics were notable by their absence. No one even suggested fine tuning, or miracles, or the Big Bang. Other topics, where they arose, did so in ways quite different from any I had seen before – such as the Greek rejection of Darwinism, not because it was red in the "tooth and claw" sense, but because it became linked to Marxism. Many topics arose repeatedly: More than one group wanted to write a chapter on our relationship to trees, rivers, and the land. More than one group did end up writing a chapter about politics.

We selected a range of topics from those suggested, and are grateful to the authors of this volume for agreeing to contribute their insights.

Many of the groups involved in this volume are relatively new, having been founded within the last decade. Christians in Science, however, can trace its history back almost a century. Its initial activities – assembling a small group of academics for lectures and discussions – bear resemblances to the initial activities of many of the other groups now just starting up. Since those early days, the group has grown and changed, learning what gets traction, and what does not work so well; they have held firm to many founding principles, while refreshing others, and moving with the times. In chapter 2, Andrew Halestrap, Keith Fox, and Paul Ewart share some of the insights gained over this long history.

A common thread that runs through this volume is the strongly interrelated nature of different areas of human endeavor. While Western thought often struggles to bring science and religion together, many other places in the world struggle to tell them apart. In chapter 3, Mike Brownnutt considers some of the ways in which people try to demarcate science from religion, and finds that things are not as simple as is often hoped or assumed.

Throughout this volume, social factors – such as community, politics, and education – are never far away. In chapter 4, Guilherme de Carvalho demonstrates that these factors are not a grubby add-on to science that should be ignored, if not done away with altogether. Rather, they must be understood as being integral to the functioning of science and of Christianity, and their relation to each other.

Politics returns in chapter 5, which looks at Orthodox engagement with Darwin as it exists in the unfolding history of the modern Greek state. Kostas Tampakis and Efthymios Nicolaidis recount how the Orthodox Church, when engaging with Darwin in Greece, necessarily also engages with ideas that have been filtered through foreign and national ideals, Marxist and socialist ideologies, and the historical political machinations of both the state and the church itself.

Chapter 6 engages with various ideas and themes that have arisen already, though now Bernard Boyo, Samuel Karenga, and Peter Kirira refract them through the prism of an African context. The holistic interpenetration of science and religion, viewed through Chinese medicine in chapter 3, is now viewed through the lens of African medicine. And the outworking of themes of empire and cultural self-determination, considered in relation to the Greek nation in chapter 5, are now considered in relation to the African continent.

In chapter 7, Nicola Hoggard Creegan outlines the situation in New Zealand, in which secularization of both the academy and the wider society hampers the cultivation of moderate Christian views, leading either to the rejection of Christianity, or to the embrace of more fringe ideas. Against this, she sees the protections given to the traditions and culture of the Māori as a seed from which wider public discourse on science and religion can be cultivated.

Via a series of biographical vignettes, chapter 8 illustrates the nature of creation care in Canada. Henry Brouwer, Edward Berkelaar, John Wood, and David Clements draw on the personal experiences of a variety of individuals, from politicians to ecologists, and authors to academics. Three are alumni, three are public intellectuals. Each is speaking from a Canadian context, and into a faith context, providing hopeful stories to inspire others to action.

Chapter 9 springs from an international collaboration, considering Christian engagement with artificial intelligence in diverse cultural contexts. Ah Chung Tsoi and Martin Ester delve into the different stances taken by Europe, North America, and Asia, and consider Christian engagement with these. They raise concerns ranging from, "What if this is used for purposes other than those intended?" through to, "What if this is used for exactly the purposes intended?" In each case, the technological developments, and Christian engagement with such, are inseparable from the region's religious, cultural, and political history.

Throughout this volume, consideration has been given to the actions of individuals, universities, nongovernmental organizations, government policymakers, and so forth. In chapter 10, Ruth Bancewicz rounds out the picture by discussing the role of the church. Drawing on her experience of working with churches in the UK, she provides a practical guide for engaging church leaders and congregations in the task of relating science and Christianity.

The authors, like the topics on which they write, form a diverse group. In addition to being based in seven different countries, they draw on disparate disciplinary backgrounds: physics, chemistry, biology, biochemistry, and medicine; computer science and control engineering; theology, history, and philosophy.

In compiling this volume, a key concern was to give the authors the freedom to present the issues that they view as important, and to present them as they see them. Naturally, given such an aim, no attempt has been made to impose consistency between the chapters. If the position taken in one chapter clashes with that taken in another, please do not view this as a flaw in the project, but rather as one of its key features.

## How Could They Think That?

The diversity of topics, and our decision to refrain from imposing consistency, has various consequences. One consequence is the near certainty that you, the reader, will likely not agree with everything that is written. Depending on your temperament, you might keep track of all the reasons why you think the author is wrong, or you might skip straight on to the next chapter in the hope that it says something more sensible, or you might hurl the book across the room in exasperation and shout out, "How could they possibly think that?"

Needless to say, the last option is the best response, and the one we would encourage. Provided you really mean it.

As soon as we step out of our own local paradigm, we will encounter ideas which seem strange, ridiculous, or downright wrong: One person claims that there are spiritual beings in your knees. Another person believes that science seeks the truth. Another person believes that we construct reality as we go.

Should you disagree with any of these positions, there is a simple and easy response, though it closes down conversations and cuts off any opportunity for discovery. It is to throw your hands up and exclaim, "How could they possibly think that?" That question, of course, is not a question at all. It means, "That is crazy. I don't need to waste my time on this. Our discussion is finished." I encounter this response often in cross-cultural communication, and it is disheartening.

However, there is another response: one which is complex and difficult, though it opens up conversations and avenues for discovery. It is to furrow your brow and wonder, "How could they possibly think that?" Because the person you are talking to clearly does think that. And, being generous, you might provisionally assume that this person is not crazy. Maybe the person knows something you don't. Maybe the person believes something you don't. What the question means is, "Our discussion has just started." When I encounter this in cross-cultural communication, I know things are about to get interesting.

If Alvin had thrown up his hands at Bunmi's vaccine skepticism and cried, "How could you possibly think that?" he would have learned nothing. However, a furrowed brow and a humble, serious question, "How could you possibly think that?" provided Bunmi space to share with him what she knew and he did not: "I think that because Pfizer came to my country and killed our children."[3] Alvin never ultimately came to agree with Bunmi's conclusion that Pfizer's COVID vaccine was unsafe. But he still came to a much richer understanding on a wide variety of issues.

It is with that hope that we offer this book: to provide a glimpse into, and even some understanding of, the rich diversity of ways in which science and Christianity relate on a global stage.

## References

Francis (pope). "Encyclical Letter *Laudato Si'* of the Holy Father Francis on Care for Our Common Home." Vatican City, 2015. https://www.vatican.va/content/francesco/en/encyclicals/documents/papa-francesco_20150524_enciclica-laudato-si.html.

Green, Gene L., Stephen T. Pardue, and K. K. Yeo, eds. *Majority World Theology: Christian Doctrine in Global Context.* Downers Grove: IVP Academic, 2020.

Lenzer, Jeanne. "Pfizer Settles with Victims of Nigerian Drug Trial." *British Medical Journal* 343, d5268 (2011).

Livingstone, David N. *Putting Science in Its Place: Geographies of Scientific Knowledge.* Chicago: University of Chicago Press, 2003.

United Nations Framework Convention on Climate Change. "Paris Agreement." 21st Conference of the Parties. United Nations, 2015. https://unfccc.int/sites/default/files/english_paris_agreement.pdf.

Wise, Jacqui. "Pfizer Accused of Testing New Drug without Ethical Approval." *British Medical Journal* 322, 194 (2001).

---

3. Jacqui Wise, "Pfizer Accused of Testing New Drug without Ethical Approval," *British Medical Journal* 322, no. 7280 (2001): 194; Jeanne Lenzer, "Pfizer Settles with Victims of Nigerian Drug Trial," *British Medical Journal* 343, no. 5268 (2011).

# 2

# The History and Future of Christians in Science

Andrew Halestrap, University of Bristol, UK
Keith R. Fox, University of Southampton, UK
Paul Ewart, University of Oxford, UK

## Abstract

In this chapter, we briefly outline the history of Christians in Science, UK (CiS), focusing on recent developments that led to employing staff, working with local groups, and being awarded our first grants.

CiS has its origins in a small group of scientists in Cambridge in 1944, which subsequently became a formal subgroup of the Inter-Varsity Fellowship (IVF); now the Universities and Colleges Christian Fellowship, (UCCF) under the name of the Research Scientists' Christian Fellowship (RSCF). The intended aims of RSCF were to support and encourage Christian research scientists in their faith; to develop a consistent Christian view on the relationship between science and faith that respected both the authority of Scripture and the findings of science; to share these insights with the wider Christian community; and to be effective witnesses to the truth of the Christian gospel in the scientific world. In 1988, as the increasing membership was no longer exclusively research based, the Research Scientists' Christian Fellowship changed its name to Christians in Science. In 1996, the society separated from UCCF, while retaining strong links, and became an independent registered charity in 2007.

Members of RSCF and CiS have always been active in publishing influential books on science and faith, and in 1989 the society launched its biannual journal, *Science & Christian Belief,* that contains original articles and book reviews. In recent years, CiS has received substantial grant funding to extend its reach into the local church and wider Christian community, to establish local CiS groups around the country, and to engage more effectively with the next generation of Christians in the sciences. Furthermore, CiS has always had a significant number of international members, some of whom have been inspired to establish similar groups in other countries, which are showcased in other chapters of this book.

## Introduction

In the early twentieth century, theologically conservative Christians in the UK were renowned for their spiritual devotion and commitment to personal evangelism, but regarded as "anti-intellectual, anti-theological and obscurantist, clinging to outmoded beliefs simply because they were afraid to face facts."[1] This was reflected in the lack of engagement with the relationship between science and Scripture, including issues such as how the theory of evolution relates to the biblical account of creation. It was in this context that, in 1928, a national Inter-Varsity Fellowship of Evangelical (Christian) Unions (IVF) was formed to support the ministry and teaching of student Christian Unions within British universities. Although occasional meetings or conferences addressed issues resulting from scientific advances, there were no formal structures to do this and there was a lack of consensus in the views held by influential leaders within IVF. While all would affirm the authority of Scripture, there were some who were ardent anti-evolutionists, some who were equivocal about Darwinism, and some who readily accepted evolution.

Today, almost a century on from the founding of IVF, there exists a variety of organizations in the UK and elsewhere, building on that original vision. Christians in Science (CiS) is one of them, comprising a network of people around the UK and beyond, including research scientists in universities, commercial and government laboratories, and hi-tech companies; engineers, theologians, and philosophers; as well as students, school teachers, administrators, and others who, for whatever reason, are interested in science and faith issues. We work to develop and promote biblical Christian views on the nature and scope of science and its interaction with the Christian faith, doing this in churches, in universities, and in wider society.

This chapter reflects on the story of the past hundred years: how we got from there to here. The journey has included successes and failures as the work of CiS continues to evolve and develop in response to the changing

---

1. Oliver R. Barclay, *Whatever Happened to the Jesus Lane Lot?* (Westmont: IVP, 1997), 95.

world in which we live. Now we have the privilege of stepping back to lay out the long game. At times, particular individuals have played a critically significant role – sometimes briefly, in a key formative moment; sometimes faithfully shepherding the work over many decades. At times, key relationships have made all the difference, be they personal relationships, institutional relationships, or organizational relationships. Key strategic decisions have had to be made – sometimes to foster relationships and partner with other groups; sometimes to recognize the need to strike out in a distinctive direction and work independently of others. Often, these relationships will shift in the course of events: a collaboration whose time had not come may – a few decades later – suddenly spring into fruitful life. And always, no matter how much we wish we could rise above such things, is the constant question of who will pay for any of it.

We rejoice that new initiatives like CiS are being set up – maybe even more new initiatives will be inspired by some of the ideas in this volume. And we are aware that in the always-on, instant-response culture of today, attention can be incessantly drawn to the pressures of short-term funding, three-year plans, and annual or quarterly targets. We offer this chapter as an account of the long path that is to be traveled, and as a testimony of what can be achieved by faithfully following God where he leads, for as long as he leads, even over the decades.

## The Birth and Early Years of Christians in Science[2]

In 1940, the IVF recognized the need to support former Christian Union members in their places of work and communities, encouraging them in their Christian witness, as well as continuing to support the ongoing work of university Christian Unions through prayer and financial giving. So it was that the Graduate Fellowship was born and, from this, there emerged groups to support Christians within their specialist professions.

One of the first of these, formed in 1944, was the Research Scientists' Christian Fellowship (RSCF), which later became Christians in Science (CiS). The driving force behind RSCF was Dr. Oliver Barclay (1919–2013), who had studied Natural Sciences at Cambridge, where he was president of the Cambridge Inter-Collegiate Christian Union (CICCU). He graduated in 1942

---

2. The content of this section is largely gleaned from two sources that can be consulted for further details: Malcolm Jeeves and R. J. (Sam) Berry, "Christians in Science: Looking Back – and Forward," *Science & Christian Belief* 27, no. 2 (2015): 125–52; and Christopher M. Rios, *After the Monkey Trial: Evangelical Scientists and a New Creationism* (New York: Fordham University Press, 2021), chs. 3 and 6.

and went on to pursue a PhD in zoology in Cambridge where, in 1943, he formed a "Scientists' Study Group." This brought together a few Christians, mainly postgraduate students, who were involved in scientific research. On the back of this he organized a "Scientific Research Workers' Conference" in 1944 and again in 1945, where papers were presented on various topics relating to Christianity and science. These conferences represented the informal start of the RSCF, which further developed when Barclay joined the staff of IVF a year after completing his PhD. The group formally adopted the name RSCF in 1950.

In its early days, membership of the RSCF was small, primarily comprising postgraduate students. However, over the next decade, the RSCF attracted a few more-established scientists with a fourfold increase in membership. A number of these early members went on to become well-known writers and speakers on science and faith, including Oliver Barclay himself, Donald MacKay (1922–87), Robert Boyd (1922–2004), Reijer Hooykaas (1906–94), and Malcolm Jeeves (1926–). The main activities of the RSCF at this time were quarterly meetings, which usually discussed a book dealing with an aspect of science and faith, such as *Miracles* by C. S. Lewis, and an annual conference at which papers from both individuals and groups were presented on a range of issues, often relating to evolution.

The RSCF was run by a small committee with Oliver Barclay as secretary, a role that he relinquished only in 1987 upon his retirement from the University and Colleges Christian Fellowship (UCCF, which IVF became in 1975). Members were required to be actively involved in scientific research and to belong to the Graduates' Fellowship, which in turn required acceptance of the IVF statement of faith. The aims of RSCF were formally agreed by the committee in 1951 and were threefold:

1. To clarify our own thinking on problems of science and faith, and to develop as far as possible a consistent Christian view on these matters;

2. To pass on to other Christians such fruits of our own activities as may help them in their own thinking and in their witness; and

3. To use such material to further witness among people of scientific training and generally help to evangelize the "scientific" world.

Underlying these three core aims was the belief that science and the evangelical Christian faith,[3] as expressed in Scripture, provide complementary – rather than conflicting – worldviews. There was no place for a "God of the Gaps" mentality, which sees God as providing the explanation for processes currently not fully understood by science. Rather, God works in his creation through processes which scientists can investigate and understand. As Johannes Kepler expressed it three centuries earlier, "Scientists are merely thinking God's thoughts after him." Or as Augustine put it even earlier still, "All truth is God's truth," whether revealed through Scripture or the scientific investigation of God's creation. Consequently, members of the RSCF were committed to both rigorous scientific inquiry and a belief that the Bible is God's written word. There should be no conflict between the two when Scripture is understood in the context and genre in which it was written. However, there were influential conservative evangelical theologians such as James Packer who, at the time (although later to change his views), expressed opposition to this position taken by the RSCF. Responding to reports of an RSCF conference in 1956 he expressed great concern that "scientific interpretations were being placed on biblically revealed fact."[4] This elicited a firm response from RSCF that summarized their attitude to biblical interpretation that remains the position of CiS today, namely,

- Scripture can never be interpreted in a vacuum: human analogy, experience, common sense, and observation are needed to understand it;
- Sometimes extrabiblical knowledge is a key to proper understanding – such as Canaanite culture or the [scientifically determined] age of the earth;
- When the Bible makes claims that are open to observation, we have a responsibility to seek out relevant facts;
- The Bible does not teach science; and
- Scientists and theologians should work together wherever appropriate.[5]

---

3. Throughout this chapter "evangelical" is used to denote a theological view that emphasizes a personal faith in Christ and accepts the authority of the Bible; it includes both noncharismatic and charismatic positions, and literalist and more traditional methods of interpreting Scripture.

4. "A Scientific Interpretation: Comments by Some Other Graduates," *The Christian Graduate* 11 (1958): 112–13.

5. Jeeves and Berry, "Christians in Science," 135.

For many years, the RSCF remained a relatively small group of Christians who were professional scientists and who, as stated in the aims of their 1965 conference, believed that across the scientific disciplines "science is a true friend of biblical faith, and not, as is often assumed, in conflict with it."[6] Further, there was a recognition that science reveals more of the wonder and glory of God's creation. Thus, pursuing a scientific career is a valid and important Christian vocation and is one way of fulfilling the command in Genesis 1:28 to be a steward of God's creation.

Several members of the RSCF were active in writing widely read books on the relationship between science and the Christian faith. These included Donald MacKay, Sam Berry, Malcolm Jeeves, Reijer Hooykaas, Colin Russell, and Denis Alexander. Papers from the annual conference, which were often the result of discussions within small local RSCF groups, were also published in the *Christian Graduate*, a journal which continued in publication until 1983. Annual conferences remained a key feature of CiS, and every few years were held jointly with the American Scientific Affiliation (ASA), a similar but totally independent organization in North America. The range of topics covered at these events continued to reflect the underlying themes described by Donald MacKay for the 1985 conference, which were as follows.

Christians should maintain a close and natural connection between realism and reverence. They have responsibilities as God's stewards which should prevent them from lapsing into pietistic passivity, instead pursuing the idea of the scientist as an active mapmaker, exploring and also foreseeing ways forward; addressing challenges – in particular the study of human personhood, artificial intelligence, personal relationships (serving or manipulating), the origin of the universe, the anthropic principle, and the consequences of population increase.

One major issue facing the RSCF during these years, and one that took a disproportionate amount of time and energy, was how to respond gracefully to those influential evangelical Christians who regarded the Genesis accounts of creation as being incompatible with the scientific view that life evolved over billions of years through evolution and natural selection. Another challenge was defending the intrinsic value of the scientific enterprise as one that Christians should be actively involved in. Despite decades of engagement, these issues remain current in some churches today.

---

6. Jeeves and Berry, 138.

## CiS Becomes an Independent Charity

As the number of students studying science at university increased during the sixties, seventies, and eighties, so did the membership of the RSCF, reaching seven hundred (mainly men) in 1982. In 1988 it changed its name to Christians in Science (CiS) to reflect the fact that many of its members were no longer research active. The change of name was accompanied by the establishment, in 1989, of a biannual scholarly journal entitled *Science & Christian Belief* (S&CB) published jointly by CiS and the Victoria Institute, now known as Faith and Thought. The journal provided an avenue for members of CiS and others to publish scholarly refereed articles on topics in the science-and-faith arena, as well as reviews of books relevant to the membership. S&CB continues to produce two issues each year and is made available to members of CiS and Faith and Thought as well as other subscribing individuals and institutions.

In order to further widen the appeal of CiS to Christians working in the sciences, it was decided in 1996 that CiS should cease to operate under the umbrella of UCCF. In 2007, Professor John Bryant, then chair of CiS, played a major role in establishing CiS as an independent charity and limited company, which is governed by a board of trustees and managed by a committee of members including a chairperson, secretary, treasurer, and membership secretary. In 2012 the organization Christians in Engineering, which was struggling as an independent entity, merged with CiS. For full membership of CiS, members must affirm their agreement with the CiS statement of faith (see below) which is based on a simplified version of that of the Evangelical Alliance. However, associate (nonvoting) membership is available for individuals who prefer not to sign this.

## CiS Statement of Faith

- I declare my belief in the triune God as creator and sustainer of the universe, and my faith in Jesus as Savior, Lord of all, and God.
- I acknowledge the Bible as the Word of God and its final authority in matters of faith and conduct.
- As a steward of God's world, I accept my responsibility to encourage the use of science and technology for the good of humanity and the environment.
- I agree with the Aims of CiS.

## Widening Horizons: CiS Develops a Broader Vision

The aims of CiS were originally those of the RSCF described above, but have broadened over recent years to incorporate the expanding vision of CiS that will be outlined below. This is reflected in points 3–5 of the current stated aims of CiS today, which are:

1. To develop and promote biblical Christian views on the nature and scope of science and its interaction with the Christian faith, bringing a biblical Christian perspective on scientific issues into the public arena;
2. To encourage Christians who are engaged in scientific work to maintain an active faith, apply it to their professional lives, and share it within the scientific community;
3. To support churches by helping congregations appreciate the harmony of science and faith and assist them with outreach activities;
4. To help Christian science students to integrate their religious beliefs with their studies and to support them as they graduate and progress in their careers; and
5. To stimulate responsible Christian attitudes and action toward care for the environment.

The effectiveness of the original vision of RSCF and CiS was (and still is) reflected in the substantial number of CiS members who are in influential positions in university, government, and research council committees, as well as the number who are members of distinguished academic societies. Furthermore, just as many RSCF members wrote and lectured widely on science and faith, this remains true of many CiS members today.

Nonetheless, at the start of the new millennium the CiS national committee, under the chairmanship of Professor John Bryant, felt it important to re-evaluate the role of the organization, and update and expand its reach in the scientific and faith communities as well as its impact on the general public. The first significant step in reaching this goal was the employment in October 2004 of a part-time salaried development officer, Dr. Ruth Bancewicz, supported by a grant from the Sir Halley Stewart Charitable Trust. Her remit was to increase recruitment to the organization, enhance awareness of its activities, improve the website and publicity material, and mobilize CiS members to form local branches. Dr. Bancewicz left in 2007 to work at the Faraday Institute, but the part-time post continued until 2010 with a further one-year grant from the Sir Halley Stewart Charitable Trust and additional support from the membership. The value of investing in a development officer was readily apparent. During this period the number of CiS local groups grew from one to eleven, recruitment of subscribing members increased more than sixfold, approximately 150 free student affiliates joined each year, and the use of the CiS website rose significantly. Moreover, through its membership of the influential Evangelical Alliance (EA) that links more than 7,000 churches and 750 organizations, CiS was also able to play a prominent role in addressing intelligent design and creationist campaigns in churches and schools.

It was also during this period (in 2006) that the Faraday Institute for Science and Religion was established in Cambridge by two active members of CiS: Dr. Denis Alexander (then editor of *S&CB*) as director, and Professor Bob White (current president of CiS) as deputy director and later director. They were joined in 2007 by Dr. Bancewicz, and the close association between the two organizations continues with Professor Paul Ewart who has been both Director of The Faraday Institute and executive chair of CiS.

## John Templeton Foundation Funding to Maintain and Expand the Work of CiS

In 2009, following the success of employing a development officer, the executive committee, chaired by Professor Keith Fox, recognized the importance of continuing the post on a full-time basis, in order to expand and diversify the work of CiS. It was clear that the finances needed to achieve this expansion could not be met from our existing membership and that external grant funding would be necessary. To this end a successful grant application was made to the John Templeton Foundation (JTF) entitled "Capacity Building on Science and Faith in the UK Evangelical Community." This funded a full-time development officer and a range of activities to fulfill the grant's aims and objectives, which are briefly outlined below.

The application acknowledged the considerable misunderstandings that existed between the scientific and religious communities. The media profile of a few prominent atheist scientists was leading many outside the faith communities wrongly to assume that science had disproved religion, or that religion was irrelevant and outdated. Several of the "New Atheists" who were at the height of their activities at this time had invoked a "straw man" that all Christians accept a literal interpretation of Genesis, providing a simple (and incorrect) target for promoting a conflict narrative. Conversely, many people within the faith communities were highly suspicious of scientific explanations, since they feared that it might undermine their worldview. Christian leaders often had little or no scientific training and, though well intentioned, were unable to address current scientific issues. They were also not equipped to offer support to scientists within their congregations, and these people often became isolated and were sometimes viewed with suspicion, especially in churches within the more evangelical and charismatic traditions. For example, when a couple of student participants at an annual CiS conference were asked, "What is the greatest challenge to your Christian faith?," they replied, "My local church"!

At this time CiS did not have a high profile within either the secular scientific or evangelical communities, though its commitment to mainstream science and orthodox evangelical belief gave it a unique platform to speak into both communities. The great majority of CiS members (and all its committee) accept evolution as the means by which God created life (theistic evolution) as opposed to either intelligent design or young earth creationism. This provides a platform for engagement that avoids some of the simplistic areas of antagonism between science and faith. Furthermore, a high proportion of CiS members were practicing scientists, with 15 percent being full professors in the scientific community across a range of disciplines and universities. However, these individuals and their work in the science-religion arena were often largely unknown in the church community, much less among the broader secular public.

A major objective of the new project was to increase the capacity of CiS, enabling it to reach out into these communities and provide more opportunities for elite scientists to have greater impact on the church and in the public domain. These formed the background to the application, which aimed to secure the longer-term financial viability of CiS. The proposal to JTF therefore included a series of projects, building on the momentum obtained during the previous development phase. The main aims were:

1. To increase the impact of the organization in educating the UK evangelical community about science and faith issues in a way that was well informed, respected, and committed to mainstream science and to evangelical Christian belief;
2. To help CiS to penetrate further into the scientific community; and
3. To synergize with other science-and-faith outreach activities to combat the inroads of unhelpful creationist and intelligent design influences in the UK churches.

We note several outcomes that we anticipated resulting from the JTF-funded work and we reflect – with full disclosure, warts and all – on what actually happened.

## *Increasing and Retaining the Membership of CiS, and Ensuring Financial Security*

It was hoped that by the completion of the JTF grant, the CiS membership would have increased sufficiently to sustain the ongoing activities of CiS and to continue employing the full-time development officer, without the need for further grant support. Achieving this would have required a threefold increase in membership from about six hundred at the time of application. We also wrote personal letters to all CiS members, asking them to commit to giving annually at levels much above the normal subscription rate. Despite major efforts at recruitment, membership increased only from six hundred to nine hundred, although this was against a trend of decreased membership of many other organizations. However, the increase fell far short of the threefold increase needed to maintain the activities and salary of the development officer without additional sources of funds, even with some members giving generously to CiS beyond their annual membership fee. By the end of the grant, we realized that it would probably not be possible to fund CiS activities solely from our membership without a massive increase in the membership fee, and that further financial support would need to come from grant funding. For many people in senior positions, we would need to move from a model of getting "value for money" to one of generously supporting the aims of the organization.

Over the course of the grant the active interest of current CiS members was maintained by the production of a regular news bulletin (five issues each year), entitled *PréCiS*, that was distributed by mail to all CiS members as well as being freely available in electronic form on the CiS website. This was supplemented by a monthly update of events by email.

## *Doubling the Number of Local Groups*

The establishment of local CiS groups, which had started when John Bryant was the CiS chair, had shown that they greatly facilitated active engagement by current CiS members and increased recruitment of new members. We therefore proposed to double the number of these with the aim of establishing a local group in each of the major cities that host a Russell Group university (the top twenty research-active universities in the UK). We made launching grants available to set up new groups whose activities might include public lectures by distinguished speakers; debates on current issues; support networks for Christians who are practicing scientists, who are often isolated and unsupported in their church environments; and support for local Christian student groups. By the end of the grant, the number of local groups had indeed doubled, from eleven to twenty-three, with CiS having a defined presence in many of the major UK cities. The size and activity of these groups varied considerably, with some hosting regular public lectures, while others focused on smaller discussion and support groups.

## *Penetrating the Evangelical Community*

We recognized that a key strength of CiS that should facilitate its engagement with evangelical churches was its membership of the Evangelical Alliance and its evangelical basis of faith. Enhancing the visibility of CiS within local churches was thus a priority. We therefore hosted a series of formal dinners for key church leaders in university cities around the country during which there was a talk on science and faith, an explanation of what CiS could offer, the opportunity to meet local CiS members, and provision of a resource pack. Following on from contacts made at the London dinner in March 2011, CiS was approached by the Evangelical Alliance to write a series of six science-and-faith articles for their bimonthly magazine, *IDEA*, under the general heading of "What I wish the church knew about . . ." The first of these appeared in January 2012 and over the next year these covered titles including "The Science vs. Faith Debate"; "Being a Christian in a Science Lab"; "The Brain and Religious Experience"; "How Scientists Seek Truth"; "Christians and the Cosmos"; and "The Science and Religion Debate."

We produced a series of leaflets entitled *Thinking about . . .*, written for the "person in the pew" and addressing key issues in the science-and-faith arena such as creation and evolution, miracles, bioethics, and natural disasters. These were each written by active CiS members who were evangelical Christians and practicing scientists in the relevant discipline. We made these freely available as print copies and online through the CiS website. In addition to these resources, we ensured that CiS had strong representation at key evangelical conferences and festivals (such as New Wine, Greenbelt, Word Alive, Spring Harvest) with provision of books and free materials. We also undertook a major enhancement of the content and appearance of the CiS website to include links to many helpful resources (text, audio, and video) on diverse aspects of the interaction between science and the Christian faith, all of which was available for free download.

By the end of the JTF grant, a significant increase in the local churches' awareness of CiS had been achieved through the establishment of local groups and by the series of dinners for local church leaders. The *Thinking about . . .* leaflets proved extremely popular, leading to the eventual production of sixteen different titles.

## *Penetrating the Student Community*

Engaging with the next generation of scientist Christians would be the focus of the next grant (to the Templeton Religion Trust, TRT, as described below), but even within the JTF grant we were already concerned to work with students to support them in their studies and scientific vocations.

CiS membership was free for students, who were provided with resources to help them in their science studies. Important among these was a series of nine subject-specific leaflets aimed at students entitled *Being a Christian in . . .* These covered subjects that included chemistry, biology, earth sciences, engineering, and physics. These were each coauthored by a senior academic and a recent graduate and proved very popular, requiring reprinting. We were also able to establish a literature fund to subsidize the provision of key science-and-faith materials and provide bursaries to help students attend key science-and-faith conferences. In addition, we distributed by email a termly student magazine addressing key student concerns relating to science and faith; and established an annual student essay competition, with the essays published in *PréCiS* and the student magazine. The introduction of free student membership of CiS for the first year attracted 220 new student members, although unfortunately many of these students did not renew their membership in subsequent years. We also held a successful student conference each year.

In addition to this work carried out on our own, we were able to further foster interactions with students by working with UCCF and attending their annual leaders' conferences.

## *Hosting a Residential Conference*

We organized a three-day residential conference, subsidized by the grant, to provide greater scope for promoting CiS activities, expanding the membership, and encouraging personal interaction and support among members. This was held in July 2012 at Queens' College, Cambridge, and was entitled "Science and Christian Faith in 2012: An Enduring Partnership," with talks given by national and international speakers. It was attended by about 150 scientists, most of whom were from the UK, although there were representatives from several other countries. A good number of students also attended, supported by bursaries. Feedback showed that the attendees found the conference to be a highly motivating and encouraging event which enabled greater networking among Christian scientists. Most of the talks were recorded and are available on the CiS website.

## Further Grant Funding from the Templeton Religion Trust

A major factor in the successful outcomes of the JTF grant was the employment of a full-time development officer who also played a key role in promoting CiS throughout the UK evangelical community. Indeed, it became increasingly clear that the continued employment of a development officer would be critical for the ongoing and expanding work of CiS. However, the modest increase in membership achieved over the duration of the grant was insufficient to generate the income required to cover a full-time salary. This was a major challenge facing the new executive chair of CiS, Andrew Halestrap, when he took office in the autumn of 2013.

It was established that requesting a second grant from JTF was unlikely to be successful, but that another Templeton body – the Templeton Religion Trust (TRT) – had started awarding grants. Informal inquiries to the TRT were encouraging, and they provided guidelines for the nature and scope of such a potential application. In the light of this advice, and following discussions at an away day with the committee, the trustees, and some local group leaders, a successful application was submitted to the TRT in 2014 under the title "Equipping and Supporting the Next Generation of Christians in Science." This provided funding to continue employing the development officer, who would oversee the three-year project. Importantly, it also allowed CiS to employ a full-time executive officer to manage the increasing administrative load of the expanding work of CiS. In addition, the grant funded modest honoraria to the CiS general secretary and treasurer, whose increasing workloads were making the previously voluntary posts difficult to fill.

The background to the TRT project was the recognition that the membership of CiS was very strongly biased to those over fifty years of age, while early-career scientists were not being recruited or retained in significant numbers. Thus, if CiS was to continue to grow and flourish it would need to engage more effectively with younger people. They would become the next generation of Christians in the sciences, including the future writers, speakers, and policymakers on issues involving the interface between science and religious faith. Key to achieving this aim would be equipping and training university students and early-career scientists in their formative years and providing practical support and advice. We anticipated that this would enable teaching on science-and-faith issues that respected both mainstream science and biblical scholarship to become integral to the life of Christian Unions and church student groups. As a result, we hoped that an increased number of students and early-career scientists would become active members of CiS, and that this would spawn a new generation of confident and competent speakers on science and faith who could tackle new issues as they arose. In the longer term, it should also result in more articulate and informed Christians in senior academic and industrial positions, professional societies and academies, the media, and as members of government science / ethics advisory panels.

The program of work funded by the grant sought to achieve these objectives through four major strands of work. The first was to establish and resource student CiS groups and student-directed lectures in the major university cities; the second, to improve access to CiS resources by upgrading the website and producing an app for use on mobile devices; third, to sponsor students, student workers, and early-career scientists to attend science-and-faith conferences and workshops, and training courses; and fourth, to host a mentoring program in which Christians in their early scientific careers were linked with mature Christian scientists who could encourage and guide their future career development.

Integral to the overall objective was hosting launch lunches in major university cities and inviting leaders of student Christian organizations such as Christian Unions, chaplaincies, and student-focused churches. In addition, a "handbook" on running a student CiS group would be produced. We recognized that engaging with Christian science students would be much easier with active collaboration with UCCF, who had large networks of students and student workers across the UK. UCCF had already started developing subject-specific ministries, of which the emerging Science Network was one, and at the time of writing and submitting the proposal, their leadership was very supportive of the concepts behind the proposed TRT grant. However, the UCCF trustees were subsequently less enthusiastic because they perceived the primary role of Christian Unions to be evangelistic and focused on students reaching other students with the gospel message. They also upheld a more conservative declaration of faith than CiS, who are keen to work with anyone who identifies as a Christian. UCCF were willing to collaborate with CiS only if the student groups operated under the leadership of the Christian Unions, but the executive committee of CiS concluded that this would diminish the reach of CiS within universities. Although a formal agreement to collaborate was therefore not possible, good relationships with UCCF have continued with increasing cooperation between their Science Network and CiS. Nevertheless, the lack of a formal agreement undoubtedly reduced the effectiveness, reach, and number of the student launches, and also delayed their rollout while negotiations with UCCF continued.

Ultimately, the grant was extended from three years to five, thanks to a no-cost extension. Most of the original objectives of the grant were met, although some were delivered on a smaller scale than originally planned. Launch lunches, and the activities that relied upon them, were hit hardest, and the mentoring did not develop to the extent that had been anticipated. Nevertheless, we achieved a number of significant outcomes.

Most notably, many students throughout the UK and Ireland were introduced to the work of CiS through university launch events, and at exhibits at Christian festivals and conferences attended by students. Several existing resources aimed at students were updated and redesigned in a consistent and more contemporary student-friendly format. These included a student-focused *Introduction to CiS*. Additionally, the *Being a Christian in . . .* and *Thinking about . . .* series discussed above were expanded to cover additional disciplines and topics. We made all of these freely available in print and electronic form and they proved to be popular, with the paper versions needing to be reprinted. We also produced a twenty-four-page color handbook on how to establish and run a student CiS group. This, together with the other printed materials, was provided for distribution to attendees at student CiS launches.

The grant also allowed us to provide financial support to students attending science-and-faith conferences, workshops, or communication training events such as those organized by the Faraday Institute. Further encouragement for students to develop their writing skills was provided by an annual essay competition with cash prizes and the publication of an online magazine for students, *Connect*. Furthermore, the grant funded an annual conference, hosted by CiS, for students and provided subsidized travel and free registration which led to increased numbers attending. Opportunities were provided for students and early-career scientists to develop their speaking skills by giving presentations at such conferences and, in collaboration with an organization called "God and the Big Bang," at workshops on science and faith in schools. An important activity for encouraging younger people to develop public speaking skills was the establishment of an annual lecture and prize, the Oliver Barclay

Lecture. This is awarded on a competitive basis to a promising science-and-faith speaker under the age of thirty-five. The lecture is given at the annual CiS southern, northern, and student conferences. Access to online CiS resources via mobile devices was greatly improved by totally redesigning the website and by developing an app which is regularly updated and had been downloaded about two thousand times by the end of the grant period. Finally, a mentoring scheme was established for students and early-career scientists, although uptake has been low.

As a prerequisite for grant funding, TRT requested a full evaluation of the effectiveness of the grant activities to be undertaken by an external organization. This concluded that, overall, the grant had enabled CiS to start a journey of better engagement with the next generation of Christians in science, highlighting those activities that had worked and those that did not. The online and printed resources we produced were clearly successful, as were the student conferences and essay competitions. However, the difficulties encountered in working closely with UCCF and the Christian Unions made establishing viable student CiS groups harder than we had hoped and, as a result, the mentoring scheme was not well used. In the light of this experience, it was recognized that new approaches would need to be developed if CiS was to more effectively engage with students and early-career scientists, encouraging, supporting, teaching, and equipping them to be the next generation of Christians in science. It also became apparent that we would need to generate additional funding from our membership to continue our work with students and early-career scientists as well as maintain the level of salaried staff that the expanding work of CiS requires. Appeal letters went out to all members to encourage regular giving toward the work of CiS and to request that members consider leaving a legacy to CiS in their wills. Measures were taken to enhance awareness of the work and resources of CiS throughout the Christian community and so increase our potential pool of donors as well as generating some income from our resources.

## Future Directions

Following the end of the TRT grant, the main priorities were to build upon the achievements of the project, notably consolidating and expanding on the progress achieved by the development officer, and to address the issue of sustainable funding for the continuation of such work. Together with developing a more reliable financial base with less dependence upon grant funding, it was decided to broaden the vision of CiS by encouraging its evolution from a "closed" group, of mostly research-based scientists discussing among themselves issues of the relationship between science and Christian faith, to a more outward-looking organization that could contribute to the work of the church more widely. The revised aims of CiS, outlined above, reflected this shift in emphasis.

A central component of the strategy was for CiS to present itself to local churches as a "partner in mission." The partnership would enhance and enrich the faith and worship within the local church by promoting a more positive view of science among believers who might otherwise view science as undermining faith. In addition, CiS could help equip and support the church in its outreach to a world where people had been led to believe science was incompatible with faith. CiS would offer its resources and its expertise in the form of nationally and internationally respected speakers on science-and-faith issues. Churches were to be invited to become a "CiS-Affiliated Church" and indicate their support for the aims of CiS by prayer and financial donations. Approaches were made at the highest levels to the central leadership of all the main denominations in the UK to endorse the affiliation of local congregations with CiS. At the lower level, members were encouraged to ask their local churches to become affiliated and to provide prayer and financial support for CiS.

To increase the sustainable income, members were encouraged to invite several Christian science colleagues to join CiS as subscribing and, it was hoped, donating members. To further broaden the support base, a new category of "Friends of CiS" was introduced for those people who were inclined to support the aims of CiS, but were not scientists and felt that full membership would be inappropriate.

No sooner had the drive to recruit more members, friends, and Affiliated Churches begun, than the COVID-19 pandemic struck the UK in early 2020. The pandemic affected all these initiatives to some extent. Church leadership at every level was faced with the urgent issues of responding to the pandemic and, understandably, few people had the time or inclination to consider the new offerings from CiS. The uptake during this time, both from churches and from individuals, was markedly lower than we had hoped, though we cannot tell at this stage if this was due simply to pandemic factors, or if there were other factors at play which must be addressed.

As the world emerges from the pandemic, some of these initiatives will be relaunched. Encouraging work is underway to renew the cooperation with UCCF, with the aim of directing graduating science students to join CiS and find spiritual support in the early stages of their careers. The annual student conference has been rebranded as the "Connect Conference" with the aim of including more early-career scientists. This is especially important to address the issue of the present age profile of the membership, which is heavily biased to the older age group. Another change has been the renaming of the former "northern" and "southern" conferences as "spring" and "autumn" conferences to counteract any suggestion of a north/south divide.

One of the first effects of the COVID pandemic was to cause the cancellation of the planned in-person student conference of 2020 and its shift, at very short notice, to an online event. The unexpected outcome, however, was that the conference reached more students than the live, in-person event would have done. The challenge of COVID and the need to operate some events online led eventually to the opportunity to use digital platforms to run hybrid events – in-person events that were simultaneously live-streamed to online audiences. This was successfully done for the 2021 autumn conference, allowing the participation of many people for whom the travel time and expense would have made attending in person difficult or impossible. The new technologies of online meeting have also allowed workshops and meetings of local group leaders to be held without the trouble and expense of venue hire and travel. Looking to the future, CiS will be further developing these hybrid events to facilitate participation of more members and attract a wider audience.

The pandemic also had a deleterious effect on some of the local groups that were not so well resourced in terms of leadership numbers, such that some became inactive. Plans are being developed to assist the growth and support for local groups by providing online lectures by well-known speakers at events organized nationally or by strong local groups. A local group can then provide an event by arranging a convenient venue with a facility to view, for example, an online lecture and have a locally based discussion or other activity around the lecture. In this way, smaller local groups can build a program around such high-profile lectures, conferences, workshops, or other events that would be beyond their capacity to provide with their own limited resources. Future possibilities include the use of such live-streamed and locally based meetings to reach out to local communities and churches with the potential to strengthen the national network of CiS groups and activities.

## We Are Not Alone

Although membership of CiS remains predominantly UK based, there are a significant number of international members and some of these have gone on to establish similar organizations in their own countries. These include

Australia, Brazil, France, Hong Kong, Kenya, New Zealand, and Spain. In North America, the American Scientific Affiliation and the Canadian Scientific and Christian Affiliation developed independently of CiS but share a common aim and occasionally hold joint conferences. Subsequent chapters in this book will describe some of the activities and distinctive challenges and opportunities found by these groups.

## Conclusions, Challenges, and Opportunities

CiS has grown since it started in 1944, and it has developed from a small group that supported Christians working as research scientists, into an organization that also engages with the church, students, and wider society. There is still much more that could be done.

We still find it difficult to penetrate some parts of the Christian community and often hear of scientist Christians who are unaware of what we do, or who don't see the need to support such an organization. In part, this reflects a lingering secular-sacred divide, in which the workplace (such as the scientist's laboratory) is not seen as an integral aspect of a Christian's vocation, serving God through science, not just in the life of the church.

Science and technology are an increasing part of people's lives and Christians need to be equipped to know how to deal with the ethical aspects that arise from emerging areas, while also rejoicing in science as God's gift to us, enabling us to understand some things about the world that he has created and continually upholds. Many church leaders have little or no scientific training and are often either unaware of the faith-related issues that are raised by science, or are disinclined to engage with such topics. As society becomes increasingly suffused by science and technology, it will become increasingly important to provide resources to help churches to engage with these matters.

The many things that we would like to do require people to do the work and funds to support it. The scale of our activities and the size of our membership require an executive officer and development officer and we struggle to generate a stable income stream to support them. We have been grateful for grant support from the Templeton Foundations (TRT and JTF) as well as local charities such as the Sir Halley Stewart Trust, but we realize that these can provide only short-term support. We will continue to face challenges with raising more funds than can be achieved from membership fees alone, unless there is a massive and sustained increase in the number of members (or a large increase in membership fees). It will be even more important to move from a membership model of getting "value for money" to one of generously supporting the aims of the organization. We also realize that, in the UK, the younger generations are often cautious about joining organizations and societies, and their work and family commitments mean that they have less time to devote to CiS activities.

Many of these things will benefit from collaboration with other science-Christian organizations, both in the UK and overseas. We have a lot to learn from each other. It is possible, also, that we could achieve more by working together, playing to our individual strengths, such that in combination we become more than the sum of the parts as we serve Christ's church together.

## References

Barclay, Oliver R. *Whatever Happened to the Jesus Lane Lot?* Westmont: IVP, 1997.
"A Scientific Interpretation: Comments by Some Other Graduates." *The Christian Graduate* 11 (1958): 112–13.

## Further Reading

This chapter draws heavily from two sources that can be consulted for further details:
Jeeves, Malcolm, and R. J. (Sam) Berry. "Christians in Science: Looking Back – and Forward." *Science & Christian Belief* 27, no. 2 (2015): 125–52.
Rios, Christopher M. *After the Monkey Trial: Evangelical Scientists and a New Creationism*. New York: Fordham University Press, 2021.

Various RSCF and CiS members were mentioned in this chapter by name as having written on science and faith. Their full publication record is too extensive to reproduce here, but we draw attention to some highlights:
Alexander, Denis. *Creation or Evolution: Do We Have to Choose?* Oxford: Monarch, 2014.
———. *Rebuilding the Matrix: Science and Faith in the 21st Century*. Oxford: Lion, 2001.
Barclay, Oliver R. *The Intellect and Beyond: Developing a Christian Mind*. Grand Rapids: Zondervan, 1985.
Berry, R. J. (Sam). *The Care of Creation: Focusing Concern and Action*. Leicester: IVP, 2000.
Boyd, Robert. "Reason, Revelation, and Faith." In *Christianity in a Mechanistic Universe: And Other Essays*, edited by Donald M. MacKay, 109–25. London: IVP, 1965.
Hooykaas, Reijer. *Fact, Faith and Fiction in the Development of Science: The Gifford Lectures Given in the University of St Andrews 1976*. Berlin: Springer Science and Business Media, 1999.

Jeeves, Malcolm A. *Why Science and Faith Belong Together: Stories of Mutual Enrichment.* Eugene: Cascade, 2021.

MacKay, Donald M. *The Clockwork Image: A Christian Perspective on Science.* Downers Grove: IVP, 1974.

Russell, Colin A. *Cross-Currents: Interactions between Science and Faith.* Leicester: IVP, 1985.

# 3

# The Blurred Boundaries between "Science" and "Religion" in Asian Thought

Mike Brownnutt, University of Hong Kong

## Abstract

In discussing science and religion, it is often assumed that there is something we can call "science" and something we can call "religion." Even if we are not sure exactly how to define such categories, we assume that the categories are both meaningful and distinct. These categories, however, are a product of the European Enlightenment project, and do not map well onto thought and practice in Asia. In order to make sense of a range of questions – from "Is acupuncture a science?" through "Is Daoism a religion?" to "What does this mean for Christians?" – it is necessary to reframe how we think about the ways of faith and the study of nature. Such considerations have implications beyond Asia. Analogous questions arise in many other cultures which struggle with importing Enlightenment dichotomies. The insights gained may in turn allow us to view Western questions in a new light, allowing us to revisit issues that had been otherwise dropped on account of seeming to be either solved or unsolvable.

## Introduction

When we talk about science and religion, there is often an implicit assumption that we know – more or less – what we are talking about. Maybe not in the details, but we imagine that, in broad outline, we at least know what science is and what religion is. And even if we cannot put that understanding into words exactly, we have a feeling that we would at least recognize science if we saw it, and recognize religion if we saw it. If the people involved in the practice have test tubes and lab coats, for example, that is science. If they have prayer beads and incense, that is religion.

Let us then consider acupuncture in this light: Is this practice scientific or is it religious? Is it both? Is it neither? The simultaneous presence of lab coats and incense makes it harder to call.

Much discussion of science and religion, particularly discussion about how science and religion relate to each other, is framed by Ian Barbour's four models. In his 1989 Gifford Lectures, Barbour outlined four ways of thinking about the interactions of science and religion:[1]

- *Conflict*: science and religion are opposed.
- *Independence*: science and religion have nothing to do with each other.
- *Dialogue*: science and religion can fruitfully engage with each other.
- *Integration*: science and religion can be brought into synthesis.

When laying out these models, Barbour made numerous caveats and provisos which tend to be ignored in the simple four-point summaries. One major assumption which is necessary for this formulation is that there is something called "science" and something else called "religion." In 1980s Scotland, there were sufficiently few acupuncturists that a person could get a long way without having to worry too much about this assumption. In twenty-first-century Hong Kong, of course, things are different.

Peter Harrison, in his 2016 Gifford Lectures, highlighted the fact that the categories of *science* and *religion* that we have in the post-Enlightenment West are inventions of the Enlightenment.[2] As such, they may variously be inappropriate, unhelpful, irrelevant, or meaningless when put to use in contexts other than the post-Enlightenment West. By way of analogy, Harrison notes that we cannot speak of the relationship between Israel and Egypt in the sixteenth century, because Israel and Egypt didn't exist in the sixteenth century. To be sure, the Jordan and Nile rivers were there, as were Jerusalem and Alexandria. There were people who lived and worked there. But there was nothing that corresponded to a modern understanding of *Egypt* or *Israel*. There

---

1. Ian G. Barbour, *Religion and Science: Historical and Contemporary Issues* (San Francisco: Harper San Francisco, 1997; repr. 2013).
2. Peter Harrison, *The Territories of Science and Religion* (Chicago: University of Chicago Press, 2017).

were simply different parts of the Ottoman Empire. Modern understandings of *science* and *religion*, says Harrison, have the same problem as *Egypt* and *Israel*.

As a historian, Harrison goes on to consider the issue diachronically, in terms of *then* and *now*: Can we talk about nonmodern contexts from the past without forcing them into modern categories? In this chapter, I want to consider the same question synchronically, in terms of *here* and *there*: Can we talk about nonmodern cultures as they find expression today without forcing them into modern categories?

The Enlightenment never happened in Asia. Modernist conceptions of the world, if they do arise in Asia, arise in their own ways, following their own contingent promptings of history, and express themselves with scant regard for following Western concerns. As such, one should not assume that the categories common in the modern West necessarily apply in Asia. Furthermore, even if such categories do seem on the surface to be broadly applicable in Asia, we might anticipate that they do not quite carve people's thinking at the joints.

The examples in this chapter will be predominantly taken from medicine and science. The branch of medicine which has historically been strongly influenced by modernity is called "Western medicine." (At least, that is what it is called in Asia. In Europe and North America, it is called "proper medicine.") Similarly, the branch of science which has historically been strongly influenced by modernity is dubbed "Western science." (This is in contrast to science that has not been strongly influenced by modernity, which Europeans and North Americans call "indigenous knowledge systems" or, more commonly, "bunkum.") It should not be imagined that such terminology is unproblematic. However, in line with such usage, and while the key contentions of this chapter concern the effect of modernity, the term "Western" will also be used to connote things tainted by modernity.

## Grouping and Ungrouping Ideas

Modernism seems to live for dichotomies: Body–Mind. Bad–Good. Sinner–Saint. Temporal–Eternal. There are two things that might be noted about these pairings. First, they are exclusive: a person cannot be bad *and* good; a thing is temporal *or* it is eternal. Second, the items can be grouped together: *Saints* are *good* because they have their *minds* set on the *eternal*. By contrast, *sinners* are *bad* because they pursue with their *bodies* that which is *temporal*. One can create extensive lists of such dichotomies. Consider, for example, the following.

| Science | Religion |
|---------|----------|
| Natural | Supernatural |
| Testable | Untestable |
| Objective | Subjective |
| Facts | Values |
| Public | Private |
| Knowledge | Faith |

The lists given here are, of course, in no way exhaustive. You should feel free to add items as they occur to you.

The pairs listed here are commonly thought of as being mutually exclusive, often necessarily so. *Natural* and *supernatural* are separate: one deals with apples, the other deals with angels. Things are either *testable* or they are *untestable*: the law of the excluded middle sees to that. Obviously, *facts* and *values* are distinct: why else would moral philosophers establish something as fundamental as the fact-value distinction? Without the *public* sphere and the *private* sphere being demonstrably different and separate, society would collapse. Self-evidently *knowledge* and *faith* are different: the more faith you have the less knowledge you need (and vice versa).

Also, working down each column, it is often thought that the things in Column 1 are related, and the things in Column 2 are related. *Facts* are *objective* because they can be *tested*. *Values* are *subjective* exactly because they *cannot be tested*. We believe in the *supernatural* by *faith*. *Religion* belongs in the *private* sphere. It is OK to teach *science* in *public* schools. These categories are all interlinked.

Within this framework of thinking, any attempt to relate science and religion is an attempt to bridge these two columns. We ask questions like, "Can we prove that God exists?" Because what we really want to know is, "Can we have *objective knowledge* (Column 1) of the *supernatural* (Column 2)? Can we bridge the two columns? Can things in the same column as religion have anything to do with things in the same column as science?"

In this chapter, I will try to shake science-and-religion discourse free of this framework. Consideration of science and religion in an Asian context forces two conclusions on us:

The first is that these columns get thoroughly mixed. *Religions* make *natural* claims. *Science* makes *untestable* claims. *Science* cannot be divorced from *values*, any more than *religion* can be divorced from *facts*.

The second is that these dichotomies are not nearly as separate as we often think. The distinction between *natural* and *supernatural* is surprisingly problematic. *Objectivity* and *subjectivity* blur into one another. *Values* are inherent in *facts*.

Science is often thought of by appeal (explicitly or implicitly) to ideas and properties relating to Column 1. Religion is often thought of by appeal (explicitly or implicitly) to ideas and properties relating to Column 2. A corollary of thoroughly mixing the two columns, as our conclusions will require, is the thorough mixing of science and religion.

While we will be provoked to these conclusions by the consideration of an Asian context, the issues that arise are no less present in Western contexts. Generations of attempts to force science and religion into a modernist Procrustean bed may have dulled us to the reality of the situation before us, but the world remains incorrigibly interconnected. Ultimately, the surprise should not be that science and religion can meaningfully relate to each other, or that we can, on occasion, seem to bridge the gap between our two lists. The surprise, rather, should be that we ever found situations in which we imagined that science and religion did not relate, or that we ever managed to convince ourselves that we could meaningfully separate out the two lists such that they might be in need of bridging.

In fairness, much has been done over the past century to deconstruct the extremes of modernism. Such work, however, is better known in departments of philosophy or social science than in departments of natural science or engineering, and it has yet to fully catch on in the science-and-religion discourse. Moreover, even disciplines which have worked to subvert some of these dichotomies may continue to embrace others. For example, a discipline may pride itself on having done away with the fact/value distinction, while leaning ever more heavily into the distinction between the natural and the supernatural.

Regardless of the stance that any individual or group takes on some or all of the modernist framework outlined here, the basic concept can be helpful to bear in mind because it has a continuing influence. Recognizing this influence can help us to understand where certain people are coming from, and why some people see the world so differently. For example, it can give us a clue as to why one person might find it strange for a Christian head of engineering to call in a Buddhist monk to check the department's flow of *qi*, while another person might see this as entirely unremarkable. But I am getting ahead of myself.

## Science or Religion? Food or Medicine?

Before getting into something as esoteric as straddling the categories of science and religion, let us warm up by considering things which straddle more mundane categories. Many visitors to Hong Kong look at shops selling dried mushrooms and ask whether the shop is selling food or medicine. It seems a simple enough question.

We know what Western medicine looks like: it comes as a tablet, or possibly a liquid to be drunk or injected. We know what Western food looks like: it comes as a chicken, possibly with some vegetables and a slice of lemon. Medicine is for healing, which is why we give it to sick people; food is for nourishing, which is why we give it to hungry people. A packet of medicine lists the active ingredients. A packet of food lists the nutritional information. No one asks how many calories an aspirin has, and no one is concerned about the side effects of a roast dinner. Medicine must go through numerous stages of scientific testing to demonstrate its efficacy. Food tastes good. The differences between medicine and food could not be more obvious or clear-cut.

Sometimes, though, we find something that is harder to classify. When you have a cold and your grandma gives you chicken soup, what is it? It is healing, but it is also nourishing. She gives it to you because you are sick, but it also fills you up. It is unregulated. It tastes good. Medical research suggests that chicken soup can indeed guard against colds.[3] Your grandma neither knows nor cares what the science says: Eat it up, it's good for you.

No one loses sleep over our inability to categorize Grandma's soup. Admitting the existence of chicken soup neither nullifies medical advances nor undermines the food industry. It might, however, give each area pause for thought regarding new opportunities open to them: What if restaurants sold food that was good for you? Or what if pharmacologists made medicine that tasted good? Academics, of course, may choose to tie their own hands and insist that they will only consider a thing to be *either* medicine *or* food, but not both. And Grandma is welcome to ignore them entirely and leave them to their folly. And shops in Hong Kong will go on selling dried mushrooms. The question "Is this food or medicine?" is quite irrelevant. It's good for you. Eat it up.

---

3. Barbara O. Rennard et al., "Chicken Soup Inhibits Neutrophil Chemotaxis in Vitro," *Chest* 118, no. 4 (2000): 1150–57.

## Questions People Ask

Moving on from dried mushrooms, let us consider acupuncture. Is it scientific or is it religious? Can Christians be involved in its practice or not? The arguments for different positions are legion. There are Christians who take opposing positions. You will also find acupuncturists disagreeing with each other over it. There is a lack of consensus even among Western medics, or among Buddhist monks, or among New Age-ers.

I am not so bold as to propose that an issue that has vexed so many before me can be conclusively settled here in a single chapter. As such, I will sidestep the question of *whether* acupuncture is OK or not OK. Instead, I shall consider the lines of argument commonly put forward for *what it is that makes* acupuncture OK or not OK. Considering these ideas without falling back on the assumptions of two-list-ism may permit us to make progress in at least understanding what are good ways to think about acupuncture.

Of the questions that are often asked when trying to evaluate whether acupuncture is scientific or religious, and when trying to evaluate how Christians should engage with acupuncture, I shall consider four:

- Does it work?
- Does it appeal to a genuine mechanism?
- What worldviews underlie the practice?
- To what extent can the practice be separated from the originating worldviews?

### *Q1: Does It Work?*

The answer to this question is surprisingly easy: Yes, it does.[4] It does not work for everything, but that is OK. Paracetamol does not work for everything. Paracetamol does not mend broken bones, for example. But we do not for that reason say that paracetamol is a sham. Paracetamol works for some things. And acupuncture works for some things. For those readers who are not convinced, I do not wish to labor the point, because the question, however it is answered, is relatively inconsequential for the line of reasoning at hand. A much more interesting and telling question is this: Even if it does work, does it *matter* that it works?

---

4. World Health Organization, *Acupuncture: Review and Analysis of Reports on Controlled Clinical Trials* (Geneva: World Health Organization, 2002).

### Does It Matter That It Works?

I have, on occasion, had the following conversation with Christians:

> "It's OK for Christians to have acupuncture."
> "Why do you say that?"
> "Because acupuncture is scientific, not religious."
> "Why do you say that?"
> "Because acupuncture has been shown to work."

Let us pause here to reflect on that reasoning: "If it has been shown to work, it cannot be religious." It might be unsurprising if a scientistic, anti-religious atheist said that. But how does a Christian come to that conclusion?

The answer, of course, is that he or she followed the logic of modernist dichotomies: If it can be *shown to work*, we are in the realm of the *objective* and the *testable*. Objective tests give us *facts*, not *subjective value* judgments which must be taken on *faith*. *Showing it to work* means its workability is *public knowledge*. By this analysis, if it can be shown to work, it unambiguously sits in Column 1: it is science. Religion has nothing to fear from it, because religion has nothing to do with it.

If we accept the standard dichotomies and the grouping of those dichotomies listed earlier, the argument is watertight. The next question we must ask is, can we accept the grouping of dichotomies listed earlier?

To help answer this, let us consider demon possession. In the biblical account of demon possession in Acts (16:16–18), Luke tells of "a slave girl who had a spirit of divination." A spirit of divination would seem to be something *supernatural* (Column 2). Luke continues that the girl "brought her owners much gain by fortune-telling." That is to say, *it worked*! At the very least, it worked in the pragmatic sense that it could be used to make money. As they went on, "she followed Paul and us, crying out, 'These men are servants of the Most High God, who proclaim to you the way of salvation.'" The girl is presenting information which is demonstrably true. Anyone who had followed Paul from Jerusalem would have known what they were proclaiming. The fortune-telling demon here is dealing in the realm of *public knowledge* and *objective facts*. The demon's claims are perfectly *testable*. These attributes are all in Column 1. If our reasoning from above holds, then we are firmly positioned in scientific territory. Religion has no concern with demonomancy, because (under two-list-ism) it is scientific and so (under two-list-ism) religion has nothing to do with it.

Why, then, does Paul say to the demon, "I command you in the name of Jesus Christ to come out of her"? It is because Paul does not care if it can be shown to work, or if it generates objectively true claims. Demon possession is not OK. Clearly, Paul does not care for our neatly separated categories.

Paul is not alone. The pattern recurs throughout the Bible. Consider what Moses says of false prophets in Deuteronomy (13:1–3).

He starts, "If a prophet ... arises among you and gives you a sign or a wonder ..." This is great stuff! Prophesy is the pinnacle of predictive claims. It is testable. It is falsifiable. Scientists should love this.

Moses continues: "... and the sign or wonder that he tells you comes to pass ..." That is to say: If – in addition to being testable – the claim passes the test and is shown to work ...

"... and if he says, 'Let us go after other gods,' which you have not known ..." Swift change of gear here. After such a scientific introduction, Moses switches (within the same sentence) to talking about gods. God-talk is religious. Open and shut.

"... you shall not listen to the words of that prophet." Moses apparently does not care whether it can be *shown to work*. If a prophet would point you to a god that is not God, Moses does not care if the truth of the factual statements can be objectively verified. It does not matter. Followers of God must have nothing to do with it.

Moses in the Old Testament and Paul in the New Testament did not care for our modern grouping of dichotomies. They had no time for the notion that "It's OK because it works." It is possible that acupuncture works. But that information, on its own, does not tell us a lot. Maybe Christians can be involved in its practice. Maybe not. But we need to ask different questions to figure that out.

## Q2: Does It Appeal to a Genuine Mechanism?

Another question that might be asked is, does it appeal to a genuine mechanism? Acupuncture talks of *qi*, *meridians*, *yin* and *yang*. While debate rages as to what exactly these are, there is little scientific evidence to suggest that any of them exists. Prima facie, acupuncture therefore seems to fail this test. Before we move on too quickly, though, let us consider what is meant here by "genuine."

### What Is Meant by "a Genuine Mechanism"?

When we talk of a genuine mechanism, we mean that the proposed mechanism should appeal to the actions of things that are "real." This, of course, only shifts the problem to wondering what is meant by "real." Let us therefore phrase the answer another way, and call out cultural biases where we see them: appeal to a "genuine mechanism" requires that the posited ontologies are commonly accepted in the modern West. The implications of this condition need some unpacking.

A mechanism could count as "genuine" if it appealed to natural entities accepted by Western science. If it could be shown that *qi* can be understood in terms of neuronal pathways and endorphins, then this could be considered a "genuine mechanism." More generally, it would be acceptable to show that it worked by means of material particles (such as atoms or electrons) and the physical interactions between them (due to things such as electrostatic or gravitational forces).

Christians, however, cannot accept such a restrictive limit on a "genuine mechanism," as they want to preserve the possibility of appealing to things such as angels, demons, the soul, and God. They must insist, for example, that when they say that the efficacy of prayer is explained by divine intervention, this is an appeal to a genuine mechanism. Naturalistic science may exclude God from consideration, but naturalistic science is limited and blinkered. It must therefore be insisted that the actions of supernatural entities accepted by Western Christianity are also counted as "genuine mechanisms."

To summarize: When we insist that something "appeals to a 'genuine mechanism,'" we require that the posited ontologies are commonly accepted by Western science or by Western Christianity. When we set it out like this, it becomes immediately obvious that the condition is tilted to favor Western thinking, to the point of being question-begging. If nothing else, the fact that Judeo-Christianity has its origins in the ancient Near East might suggest to us that any system giving priority to modern European thinking is a later imposition, rather than one inherent to Christianity per se.

## Does Gravity Appeal to a "Genuine Mechanism"?

In addition to risking unnecessarily excluding ideas from outside the modern West, the condition of requiring appeal to a "genuine mechanism" risks unnecessarily excluding ideas from within the modern West. This can be illustrated by considering the status of gravity under such a condition. Does our scientific understanding of gravity appeal to a "genuine mechanism"? Alternatively stated, does the mechanism proposed by science for gravity posit ontologies which are commonly accepted in Western science?

Phenomenologically, gravity is hard to argue with: things fall. But we are concerned here with the mechanism: *Why* do things fall? What *makes* them fall? What mechanism does Western science accept for this? Western science has, over the course of time, given a number of different answers to this question.

Descartes proposed that objects fall due to *vortices* in the gravitational ether. He considered gravitational ether to be a dense homogeneous fluid. Subsequently, and by contrast, Newton proposed that objects fall due to *streams* of gravitational ether. Moreover, in Newton's thinking, gravitational ether was rarefied, inhomogeneous, and corpuscular. The consensus changed. It would seem strange to insist that laggard adherents to the Cartesian view were somehow deficient in their Christianity for not embracing the new scientific consensus. And certainly, Newtonian Christians could not retroactively declare Descartes to have been heretical for having embraced a mechanism that was no longer accepted.

The situation today is even more tricky. Einstein's theory of Relativity posits a mechanism for gravity involving curved space-time. This would have been unthinkable to both Descartes and Newton. By contrast, the Standard Model of particle physics posits a mechanism for gravity involving a carrier particle which they call a "graviton." Particle physicists' interest in gravitons is largely undamped by the theoretical difficulties of renormalizing them, the experimental difficulties of detecting them, or the successful experimental observation of gravitational waves in line with relativity. If we look today at what ontologies are "commonly accepted by Western science," we find two distinct communities, at odds with each other, and both at odds with what was commonly accepted historically by Western science.

It must be noted just how radical these breaks in the scientific explanations are. It is often pointed out that scientific results converge over time. Older theories, it is said, are approximations of newer ones. Newtonian mechanics gives the same answers as relativity in the limit of low velocity and low space-time curvature. This convergence, when it holds, tends to hold for phenomenological questions: questions about *what* result I will observe. If the question is, "Will I observe the axis of Mercury's orbit around the Sun to shift by 56 arcseconds per year?" the answers from Newton and Einstein are, respectively, "Approximately yes" and "Yes."

By contrast, answers to questions regarding the underlying mechanism – questions about *why* I will observe a particular result – do not tend to converge. If the question is, "Will Mercury orbit the Sun because it is caught up in streams of gravitational ether?" the answers from Newton and Einstein are, respectively, "Yes" and "No." If Einstein held that gravitational ether was a little less rarefied than Newton had thought, then the mechanism in one theory would be an approximation of the mechanism in the other. But "gravitational ether exists" is not an approximation of "gravitational ether does not exist." Clearly, the notion of a "genuine mechanism" is a moving target in science.

How do Christians respond to all this? Do Christian parents object to schools teaching their children Newtonian gravity? Not at all. The failure of Newton to appeal to anything we would now consider to be a "genuine mechanism" is quite irrelevant. Do Christian physicists view research into the Standard Model as off-limits? Absolutely not. They may even embrace the topic exactly because of the opportunities they see afforded by the contrarian position.

Our notion of what constitutes a "genuine mechanism" is Western-centric and fuzzy at best. We should hold onto it lightly, if we hold onto it at all. Given these cautions, let us return to the consideration of acupuncture.

### Does Acupuncture Appeal to a Genuine Mechanism?

We have established that an appeal to a "genuine mechanism" is not the cut-and-dried decider that we might have hoped. Still, it may be informative to consider whether or not there are circumstances under which acupuncture might be said to appeal to a "genuine mechanism," and whether the appeal (or failure to appeal) to a "genuine mechanism" is of any significance to the concerns at hand regarding Christian engagement.

Even among those who believe that acupuncture works, the exact mechanism by which it works is hotly debated. For the purposes of illustration, I will consider the view that acupuncture works by manipulating the flow of *qi* around the body. Even among those who accept this explanation, the exact nature of *qi* is still hotly debated. For the purposes of illustration, I will consider the view that *qi* is some immaterial "life force." The modern West does not currently accept that such a life force exists. In a simplistic view, such an account of acupuncture therefore does not appeal to a "genuine mechanism." Let us therefore move beyond a simplistic view.

Western medicine has not historically had any in-principle objections to invoking a life force. Galen, for example, held that living beings were animated by "vital spirits." Vitalism continued as a highly respected view – indeed the prevailing scientific view – across the West for centuries. It was not viewed as being anti-Christian. Quite the contrary, in fact. Faced, on the one hand, with a vitalist theory which says that life is more than matter in motion, and, on the other, with a mechanistic theory which insists that the universe simply consists of nothing but inert *stuff*, the Christian objection should surely be raised against the inability of modern materialistic science to grasp the nonphysical.

It may be that Christians should object to the life force invoked in acupuncture. But if they do, it should not be on the basis that modern science – naturalistic, thoroughly physicalist, modern science – a priori rejects the metaphysical and, as such, would not recognize something spiritual if it was staring it in the face.

**Does Appeal to a "Genuine Mechanism" Make Something OK?**
We have established that an *inability* to point to a "genuine mechanism" (in some narrow modern Western sense) does *not* require Christians to reject a practice. Now let us consider the inverse question: Does an *ability* to point to a "genuine mechanism" indicate that Christians *should* accept a practice? If there were universal agreement on the science, and if the mechanism by which it operated were perfectly understood, would that make a practice acceptable?

This is no hypothetical question. It has been scientifically demonstrated that castration of people from racial minorities leads to fewer births of people from racial minorities. As scientifically established facts go, this is about as firmly established as one could hope for. The mechanism by which this effect works is beyond doubt. Nonetheless, Christians should be at the front of the line to object to this practice.

If you want to eradicate racial minorities, enforced sterilization works (cf. Q1), and the practice without doubt appeals to a "genuine mechanism" (cf. Q2). By the reasoning outlined above in discussion of Question 1, the claim that it works is not sufficient to make eugenics acceptable to Christians. By the reasoning outlined here in discussion of Question 2, the claim that it appeals to a "genuine mechanism" is not sufficient to make eugenics acceptable to Christians.

The failure to appeal to a "genuine mechanism" for gravity does not upend the case for space exploration, and does not provide a reason for Christians to reject it. The successful appeal to a "genuine mechanism" for heredity does not create a case for eugenics, and does not provide a case for Christians to accept it. In light of this, let us leave the question of mechanism behind, and move on.

## *Q3: What Worldviews Underlie the Practice?*

In analyzing the worldviews that underlie the practice, there are two sets of considerations to be tackled. One set of considerations is nonrealist, by which I mean that the key issues and responses to them depend on people's opinions. The other set of considerations is realist, by which I mean that the key issues and responses to them do not depend on people's opinions.

An example of Christian concern for nonrealist considerations can be found when Paul writes to the church in Corinth that "if food makes my brother stumble, I will never eat meat, lest I make my brother stumble" (1 Cor 8:13).

Paul's actions here had nothing to do with the meat itself, and everything to do with his brother's opinion of the meat.

An example of Christian concern for realist considerations can be found when Paul writes to the church in Corinth that "what pagans sacrifice they offer to demons and not to God. I do not want you to be participants with demons" (1 Cor 10:20). Paul's actions here are made on account of demons. And the demons' existence is quite independent of your opinion of them.

**Nonrealist Considerations**

To get a handle on a Christian approach to nonrealist considerations, one helpful question to ask is, "Is there anything in this that will distract people from an appropriate relationship with God?" If the answer is "Yes," that is a red flag. To paraphrase Paul's comments from 1 Corinthians 8, if meat does not distract my brother from his relationship with God, great; if meat does distract my brother from his relationship with God, throw it out.

How might this apply to acupuncture? If your brother is steeped in a Buddhist worldview and on that account is having difficulty embracing God's total care, then your involvement with acupuncture could distract him from engaging fully and properly in his relationship with God. In that context, a Christian should approach acupuncture with caution, to the point of declaring, "I will never have acupuncture, lest I make my brother stumble."

If we grant that acupuncture can distract a person from God, and that under such circumstances a Christian should avoid it on religious grounds, does this settle the discussion on whether acupuncture should be classed as scientific or religious? No, it does not! Rather, it places one more nail in the coffin of the distinction that some would like to draw between science and religion.

To see how this is so, let us move on from acupuncture, and ask the same nonrealist question about Western medicine. Is there any aspect of Western medicine that might distract a person from an appropriate relationship with God?

Consider a person who believes that their pills keep them healthy. That is fair enough, as far as it goes. But what if that person, remembering that their pills keep them healthy, forgets that the universe exists moment by moment because God chooses for it to exist? What if they forget that, should God want them to die tonight, then there is nothing their pills can do to prevent it? What if they forget that, should God want them to live to be a thousand, then taking away their pills will not prevent that? From a Christian perspective, their medicine, on which they have come to believe that they rely, has distracted them from an appropriate relationship with God.

Obviously, idols are religious. Obviously, medicine is scientific. But, with respect to the question of a person's relationship with God, it is totally irrelevant whether a practice is classified as scientific or religious. Given this, it is irrelevant whether acupuncture is scientific, or religious, or both, or neither. That categorization is quite inconsequential when considering whether it will cause someone to stumble.

Lest the parallel drawn here between the perils of traditional Chinese medicine and the perils of Western medicine seem contrived, the following objection by a Christian writer to the attitudes of certain medical practitioners may throw the situation into sharper relief: "The entire universe, [the practitioner] feels, works to such a precise orderly fashion that it contains no mysteries beyond the scope of understanding. Because no supreme power, no Lord of Hosts, created the world, the forces behind life and death and illness and health are not beyond man's comprehension."[5]

This objection – that the practitioner has shorn the world of all that is mystical, ineffable, or transcendent, and reduced life to that which is understood and controlled by humankind – might have been leveled at the most materialistic, naturalistic, scientistic medic there is. It was, however, leveled against acupuncturists. Damned, not for being too religious, but for being too scientific.

**Realist Considerations in Religion**

Not all issues come down to how a person thinks about the situation. There exists an external world against which we beat ourselves, and we must reckon with that.

Consider the actions of Uzzah (as recorded in 2 Sam 6). When God gave the command "Do not touch the ark of the covenant or you will die" (see Num 4:15), he did not add, "unless your motivation is pure and you are trying to protect the ark." It was not Uzzah's fault that King David had chosen to sling the ark on an ox cart, instead of having it carried carefully by priests. Uzzah, to his credit, was trying to stop the ark from falling into the mud. Still, whatever his intentions, he met an external, opinion-independent reality. Just as surely as a person with pure intentions who touches a mains cable will die, Uzzah died.

**Realist Considerations in Acupuncture**

What, then, is the reality behind acupuncture? This is a highly contentious topic on which there is much disagreement. Some say there is nothing more

---

5. Marc Duke, *Acupuncture* (New York: Pyramid House, 1972), 164.

happening than the natural release of endorphins in response to the needles. Others say that the needles better direct *qi* to the various spirits that live within the human body. Still others say that the effects of acupuncture are due to the intervention of demons.

For the sake of discussion, let us start by taking the proposed existence of spirits and redirection of *qi* at face value, and assume such accounts to be correct. This is a view adopted by some texts within acupuncture's originating cultures. If this view were true, what would be the implications for Christians? The spirits are there. Acupuncture does not conjure them up, any more than having stitches conjures up red blood cells. We worship neither the blood in our veins nor the spirits in our organs. Using a needle to sew up a wound allows the blood to do its job. Using a needle to redirect *qi* allows the spirits to do their job.

This account raises a number of new questions: What reasons might there be to believe that the account of spirits and *qi* is correct? If it is correct, should that cause any problems for Christians? How then should Christians respond? I will not attempt to answer these questions here. I simply point out that these are reasonable questions. Significantly, when considering how Christians should engage with acupuncture, these are much better questions than asking, "Is acupuncture religious or scientific?," and they are very much better questions than asking, "Does acupuncture work?"

Next, let us consider the view that acupuncture works by the actions of demons. This is a quite different scenario from the case of spirits considered above. Demons are not simply there, but are conjured by the practice of acupuncture. It should be noted that, while some Christians take this view, it is not a position held within acupuncture's originating cultures.

It is not necessarily problematic or wrong to reject the ontology which had been adopted by the originating culture. Most people, for example, are happy to use Newton's law of gravitation without feeling the need to believe that the law functions because of gravitational ether. Similarly, some people are willing to adopt a naturalistic view of acupuncture, insisting that when the *Yellow Emperor's Inner Canon* refers to the "Transportation Official," it simply means the large intestine, and the "Receiving Official" is nothing more nor less than the small intestine. In this naturalistic view, one rejects the original ontology of spirits, and adopts instead the materialistic ontology of biology and chemistry. It is in like fashion that someone may reject the original ontology of spirits and claim instead that acupuncture works by demons. Claims of demonic involvement are not trivially defeated by pointing out that the originating worldview did not invoke demons, any more than claims of curved space-time are defeated by an appeal to Newton.

Faced, then, with the possibility of demons, one might reasonably ask, What reasons might there be to believe that such an account is correct? If it is correct, should that cause any problems for Christians? How then should Christians respond? Again, I will not attempt to answer these questions here, but they are reasonable questions. Once again, they function entirely well as questions, independent of whether we can or do categorize the subject as science or religion.

On reading the above sections, some people may think that there exists no conclusive evidence for either spirits or demons. As such, they may conclude that they should fall back on the naturalistic default: there is probably nothing more happening than the natural release of endorphins in response to the needles. Such a person faces (at least) three questions: What reasons might there be to believe that such an account is correct? If it is correct, should that cause any problems for Christians? How then should Christians respond? An appeal to naturalism does not let us off the hook of answering these questions.

In answering the first question – What reasons might there be to believe that the naturalistic account is correct? – a proponent of the naturalistic view may argue that science has shown that there are no such things as spirits or demons. For the Christian, this response runs into the difficulty that (by some accounts) science has also shown that there are no such things as the soul, purpose, moral evil, heaven, or God. If science has proven that there are no demons, then it has also proven that there is no God, and Christianity is hollow. If the Christian rejects the claim that Christianity is hollow, he or she must also accept that science is not as good at "proving" things as some would hope, and so the jury on demonic involvement in acupuncture might still be out. Naturalist physicalism is not the default to which the neutral observer must return when there is no evidence of anything else. It may be the default to which educated Westerners return, but that simply shows that educated Westerners are not as neutral as they might suppose. Certainly, naturalist physicalism should not be the default to which Christians return.

As ever, I do not attempt here to answer the question of what reasons one might have to believe that acupuncture is naturalistic, or why that might (or might not) be problematic for Christians, or how Christians should respond. I wish only to highlight that these are reasonable questions to ask, and they do not require the assignation of labels like "science" or "religion."

## Realist Considerations in Science

We have seen that acupuncture (regardless of how we classify it with respect to the categories of science and religion) raises realist considerations about which Christians should care. Religion, as we saw with Uzzah, faces realist questions. For symmetry, we shall now briefly consider realist questions raised by science, about which Christians should care.

Consider the reality (or otherwise) of *personhood*: Is someone a person independent of social conventions on the subject? Under a nonrealist conception of personhood, the answer would be "No." Under a realist conception of personhood, the answer would be "Yes."

To get a handle on this, let us start with questions that science is reasonably good at. Consider the question "Is this baby a living organism?" Science treats this question realistically. Based on observation, we can assert that the baby under consideration is living. We do not hold a referendum on the issue. We appeal to the state of the universe itself and say that this baby *is* alive. We can go so far as to specify the reason why we consider it to be alive: it respires, it moves, and so on.

The same situation holds for questions like "Is this patient in pain?" The experience of pain may be subjective. We may not be able to ascertain with certainty what the answer to the question is. But there is an answer. The answer may be "Yes," "No," or "A bit, if I put weight on it like this." And the answer lies with the patient with a broken leg, not with the opinion of the assembled onlookers. When specifying the reasons for the pain, people may variously appeal to the patient's broken leg, or to the patient's neuronal oscillations, but they do not appeal to societal convention.

Without wishing to multiply examples, consider the question "Is this immigrant economically productive? And for what reasons is this immigrant economically productive (or not)?" The answers to these questions are independent of our opinion. People may not know the answers. People may disagree about the answers. But the answer is "out there."

Consider now, for each case – a baby, a patient, an immigrant – the question, "Are they a person? And for what reasons are they a person (or not)?" Science – which was so good at assessing life, pain, and economic productivity, and is so willing to treat such topics realistically – suddenly balks. We come up with conventions. We canvass for opinion. We ask lawyers. After a while, there creeps upon us the feeling that maybe the answer is *only* conventional. Any given being is a person because we (or the government, or "society") has *decided* he or she qualifies for personhood.

Christians hold that there is a *reality* to personhood. We are not free to choose the answer. Sure, we might not know the answer, or we might disagree with people about the answer, but the answer is not set by individual or collective opinion. When we do harm to a person, we do not pit ourselves against socially agreed convention. We pit ourselves against an aspect of reality, for which there will be a reckoning. If science is not able to get a handle on personhood, too bad for science.

In summary: The reality (or otherwise) of God's judgment is not a social convention. The reality (or otherwise) of demons is not a social convention. The reality (or otherwise) of personhood is not a social convention.

None of these realist claims is changed by whether the topic at hand is categorized as "science" or "religion." There are many interesting questions that can be asked in connection to these claims, but "Is it science or is it religion?" is not one of them.

## Q4: To What Extent Can the Practice Be Separated from the Originating Worldviews?

In considering Question 3, we alluded to the fact that it is possible, to some extent and under certain conditions, to adopt a practice without being bound to the fullness of the originating worldview. Acupuncture has historical connections to the "Three Teachings" of Buddhism, Confucianism, and Daoism. However, it has, in some respects, distanced itself from those historical ties. It is reasonable for Christians to consider these historical ties, both those which are broken and those which remain, and to ask what would be an appropriate engagement with acupuncture. Are the historic connections to the Three Teachings so indelible that acupuncture is forever anathema to Christianity? Might acupuncture be anathema for other reasons? What might those other reasons be? Under what circumstances, if any, might the practice of acupuncture be acceptable?

Before getting into such questions, let us consider the ways in which Western medical practice has been separated from wider, particularly religious, worldview considerations. In the West, modernism has separated science from religion and (the concerns of this chapter notwithstanding) many people think that it has done a good job of it. Medicine is placed firmly in the science category and as such, so the argument goes, can be of no concern to Christianity. The doctor who gives you an injection does not tell you how to live your life. A doctor may have an opinion on morality, or the afterlife, or transubstantiation, but none of those opinions are relevant to how he or she gives you an injection.

Even under modernism, however, the separation has not been total. Religious concerns about questions such as morality and the sanctity of life creep in for certain liminal cases. Nonetheless, says modernism, such concerns can be dealt with under a separate topic of "medical ethics." Ethicists work out the tricky questions regarding abortion, euthanasia, stem cell research, animal testing, and the like. The answers that they come up with can then be bolted onto medicine, without impacting on the scientific core that makes up medicine proper. The religious content of medicine is (under this picture) little more than the ethical content, and the ethical content is little more than a list of checkboxes to make sure we are operating within the required guidelines.

How did we get to this point? Thousands of years ago, medicine in the West (to which contemporary Western medicine can trace some of its roots) looked very different. It was, like Chinese medicine, founded in antiquity by pagans. Like Chinese medicine, its practice was connected to healing, cultic rituals, and pagan worldviews. As with Chinese medicine, the boundaries between such categories were, at the time, somewhere between highly porous and nonexistent. Over time, Western medicine has dropped various ideas, such as appeals to correspondence: the notion that something's shape provides information about its medicinal use. In like manner, contemporary Chinese medicine has also dropped various ideas, including its earlier appeals to correspondence. While dropping some ideas, Western medicine, like Chinese medicine, has introduced new ideas which would have been incomprehensible to earlier practitioners. For Western medicine these include the existence of vitamins. For Chinese medicine these include the existence of external *qi*.

Within contemporary Western medicine, there are various aspects which a sceptic might take as cause for concern, but which are usually ignored as broadly unproblematic. For instance, there are multiple, sometimes contradictory, strands: concerning any given ailment, different practitioners may claim its cause is predominantly genetic, or environmental, or social. Western medicine uses terms which have meanings different from those used in the physical sciences: medics may talk about a person being "under stress," or "under strain," without regard for a physicist's thoughts on *force divided by area*, or *fractional linear extension*. Additionally, while Western medicine has some scientific backing, it faces a more significant reproducibility crisis than its proponents are comfortable admitting.

Again, point by point, similar concerns hold regarding Chinese medicine: there is a contradiction between those who view *qi* as something physical and those who view it as something nonphysical. Those who refer to *qi* as an "energy" do not feel bound to anything that physicists would measure in joules. Research papers abound confirming many aspects of Chinese medicine, and research papers abound debunking many other aspects.

As with Questions 1 to 3, it is not my intention here to unpick the many issues at stake, much less provide a definitive answer. It may be that contemporary Asian practices are so far removed from the Daoism of the Yellow Emperor, and Western practices are so far removed from the Paganism of Galen, that such connections are no longer of concern. It may be that other issues of concern have crept in in the meantime. Such discussions are beyond the scope of this chapter.

It is my intention, however, to indicate that we cannot claim that a practice is unproblematic for Christians simply because it is scientific, or because it is unrelated to religion. Similarly, we cannot claim that a practice is problematic for Christians simply because it is unscientific, or because it is related to religion.

## Moving beyond Asia

Over the course of this chapter, I have argued that the categories of science and religion that people are used to using in the modern West – and the many other dichotomies that are often associated with them – are ill-fitting for engaging with contemporary Chinese thought. I have illustrated this by appeal to Chinese medicine. Along the way, I have also argued that the categories of "science" and "religion" are similarly ill-fitting for engagement with at least some contemporary Western thought, as illustrated by appeal to Western medicine. The examples used are not the results of careful cherry-picking, but exemplify a general situation. To indicate the ubiquity of the blurring of boundaries between science and religion, let me sketch further examples: one taken from another place, and one taken from another time.

Looking to other places – beyond "East" and "West" – the above discussion about medicine has many parallels with thinking about how Christians should engage with medicine in Africa. What is the difference between a potion prepared by a sangoma, the same herbal remedy prescribed by a traditional African healer, and the same active ingredient isolated in a white pill and administered by a doctor in a lab coat? What difference does it make (if any) if the traditional healer is an atheist? Or if the doctor in a lab coat is, on occasion, possessed by her ancestors? Does it make a difference if, on different days, one and the same person acts as doctor, traditional healer, and sangoma? In asking such questions, it is clear that the discussion has moved from one in which we are uncertain how to bring science and religion together, to one in which we are uncertain how to tease them apart, or even tell them apart.

Looking to other times, the above discussions about the desacralization of medicine (Q4) have interesting parallels with mathematics. When Pythagoras is taught today, we are happy to present his theorem without reference to the sects of Pythagoreans who worshipped him. A math curriculum today may mention Pythagoras's ideas on the geometrical basis of harmony in music, while passing over his ideas on the geometrical basis of harmony in justice. It would almost certainly not mention his views of the transmigration of souls. Pythagoras, like us, viewed numbers as somehow immanently present in objects (there is a *three* in three apples), and yet also saw that they transcended mere objects (the number *three* does not require apples in order to be *three*); he saw that numbers somehow existed immaterially, and always existed from eternity past to eternity future. Like us, he recognized that confrontation with an immanent, transcendent, immaterial, and eternal entity is something special. But, unlike us, he did not suppress the obvious conclusion: that mathematics is inherently entwined with religion. However clear his logical reasoning, we find it hard to follow, simply because we have been enculturated in the idea that math and religion "don't go together."

Shoehorning practices into categories of what is "scientific" and what is "religious" may provide an interesting (if potentially ultimately futile) academic pastime. That being said, questions surrounding whether to categorize an idea or practice as "science" or "religion" are broadly irrelevant to the much more interesting questions surrounding how Christians are to engage with any given idea or practice. In the process of arriving at this conclusion in the context of Asian thought and practice, we have found along the way that similar conclusions hold in the context of contemporary Western thought and practice. Moreover, once alerted to the possibility, there is reason to believe that the blurring of boundaries between what is scientific and what is religious is not limited to a few situations. Rather, the thorough mixing arises ubiquitously across times, places, and disciplines.

## References

Barbour, Ian G. *Religion and Science: Historical and Contemporary Issues*. San Francisco: Harper San Francisco, 1997; repr. 2013.
Duke, Marc. *Acupuncture*. New York: Pyramid House, 1972.
Rennard, Barbara O., et al. "Chicken Soup Inhibits Neutrophil Chemotaxis in Vitro." *Chest* 118, no. 4 (2000): 1150–57.

World Health Organization. *Acupuncture: Review and Analysis of Reports on Controlled Clinical Trials*. Geneva: World Health Organization, 2002.

## Further Reading

John Walton has authored a series of books framed by the categories typically adopted by cultures in the ancient Near East. To this end, he does not so much "blur the boundaries" between science and religion, as ignore the categories of science and religion altogether and roll with what Hebrew thought considered important when the Bible was being written.

Walton, John H. *The Lost World of Genesis One: Ancient Cosmology and the Origins Debate*. Downers Grove: IVP Academic, 2010.

———. *The Lost World of Adam and Eve: Genesis 2–3 and the Human Origins Debate*. Downers Grove: IVP Academic, 2015.

Longman, Tremper, III, and John H. Walton. *The Lost World of the Flood: Mythology, Theology, and the Deluge Debate*. Downers Grove: IVP Academic, 2018.

Paul Unschuld has provided an annotated translation of the *Yellow Emperor's Inner Canon*, one of the earliest Chinese medical texts. Susan Huang traces, in two volumes, how Daoist conceptions of body gods and spirits evolved over time. Hsiang-lin Lei provides an account of the radical changes which took place in Chinese medicine in the twentieth century, to create the disciplines and practices we have today.

Unschuld, Paul U. *Huang Di Nei Jing Su Wen: Nature, Knowledge, Imagery in an Ancient Chinese Medical Text*. Los Angeles: University of California Press, 2003.

Huang, Shih-Shan Susan. "Daoist Imagery of Body and Cosmos, Part 1: Body Gods and Starry Travel." *Journal of Daoist Studies* 3 (2010): 57–90.

———. "Daoist Imagery of Body and Cosmos, Part 2: Body Worms and Internal Alchemy." *Journal of Daoist Studies* 4 (2011): 32–62.

Lei, Sean Hsiang-lin. *Neither Donkey Nor Horse: Medicine in the Struggle over China's Modernity*. Chicago: University of Chicago Press, 2016.

In recent decades, *qigong* has been officially classified in China as science, medicine, sport, pseudoscience, religion, cult, and fomenter of terrorist activity. David Palmer recounts China's struggles to position *qigong* within Western categories. Different parts of Asia have developed categories of science and religion at different times and for different reasons. Jason Ānanda Josephson documents the historical, political, and economic considerations behind creating the category of "religion" in Japan.

Palmer, David A. *Qigong Fever: Body, Science, and Utopia in China*. New York: Columbia University Press, 2007.

Josephson, Jason Ānanda. *The Invention of Religion in Japan*. Chicago: University of Chicago Press, 2012.

Peter Harrison has provided an account of how the categories of science and religion emerged in European thought. Mary Midgley and Bruno Latour look at attempts to compartmentalize and dichotomize thought and explain why, despite our best efforts, such compartmentalization does not and cannot ultimately work.

Harrison, Peter. *The Territories of Science and Religion*. Chicago: University of Chicago Press, 2017.

Midgley, Mary. *Evolution as a Religion*. London: Routledge, 2002.

Latour, Bruno. *We Have Never Been Modern*. Cambridge: Harvard University Press, 1993.

# 4

# The Quest for Presence: Social and Theological Aspects of Science-Faith Dialogue in Brazil

Guilherme de Carvalho, Brazilian Association of Christians in Science, Brazil

## Abstract

Building bridges between science and Christianity should reveal inner harmony and cross-fertilization between the core ideas of the two realms. Because Christianity and science are practiced by two similar-yet-different communities, this has an important social dimension. Some regulative ideas about what a community is, and specific models for understanding the scientific and religious communities, are therefore necessary for strategic thinking in the process of bridge-building. Today, the Brazilian Association of Christians in Science (ABC$^2$), has about seventy work groups, comprising local chapters and thematic groups, that are spread across the country. From the beginning of the ABC$^2$ initiative, we arranged our activities around the view that science and Christianity are both *learning communities* that focus on different dimensions of reality and distinct human goods. This approach called for political diplomacy when balancing frontiers, discourses, and authorities.

> A theology of faithful presence obligates us to do what we are able, under the sovereignty of God, to shape the patterns of life and work and relationship – that is, the institutions of which our lives are constituted – toward a shalom that seeks the welfare not only of those of the household of God but of all.[1]
>
> James Davison Hunter

## Introduction

The Associação Brasileira de Cristãos na Ciência (ABC², Brazilian Association of Christians in Science) was founded in November 2016, and the first ABC² national conference was held in the main hall of Mackenzie Presbyterian University in São Paulo. This was a first step in the search for a faithful Christian presence within the Brazilian academe.

I had been haunted by that idea since the beginning of the 2000s, receiving crucial encouragement through the efforts of Dr. Denis Alexander and the team at The Faraday Institute for Science and Religion in Cambridge. It gained traction in September 2013 while we were in Campinas with Dr. Ruth Bancewicz, during a seventeen-day tour, launching the Test of Faith Brazil Project. During a break-time chat, Roberto Covolan and I discovered that we had the same dreams about a Brazilian Christians in Science. With the stimulus of Dr. Andrew Briggs and the support of other Brazilian academic friends, we wrote down our ideas and sent a proposal to the Templeton World Charity Foundation (TWCF).

The grant proposal – under the title "ABC²: Proposal for Establishment and Full Implementation of the Brazilian Association of Christians in Science" – was accepted, and the project started officially on 20 March 2015. Dr. Roberto Covolan (physics, Unicamp) was the leader; Dr. Gustavo Assi (naval engineering, University of São Paulo), and I (the "chaplain") were co-leaders; Jonathan Simões (administration, Federal University of Minas Gerais) was executive secretary; and Ana Flávia Vieira assisted us all. The project worked on three fronts: *networking, engagement,* and *content*.

The Networking Initiative, run by Dr. Covolan, aimed to identify and connect university students and professors, to spread the basics about faith and science, and to establish a small network from our visits to twelve important

---

1. James Davison Hunter, *To Change the World: The Irony, Tragedy, and Possibility of Christianity in the Late Modern World* (Oxford: Oxford University Press, 2010), 254.

cities. These twelve cities provided the name of this part of the project: Dodecapolis. The Engagement Initiative, with Dr. Assi, was responsible for formation, local leadership training, and commitment-building. The Content Initiative, which I headed, focused on the production and distribution of high-quality content through a book series, videos, a minidocumentary, a web page, and a series of articles.

The project went well, and we established reading groups on faith and science which were being formed through the Dodecapolis. Since the beginning of the project, we had in mind to build what I called a "bridge community": an intellectual community with a mediatory function between churches and universities. I therefore proposed that we create the role of a network manager within our team, with the specific task of building a university culture and expanding the net of local groups. For this we recruited Marcelo Cabral – economist, philosopher, and, at that time, a graduate student at Calvin Theological Seminary in Grand Rapids, Michigan – to integrate the team.

From the initial twelve groups, we expanded to more than seventy local groups in many capitals and university cities, with regional leaders, and almost six hundred associates. These groups promote the basics about religion and science, philosophy, and humanities in university and religious contexts; organize in-person and online local events; and provide environments of friendship to stimulate intellectual life among Christians. We have also seen the steady emergence of thematic groups with a sharper academic focus. These have formed in fields such as medicine, chemistry and biology, computer science, philosophy of technology, business administration, and history, with a forthcoming physics group.

Cultivating intellectual and spiritual friendships has been, for us, a matter of principle. It has taken us to a deep reflection about the virtues of life and mind. This is worked out practically in cultivating a creative and cooperative community which is committed to education and persuaded of the value of intellectual life and science. In this context, faith does not become a regressive force within the Brazilian academic sphere but, rather, a progressive one.

This chapter is an effort to explain the concept and "theory of change" behind the ABC² initiative – not merely in strategy, but in terms of the normative social architecture that we presupposed throughout the project, and the social-theological perspectives behind the idea of building bridge communities for science-faith dialogue.

Section 1 of this chapter considers the cultural and historic context of science and religion within the Brazilian academy. Efforts to fruitfully relate science and religion within the academy have been rare in Brazil and broadly unsuccessful. This provides us with motivation for the analysis in the rest of the chapter: We cannot simply repeat what has been done before, and we ought not to rest too heavily on our intuition alone. Rather, we set about carefully analyzing how science and religion can and should appropriately engage with one another within the academy, and in wider society. This provides us with a theoretical framework within which to formulate the work of ABC$^2$

In section 2, we set out what we mean by science and religion. We draw on insights from social sciences, philosophy, and theology, and we show how and why science and religion – along with politics, art, education, and so forth – can be meaningfully differentiated. On this analysis, we find them to be relatively independent spheres, each with its own goods, institutions, power structures, capitals, and economies.

In an undifferentiated world, one cannot say, "I am, first and foremost, a scientist," or "religion is more important than science." However, once the spheres of science and religion have been differentiated, very human issues concerning identity and power arise immediately, and must be reckoned with. This is dealt with in section 3.

While different spheres of endeavor are relatively independent, they cannot ever be absolutely independent. Section 4 considers the tension that necessarily exists between the need for a field to protect the integrity of its own goods and capitals, and the need for a field to exchange goods and capitals with other fields. All fields need so-called transversalist communities, acting at the boundaries. There are common lessons to be learned from and for such communities, be they politicians engaging with science, scientists engaging with religion, or even biologists engaging with physics.

Section 5 then explicitly addresses this tension with respect to science and religion. Science, if it is to be science, must remain essentially autonomous and independent of religion. And yet science – when done well – must necessarily draw on religious capital. Scientists with no understanding of religion are not in a position to mediate this necessary interaction, and so a transversalist community is required to enable science to be – in all senses of the term – good science.

Finally, in section 6, these thoughts are drawn together, and the argument comes full circle. The social-theological ethics for science-and-religion dialogue that we painstaking develop through the chapter can be held up alongside the vision we had for ABC$^2$. Our initial intuitions are supported, but now also enriched and deepened. A transversalist community – that is, a bridging community – is both appropriate and necessary for the flourishing of the academy and the life of the nation. Religion has a place within the university:

not to dominate, compete with, or subsume other disciplines, but to support them to practice their disciplines well. Not to stand aloof, but to come alongside them, incarnating faithful presence within the university. This is not a simple matter, and it requires time, space, skill, and love to develop it. This, then, is part of the task of ABC².

## Incarnation and Presence

From the beginning of our initiative, relationships and real presence have played an especially important role. The original conversation between Roberto Covolan and me that resulted in the creation of ABC² took place through the philosopher Marcelo Cabral, a mutual friend who, at the time, was still an undergraduate student. The network of friendships has continued to play an important role in this initiative.

We have always intended that our bridge-building should be about more than just promoting ideas and stimulating intellectual creativity: it should also involve being present and building communities. The focus of an "intellectual community" is friendship around *ideas* but must still contain elements of social friendship and companionship, since our intellects emerge among real people who speak, communicate, and hug. It is no coincidence that the divine *Logos* became flesh and could be touched by human persons.[2]

After many years of theological teaching in Belo Horizonte, I was inclined to think about that task in missiological and incarnational terms. The theme of incarnation was one of the keys for Latin American mission theology, which had a significant impact on the Lausanne '74 conference and on the subsequent debates in the Lausanne Movement. The idea of building bridges between religion and science therefore contained this missiological and incarnational element. If the Christian mission involves both evangelism and social responsibility, each of which is indispensable, should this not be practiced also in the academy, as a place of presence, demonstration, and transformation, signaling the reign of Christ?

The theological and missiological task of building bridges had a very specific empirical connection. In a nation like the United Kingdom, where the oldest universities have historical links with the Anglican Church, there has been a Christian presence since the beginning of the scientific revolution.

---

2. For an excellent explanation of the social nature of the religious life from a neuroscientific perspective, see Brad D. Straw and Warren S. Brown, *Enhancing Christian Life: How Extended Cognition Augments Religious Community* (Downers Grove: IVP Academic, 2020).

The substructure for maintaining bridges has therefore always been present. But in Brazil, things are much more complicated.

First, Brazilian intellectual life has developed with an intense polarity between the Catholic mind and successive waves of European secularism. At the time of the constitution of the Republic in 1889, under the influence of French positivism, a strong secular discourse was established, which was averse to any religious presence in the academy. Successive varieties of the French secular mentality have shown their strength since then. The University of São Paulo (USP), the largest and most important Brazilian university, was formed from the demand for the constitution of a new cultural elite in the 1930s. It was inspired by the French academic model and had famous guest professors such as Claude Lévi-Strauss and Fernand Braudel. Other regional and federal public universities developed under the same secularist bias. An emblematic case is that of the University of Brasilia, which was founded in 1962 by the writer and politician Darcy Ribeiro, its first rector. Ribeiro attempted to include theology among the arts and sciences, but saw his efforts frustrated:

> I searched in São Paulo for the General of the Order, in Brazil, who was Friar Mateus Rocha, and I explained my problem to him. I argued that Brazil had eight Catholic universities, four of them pontifical, which trained thousands of pharmacists and dentists, but did not train any theologians. I proposed to hand over to the Dominicans the creation of an Institute of Catholic Theology within the University of Brasilia. It would be a revolutionary act, because theology, expelled from public universities since the French Revolution, would return to them, precisely in the most modern university that was being created in those years. There were adverse reactions to my initiative, including that of an eminent scientist, who accused me of betraying the secular tradition of education.[3]

Despite initial support, the project did not happen. To this day, the University of Brasilia does not have any theology courses, nor do any of the Brazilian public universities. Although the country has a good system of private and confessional universities – notably Catholic, Lutheran, and Presbyterian

---

3. Darcy Ribeiro, "Prólogo," *Carta*: *Falas, Reflexões, Memórias: 1961–1995: A Invenção Da Universidade de Brasília* [1961–1995: The Invention of the University of Brasilia] 14 (April 1995): 8. Unless otherwise stated, translations of quotes into English in this chapter are my own.

ones – reflections on religion and culture have been effectively excluded from the inner circles of Brazilian academia.

Traditional Brazilian Protestantism, which was initially aligned with progressive cultural attitudes, was gradually supplanted in size and influence by evangelical mission churches, such as Baptists, and later by Pentecostal, charismatic, and neo-Pentecostal movements, which were composed mainly of less-educated people. Only in the last twenty years has the Protestant mind started to work in contexts previously dominated by secular elites, such as the press, politics, the arts and cultural media, the literary market, and, timidly, the academy.

The immense number of evangelicals – about 65 million people (31 percent of the population) – did not translate into an effective public presence, and there was an absence of intentional theological, catechetical, and pastoral activity. Negative attitudes toward science and a lack of interest in academic training are quite common, even in traditional denominations, such as Baptists. So-called "scientific creationism" continues to expand. Even among Roman Catholics, who make up 50 percent of the population, the Catholic Social Teaching is less influential than liberation theology, and Catholic universities do not have good systematic projects for dialogue between religion and science. The Brazilian Society of Catholic Scientists, for example, was founded only in October 2018, the recency of this development underscoring the fact that Brazil does not have a tradition of dialogue between religion and science.

This does not mean that there has been no cooperation. Almost thirty years ago, Dr. Geraldo José de Paiva, from USP's Institute of Psychology, published the results of an investigation involving scientists from the fields of physics, biosciences, and humanities at his university which indicated a significant opening for compatibility between religion and science.[4] This seems consonant with the popularity of religion among Brazilians.

However, Paiva also discovered a trend of religious disaffiliation among academics, following the increasing proportion of the population "without religion." At the same time, the disconnect between secularized cultural elites and religious communities, and the acute politicization of religion in Brazil, favored defensive and reactive views between academia and the church. For example, one of the main effects of "scientific creationism" was to strengthen the counternarrative of evangelical communities against these elites. The combination of a lack of tradition in the dialogue of faith and science, and

---

4. Geraldo José de Paiva, "Itinerários Religiosos de Acadêmicos: Um Enfoque Psicológico" (diss., University of São Paulo, 1993).

a climate of tension between secularism and organized religion, meant that there were few opportunities for exchanges between religious communities and the academy.

In such a context, it was evident that the construction of bridges between religion and science would require a lot of groundwork: creation of safe spaces for intellectual formation in harmony with faith, intense diplomatic conversations with religious communities in order to facilitate the opening of borders, academic training for people of faith, and availability of high-quality content presented for various levels of intellectual and scientific maturity. All this groundwork was necessary to enable faith to have a positive presence in the Brazilian academy.

This complex movement must be christological in approach. According to the Gospel of John, "the Word became flesh and dwelt among us" (John 1:14): Christ's example involved both *incarnation* and *presence*. In like manner, our efforts involved intentional encounters: going to different cities and contexts; connecting with people face-to-face; building relationships; inhabiting the church and the academy; being present relationally, culturally, and institutionally.

James Davison Hunter has done invaluable work developing the concept of "faithful presence" to express the understanding of acting collectively in cultural leadership through service, bringing shalom in the places where we practice our faith. His rendering expresses the core theological motivations of our initiative: "Faithful presence in the world means that Christians are fully present and committed in their spheres of social influence, whatever they may be: their families, neighborhoods, voluntary activities, and places of work."[5]

For science-faith work in Brazil, this involved two movements, corresponding to the two banks of the river that we intend to bridge: a dialogue of faith and science within churches, media organizations and Brazilian Christian imagination, as well as a Christian presence in the academy itself.

Our networking initiatives within the project were not just pragmatic but fundamentally missiological. Communities needed to be woven, and commitments and bonds of trust needed to be built. With that in mind, what was initially called "Dodecapolis" was the concerted action to announce the "good news" and bring people together, first in twelve capitals and then in smaller cities.

In strategic terms, such groups are the seeds of a multidisciplinary evangelical intellectual community, operating at the borders between churches

---

5. Hunter, *Change the World*, 247.

and academia. Our experience has been that they have multiplied to fulfill this function very well.

## Differentiation, Spheres, and Social Fields

One of our chief concerns was to obtain a clear grasp of the type of society in which faith should be incarnated. The mission is addressed to "all peoples and languages," but this may have different applications for our complex modern societies. In what sense, if any, are academic scientists "a people"? In this section we draw on insights from social sciences, philosophy, and theology to understand what makes science – or any other part of society – distinctive.

Max Weber is considered to be one of the founding fathers of modern sociology. He discerned a process of rationalization, following an instrumental logic of control and efficiency, which led to the differentiation of society into distinct fields of activity, with different specialties, logics, and institutions. Thus, the West saw the rise of many autonomous "fields": the Renaissance introduced a separation between art and religion; the Reformation brought the principle of separating church and state; the scientific revolution allowed the emergence of scientific fields and the professionalization of science; then came the birth of the free press and modern journalism; and, finally, there arose a plethora of new professional classes.

According to the metaphor developed by the French sociologist Pierre Bourdieu, the spheres of power in modern societies have a complex structure and engage in exchanges based on their goods and capital. Michael Walzer calls these fields "spheres of justice": art, science, politics, communications, affectivity, religion, health, education. All of these activities are organized in distinct and relatively independent symbolic fields.

These same fields were called "spheres of sovereignty" by the theologian Abraham Kuyper, who interpreted the emergence of these diverse modes of human activity and authority as the result of a divinely established creation order. He defended the sovereignty of each sphere of social life before God, and their mutual relative autonomy. This distinctly theological look at the question of social architecture was incorporated into the theory of social institutions developed by the Dutch philosopher Herman Dooyeweerd. According to Dooyeweerd, the differentiation between such spheres of life and social activity reflects the nature of the created universe, as a temporal process that begins in God and is directed to him. Thus, it is argued that – the historical-critical evaluations of the model's shortcomings notwithstanding –

we should honor these structures and assume them as normative references for our creative activity.

Taking the Kuyperian conception of social architecture[6] as a starting point, we describe the broader phenomenon of differentiation as the formation of social "spheres." However, we need something conceptually more refined to describe the actual way these "spheres" work. Here, Bourdieu's idea of "fields" seems to fit the job. The "fields" are concrete phenomena of social coherence, bringing together institutions, discourses, subcommunities, and internal social practices. Strictly speaking, the fields are communities and social spaces for scientific cooperation and conflict. Metaphorically, we could call the spheres "social orbits," with the various social fields being the "social bodies" that travel through these orbits. We can also say that the "fields" are autonomous and structured communities that instantiate the broader, fragmentary reality of the larger social "spheres." Each sphere, instantiated in its social fields, involves (1) *an internal language*, setting the field as a distinct symbolic universe; (2) a set of *human goods* gathered, cultivated, and described as being covered by that field; (3) *institutions and power structures* specific to that field, including a dominant elite; (4) and an *economy* intrinsic to that field, given that symbolic capital always involves credibility and influence.

The language of *goods* is lifted from moral discourse and refers to the forms of goods that together constitute human flourishing. The language of *capitals*, on the other hand, is an economic metaphor and refers to the credibility, authority, and competences that are available in a field that cultivates its internal goods.[7] By way of example, scientific capital sets out the rules of the scientific game, and recognizes skill in navigating such: choosing topics to research, identifying significant results, selecting where to publish. But scientific capitals cannot be the purpose of the scientific field. Rather, science exists for scientific goods. Scientific capitals simply regulate the processes of accumulating and distributing scientific goods. This relationship holds similarly between goods and capitals in other fields, such as religion, politics, and art.

---

6. There is a diversity of conceptions about the internal organization of these social fields. Our view will be explicated in this chapter, though it might be summarized as being a Kuyperian-Dooyeweerdian-inspired composition, in dialogue with Pierre Bourdieu's theory of symbolic fields and capitals, Michael Walzer's notion of "spheres of justice," Michael Polanyi's thesis on spontaneous systems, and elements of John Finnis's theory of goods.

7. Pierre Bourdieu, *Os Usos Sociais da Ciência: Por Uma Sociologia Clínica do Campo Científico* [The social uses of science: A clinical sociology of the scientific field] (São Paulo: Unesp, 2003), 27.

It is important to keep in mind that different forms of capital and goods existed prior to the historical differentiation of social fields. However, with the historical formation of these social fields, forms of capital and goods started to be *described* and to have *their flow controlled* in a systematic way. This was done through the process of cultural opening, described by Dooyeweerd as "differentiation and integration."[8] Thus, for example, political capital has existed since human beings negotiated the conditions of common life and interests of groups from time immemorial; but the scientific description and management of this form of capital is simultaneous with the birth of modern politics.

The main point of our explanation of these spheres and fields is to make clear that effective and mutually beneficial communication between religion and culture depends on recognizing the complexity of modern societies. Differentiated fields have emerged with internal governance centers, borders, economies, and their own languages. Such differentiated fields should receive from religious communities all the respect they deserve, so that their internal meaning is recognized, and their symbolic exchanges are enriched. We could think of each field as a "people" with its own "language," which must be understood by ambassadors and diplomats of modern religion.

Thus, it is not enough to speak of a dialogue between "religion" and "science," considered abstractly as theoretical and parallel universes; it is necessary to descend to the concreteness of communication between scientific and religious social fields. Given the complexity of modern societies, the challenges of communication between different fields cannot simply be done away with. They are inherent – pathological – to the system. It is to these pathologies that we now turn.

## The Pathologies of Differentiation

The incarnational challenge of the Christian mission of translation and diplomatic negotiation is not the whole story. The task becomes more complicated when we recognize that the internal life and external relations in these fields are dynamic and often dysfunctional. There is a significant gap between thinking about things as being just *different*, and declaring them *wrong*, or *better*, or *more important*. Fallen humans, however, are all too ready to make this leap, choosing one of the "different" things to champion, and

---

8. Herman Dooyeweerd, "The Criteria of Progressive and Reactionary Tendencies in History," in *Christian Philosophy and the Meaning of History*, vol. 13, series B of *Collected Works of Herman Dooyeweerd* (Lewiston: Edwin Mellen, 1996), 47–66.

another to disparage. In any real-world situation, we must face both functional and dysfunctional human tendencies, and so here we consider two pathologies of differentiation: identity and power.

## *Identity Pathologies*

The diversity of these social spheres is sometimes called, in the Weberian tradition, "social polytheism": each field develops specific rules distinct from those of other fields; and devotion to these rules is demanded of the individuals practicing within that field. This condition feeds fragmentation, stimulates a "fundamentalist" devotion, and promotes overspecialization.

An important effect of this dynamic is that individuals tend to identify with institutions, activities, or goods that belong to their own field. Thus, scientists will tend to see science as the most valuable activity and construct their image of humanity, the world, and the good through scientific symbols and scientific goods. The same will hold for artists in relation to art, and militants in relation to politics. The problem of identity is crucial in the contemporary world. Addressing the demand for self-awareness and self-constitution of identity is difficult, but the task is unavoidable. One of the main resources for this activity is psychology.

By way of example, I will quote one of the dominant narratives for constructing contemporary identities: that of affective-centered relationships. In this narrative, in which individual happiness is prioritized, the individual is integrated into the field of affective power, and becomes its representative. The emergence of the modern affective fields, as described by the sociologist Eva Illouz, legitimizes and catalyzes the affective search as a privileged way for human flourishing and happiness. However, other ways of constituting identity coexist with the affective path: we could mention here political power, knowledge, philosophical life, the way of science, and the way of religious experience.

This all implies that the religious field and the affective field can develop a conflicting relationship, since their own goods are treated by their "devotees" as having unconditional value, thus becoming immeasurable and irreducible social subsystems. The actors in each field will tend to consider the goods of other fields as "sacrilegious," or "immoral," or "little clarified" actions. To understand the affective field, it is therefore useful to look for occasional signs of an artificial or exaggerated rise in affectivity to the detriment of values from other social spheres.

In *Consuming the Romantic Utopia* (1997), Eva Illouz described this dynamic within the affective field itself:

> In capitalist societies, love contains a utopian dimension that cannot be easily reduced to "false consciousness" or the alleged power of "ideology" to recruit people's desires. Rather, the yearning for utopia that lies at the heart of romantic love has deep affinities with the experience of the sacred. As Durkheim suggested, such an experience did not disappear from secular societies, but emigrated from religion itself to other domains of culture. Romantic love is one of the places of this displacement.[9]

Illouz's observation is insightful. It indicates the religious nature of identity-seeking activity through the route of the romantic encounter. It is this "divine" vocation that can explain the unconditional relationship some social movements have with affective happiness, and their tendency to seek the submission of other social spheres.

## *Pathologies of Power*

Political philosopher Michael Walzer distinguishes between two types of domination that can lead to injustice: "dominance" and "monopoly."[10] Monopoly occurs when a social group controls a particular good (e.g. the tycoons of industrial capitalism who control private property). The dominance occurs when a good, monopolized by one group, is elevated to the position of a "gold standard," as if it has a greater value, or is preeminent among other goods.

To promote a just society, it is not enough merely to undo monopolies of power. For Walzer, it is especially important to reduce the dominance of one set of social goods over the others. The dominance of one set of social goods over others is seen in society when, for example, education becomes a mere commodity, or emotional well-being replaces virtue, or religious traditions stifle scientific research. From this, Walzer introduces his concept of "complex equality": "Equality is a complex relation of persons, mediated by goods we make, share, and divide among ourselves; it is not an identity of possessions.

---

9. Eva Illouz, *Consuming the Romantic Utopia: Love and the Cultural Contradictions of Capitalism* (Berkeley: University of California Press, 1997), 7–8.

10. Michael Walzer, *Spheres of Justice: A Defense of Pluralism and Equality* (New York: Basic, 1983).

It requires, then, a diversity of distributive criteria that mirrors the diversity of social goods."[11]

Walzer illustrates this concept with thoughts from the seventeenth-century Christian mathematician and philosopher Blaise Pascal:

> The nature of tyranny is to desire power over the whole world and outside its own sphere. . . . There are different companies – the strong, the handsome, the intelligent, the devout – and each man reigns in his own, not elsewhere. But sometimes they meet, and the strong and the handsome fight for mastery – foolishly, for their mastery is of different kinds. They misunderstand one another and make the mistake of each aiming at universal dominion. Nothing can win this, not even strength, for it is powerless in the kingdom of the wise. . . . The following statements, therefore, are false and tyrannical: "Because I am handsome . . . I should command respect." "I am strong; therefore, man should love me." . . . Tyranny is the wish to obtain by one means what can only be had by another. We owe different duties to different qualities: love is the proper response to charm, fear to strength, and belief to learning.[12]

This coheres with the thinking of Dooyeweerd, who developed a philosophical analysis of society to show how different spheres relate to each other. Unlike Walzer, Dooyeweerd explained the efforts to establish the dominance of one sphere over others as a distorted spiritual impulse. For Dooyeweerd, when the mind closes to the absolute and divine source of meaning, it will seek a temporal reality to fulfill divine functions. This leads to a distortion in the mind's perception of how the spheres of life are related, which can result in an unbalanced theory of good.

This has important implications for human communities in situations like ours, in which the cultivation of human goods has reached a high degree of differentiation and specialization. In searching for a source of meaning and identity, we will tend to choose one or another sphere of social goods as a kind of spiritual idol, and to establish it as dominant over other spheres. "Devotees" of each sphere will then evaluate each type of good according to its own "gold standard."

---

11. Walzer, *Spheres of Justice*, 18.
12. Blaise Pascal, *Pensées*, cited in Walzer, 18.

This means that, as we try to build bridges, we will find situations in which political interests (from the state), economic interests (from the market), and even ethical interests (from social activism) will show predatory attitudes toward some scientific fields. In like manner, we will find that scientistic practices and agendas may project from scientific fields to society, apparently legitimizing the predation of ordinary life by the priorities and devotions of the academy.

Armed with these basic categories, we can discuss more specifically the structure of scientific fields, and what this means for diplomacy between fields.

## The Formation of Scientific Fields

Consideration of the universe of science as a distinct sphere, with its own logic, has among its historical defenders the social scientist Robert K. Merton. In a classic 1942 article, "The Normative Structure of Science," Merton summarized the evolution of self-awareness in scientific fields, pointing out that science started as dependent on religious and social sanction, then proved its independence, as if it was above society, finally to find itself under opposition and with the need to explain and affirm socially its own ethos.[13] Merton notes that the scientific field has real autonomy, related to its internal ethos and the institutions that support it. At the same time, he notes that this autonomy is not absolute, since science cannot operate completely independently of society.

In this sense, there is an ambivalence in the scientist's desire for a "purity of science":

> One sentiment which is assimilated by the scientist from the very outset of his training pertains to the purity of science. Science must not suffer itself to become the handmaiden of theology or economy or state. The function of this sentiment is to preserve the autonomy of science. For if such extrascientific criteria of the value of science as presumable consonance with religious doctrines or economic utility or political appropriateness are adopted, science becomes acceptable only insofar as it meets these criteria. In other words, as the pure science sentiment is eliminated, science becomes subject

---

13. Robert K. Merton, "The Normative Structure of Science," in *The Sociology of Science: Theoretical and Empirical Investigations*, eds. Robert K. Merton and Norman W. Storer (Chicago: University of Chicago Press, 1979), 228–80.

to the direct control of other institutional agencies and its place in society becomes increasingly uncertain.[14]

These desires, which we will discuss later, indicate that scientific fields have their internal goods, along with the responsibility to protect and cultivate them for the benefit of society as a whole. On the other hand, as the sociologist notes, this exaltation of the purity of science can set society against it, when its results interfere with other fields. In addition, its successes can stimulate movements of dominance and external control over science. In this way scientific institutions may fail to integrate with much larger social structures, although they are an integral part of them.

The dilemmas of autonomy and integration force a deep self-understanding of each social field. Merton himself showed that the scientific field has an internal structure and a distinct ethos, which gives it a unique and irreducible character. Merton also believed that the contents of science cannot be reduced to general sociological processes. His position, for example, against political interventions on scientific activity is unequivocal.[15] Merton's view of the scientific sphere is therefore normative. His ideas on the autonomy of science were central to the paradigm called *differentiationism*, with a clear focus on the ethos of science and the need to defend it against external interference. This paradigm was dominant between the 1940s and 1970s.

But in the 1970s, this hegemony was challenged. *Antidifferentiationism* in sociology of science sought to demonstrate the continuity of symbolic processes internal to science with external processes, denying the field's autonomy. One of the first and most influential names in antidifferentiation was the historian and philosopher of science Thomas Kuhn, particularly in *The Structure of Scientific Revolutions* (1962). Kuhn's argument was basically that the advancement of science does not occur in a progressive and linear way, but through qualitative leaps, with conflict between incompatible paradigms leading to the victory of the new paradigm and reorganization of the scientific field. These criticisms sought to show that extrascientific factors (historical, sociological, political, and economic) affect the theoretical process.

More recently, the antidifferentiation argument has lost some of its potency, in part because of the realist tendencies of the scientific community itself. The admission that scientific knowledge could not be "pure" fueled mediatory solutions such as Roy Bhaskar's critical realism. According to Terry Shinn and

---

14. Merton, "Normative Structure," 260.
15. Merton, 258–59.

Pascal Ragouet, criticism of the Mertonian model of the autonomy of science and the scientific ethos is not enough to dissolve differentiation, since "the scientific field profits by being distinct from other social fields."[16] Nonetheless, the internal structure of scientific fields is not *purely* scientific. Shinn and Ragouet follow a model of the scientific field inspired by Bourdieu as being structured from two types of capital: *properly scientific capital*, consisting of academic successes and peer recognition; and *temporal capital*, constituted by institutional power, access to financing, political force, and all control over the means of production and reproduction of science. Bourdieu's view helps us to recognize what is missing from the Mertonian discussion of scientific ethos: it is not only composed of habits directly linked to the production of properly scientific capital – that is, to the internal goods of science – but it is also influenced by practices arising from the temporal structure of science.

How is this temporal structure formed? The description of the various capitals and goods presented at the beginning of our discussion can be extended: while there are different types of capitals and goods, in each field, they are not forever independent. Cooperation permits relative convertibility of capitals and goods between fields.

Scientific fields therefore have a *porosity*. Financial, political, and moral capitals, constituted from the exchange with other social fields, also make up the scientific field. This circulation of capitals is necessary for the production of scientific goods. And yet, paradoxically, such circulation can also distort the intrinsic economy of the scientific field, and so harm the cultivation of scientific goods. Circulated capitals can even be vectors for dominance of other social fields over the scientific field.

This porosity is also true of all other fields: scientific, economic, and moral capitals are necessary in – and also distort – political fields; likewise for scientific, economic, and political capitals in the religious field; and so on. This porosity means that each field exhibits a search for a center of unity and universality, within a complex, dynamic, and fragmentary structure.

Given that all fields – including scientific and religious fields – have structural substrates in which capitals from other fields circulate, the porosities between fields must be understood and managed wisely. This is necessary so that the internal goods which define each field can function appropriately.

---

16. Terry Shinn and Pascal Ragouet, *Controvérsias Sobre a Ciência: Por uma Sociologia Transversalista da Atividade Científica* [Controversies about science: Toward a transversalist sociology of scientific activity] (São Paulo: Editora 34 / Associação Filosófica Scientiae Studia, 2008), 16.

Diving a little deeper into the complexity of these structures, Shinn and Ragouet discuss the role of scientific microcultures and different regimes of work within scientific fields. From this they note that there is a lot of *transitional activity* within scientific fields. One of these regimes identified by Shinn and Ragouet – and which directly interests us here – is called the "transversal" regime. Practitioners of the transversal regime focus on mediation between a scientific field and broader social interests. Operating in interstitial arenas, their identity is not linked to a discipline or to a particular employer.

> In addition, practitioners of the transversal regime do not detain themselves on institutional and cognitive boundaries. Their permanence within specialized groups lasts the time required for the importation of ideas and data necessary for the elaboration of new utensils; it also lasts as long as it takes to indicate . . . how to appropriate the fundamental principles of these technologies in order to adapt them as adequately as possible to their own needs.[17]

An example of a person working in such a regime would be Jesse Beams (1898–1977), a multi-institutional technical-instrumental researcher, inventor of the modern ultracentrifuge and other equipment, with diverse scientific interests and inventions that enabled cooperation between people from very different fields. Practitioners of this type are essential for the development of science, but their activity is neglected by historians and sociologists of science. They also contribute, in the process of "decontextualizing" and "recontextualizing" knowledge, carrying out what Shinn and Ragouet call "practical universality"[18] and using a kind of lingua franca between scientific fields and social spheres.

This recent sociology of science interests us because how work is carried out in the transversal regime between scientific microcultures operating at the borders of different scientific fields can shed light on the dialogue needed in the transversal regime between religion and science.

To avoid predation of one field on another, it is necessary that agents operating in transversal regimes are creative and parsimonious, cultivating what Roel Kuiper calls *social symbiosis*. This brings us closer to the central argument of this chapter: societies dedicated to the dialogue of religion and science are corridors of the transversal regime, dedicated to the construction

---

17. Shinn and Ragouet, *Controvérsias Sobre a Ciência*, 146.
18. Shinn and Ragouet, 153.

of symbiotic relationships between academic fields (such as theology and the sciences) and between social spheres (such as churches and the academy).

## Good in Science, for Science, and through Science

A way must be found to prudently manage the transverse porosity of scientific fields. To this end, we shall consider a key Mertonian idea: that it is necessary to protect the scientific ethos and the autonomy of the scientific field. However, we shall modify Merton's interpretation of what such an ethos is and what such an autonomy would be.

An important voice from the philosophy of science which can contribute to the discussion is that of the scientist and polymath Michael Polanyi (1891–1976). Polanyi's description of the personal nature of knowledge has immediate relevance to a critical review of the Mertonian scientific ethos, particularly regarding the excessive weight given by the sociologist to "organized skepticism" as a normative aspect of science. Polanyi shows the importance of the fiducial dimension in all cognitive experience and, particularly, in scientific activity. This idea has been widely explored in faith-and-science dialogue, especially by Thomas Torrance, the pioneer of Scientific Theology:

> It would be irrational to contrast faith and reason, for faith is the very mode of rationality adopted by the reason in its fidelity to what it seeks to understand. . . . In showing that all knowledge rests upon faith and develops under the guidance of a framework of belief, Michael Polanyi has much to offer us in elucidating the nature and functioning of faith in the understanding and life of Church today.[19]

The point of greatest interest to us here is the fact that Polanyi uses the language of the "purity" of science and, like Merton, is concerned with heteronomous interference with scientific fields. However, unlike Merton, Polanyi opened scientific activity up to the *tacit* dimensions of the cognitive gesture and spoke freely about the moral foundations of the scientific enterprise. He thereby integrates his thinking by circulating capitals from outside the scientific field.

---

19. Thomas F. Torrance, "The Framework of Belief," in *Belief in Science and in Christian Life: The Relevance of Michael Polanyi's Thought for Christian Faith and Life*, ed. Thomas F. Torrance (Edinburgh: Handsel, 1980), 10–11.

With exceptional strength and beauty, and with the combined authority of the scientific world and his experience of confronting the antiscientific impulses of communism and Nazism, Polanyi sought to unveil the sources of the scientific field beyond itself, in a way that is rooted in its life and its greatest values.[20] We now speak of *passions* and *loves*, and, therefore, of *goods*. If love is the supreme guide and the cohering force of various forms of coexistence and our common life, would it not also be an engine for the scientific community?

In this regard, it is appropriate to consider the Augustinian conception of society expressed in *The City of God*:

> But if we . . . say that a people is an assemblage of reasonable beings bound together by a common agreement as to the objects of their love, then, in order to discover the character of any people, we have only to observe what they love. . . . It will be a superior people in proportion as it is bound together by higher interests, inferior in proportion as it is bound together by lower.[21]

The British moral theologian Oliver O'Donovan borrowed the expression "our common objects of love" from Augustine as the title for his 2001 Stob Lectures,[22] in which he argued that human agents come together in communities of action and joint experience, supporting this over time, identifying and caring for common objects of love together. The things that we love and associate with them are what create communities. Augustine applied it to entire peoples, yet it can also be applied to modern social fields.

This is a feature of the most diverse forms of human association: families, parties, churches, universities, artistic collectives, neighborhood associations, professional societies, and so on – they all have centers of gravity that make us orbit around them. These centers of gravity are collectively recognized human goods, which can be affection, children, faith and religious traditions, science, poetry, the environment, culinary traditions, the education of children, a profession, and so on. We could also say that these goods loved by their corresponding communities constitute the ends of these communities. Thus, communities of love are also communities of purpose.

---

20. Michael Polanyi, *Personal Knowledge: Towards a Post-critical Philosophy* (Abingdon: Routledge, 1962).

21. Augustine of Hippo, *The City of God* 19.24. Translated by Marcus Dods (Edinburgh: T&T Clark 1913).

22. Oliver O'Donovan, *Common Objects of Love: Moral Reflection and the Shaping of Community; The 2001 Stob Lectures* (Grand Rapids: Eerdmans, 2002).

In addition to this "horizontal" distinction between types of association that deal with different human goods, establishing what we have called social spheres and fields, there is a "vertical" distinction, in terms of levels of responsibility. This tradition, of "gradual orders" of power, has one of its sources in Thomas Aquinas, finding its way into more recent thought through the encyclical letter *Rerum Novarum* by Pope Leo XIII (1891). Another source is Johannes Althusius, a political thinker of the sixteenth century, and one of the precursors of modern federalism. Althusius's ideas were renewed by the Dutch statesman Abraham Kuyper, who also wrote in 1891 on tackling social issues through a pluralist and symbiotic view of society.

According to pluralistic views of modern social structures,[23] spheres or fields of social life have their own autonomy – their own particular sovereignty – by virtue of their capacities, arts, and techniques for cultivating their own internal goods. It is this sovereignty which guarantees, for example, the right of parents to guide their children morally, or the sovereignty of the field of the arts against state control, or the autonomy of universities and the academic freedom of professors, or the relative autonomy of states in the federative system.

The different forms of community association, or spheres of social life, that are distributed between the individual and the state composing *civil society* should not be seen as submitted to the state, nor to the individual, but preserved as systems of a spontaneous order,[24] which emerge from natural human needs and from optimized and efficient practices of cultivation of different human goods, such as conjugal and family love, parenting, art, science, trade, and free enterprise. In this regard, the contribution of Polanyi in *The Logic of Liberty* is useful:

> When order is achieved among human beings by allowing them to interact with each other on their own initiative – subject only to laws which uniformly apply to all of them – we have a system of spontaneous order in society. We may then say that the efforts of these individuals are coordinated by exercising their individual

---

23. Manfred Svensson, "Subsidiariedad y Ordopluralismo," in *Subsidiariedad: Más Allá del Estado y del Mercado*, eds. Pablo Ortúzar and Santiago Ortúzar (Santiago: Instituto de estudios de la sociedad, 2015), 77–94.

24. D. M. Yeager, "Taylor and Polanyi on Moral Sources and Social Systems," in *Michael Polanyi and the Critique of Modernity: Pluralist and Emergentist Directions*, ed. Charles W. Lowney II (Cham: Palgrave Macmillan, 2017), 189–214.

initiative and that this self-coordination justifies their liberty on public grounds.[25]

Therefore, civil society becomes a symbiotic network of communities and fields, with shared responsibilities, with a dynamic structure that Polanyi calls "polycentricity."[26] In this perspective, the advance of civilization will be marked by a process of diversification, integration, and complexification, in which the subsidiary authorities in the various fields and levels of governance coordinate themselves by respecting their limits and competences, admitting the rules of the game of cooperation and competition, and contributing toward the common good. As for the state, its function would be supplementary and regulatory, measured by the capacity to stimulate and preserve the vitality of civil society.

Considered from the point of view of its ends rather than its methods, the scientific field can be seen as part of a larger movement of a people toward what they love: in other words, an ethical and spiritual law which engenders a spontaneous ordering process. Knowledge in general, scientific knowledge, and the various secondary goods necessary for attaining and cultivating fundamental goods would, as a whole, be a part of the garden for which people are summoned to plow and guard.

Now here we have a conception of scientific activity that seems to be compatible with Augustinian Christianity: that in some way we are what we love, and that we form communities around these objects of love. If love for the basic forms of good sets us in motion and has the power to bring us together in social life, can we find there the spiritual origin of the scientific institute itself?

The fact is that scientific fields, as subcommunities of our modern societies, have their own ends and internal goods, and contribute to society as a whole when they act in a fair and optimal way in the cultivation and pursuit of those ends. And these ends are no different from the objects of scientific passion noted by Polanyi. As early as 1945, in his article "The Social Message of Pure Science," he made clear the moral core of scientific life:

> We must reassert that the essence of science is the love of knowledge and that the utility of knowledge does not concern us primarily. We should demand once more for science that public respect and support which is due to it as a pursuit of knowledge

---

25. Michael Polanyi, *The Logic of Liberty: Reflections and Rejoinders* (Oxford: Routledge, 1951), 159.

26. Polanyi, *Logic of Liberty*, 170.

and of knowledge alone. For we scientists are pledged to values more precious than material welfare and to a service more urgent than that of material welfare.[27]

We have thus explicitly stated the love of knowledge as the essence of scientific life and perhaps as the missing spiritual component in the Mertonian description of the scientific ethos.

It is curious to think that not a few members of the academic community think that scientific activity itself should not have a definite moral character or relationship with "values," since scientists deal with "facts." However, the scientific institution does not exist abstracted from human reality, and could not have been established if it were not considered to be the bearer of some human good.

It is also curious that many sociologists, as well as scientists and philosophers of science, abstain completely from the language of goods, adopting one or another version of what Charles Taylor describes as "projection theories."[28] According to such theories, the language of goods has no correspondence with the order of reality, consisting only of symbolic systems designed by consciousness and culture. The popularity of these theories is unjustifiable, given their theoretical and operational unsustainability. For even in the defense of itself, projectivism is self-refuting. In science's search for self-reflection, it is essential that it recovers its own sources, which are unavoidably moral.

An important philosophical contribution that can help to clarify the spiritual rooting of the scientific sphere is that of the philosopher John Finnis, in his seminal work *Natural Law and Natural Rights*.[29] Finnis makes a distinction between, on the one hand, what we could call properly moral issues, referring to "right and wrong"; and, on the other, the basic forms of good, onto which such a debate of "right and wrong" does not fit, since the benevolence of such realities is universal and self-evident. Finnis presents a series of seven basic forms of good: life, knowledge, play, aesthetic experience, sociability, practical reasonableness, and religion.

The list could be extended, and there are also secondary goods associated with each of these basic forms of good. Finnis's position is that there are "countless objectives and forms of the good," but always based on their seven basic modalities. I would say that flow systems of symbolic capital necessarily

---

27. Michael Polanyi, "Social Message of Pure Science," in *Logic of Liberty*, 6.

28. Charles Taylor, *Sources of the Self: The Making of the Modern Identity* (Cambridge: Harvard University Press, 1989).

29. John Finnis, *Natural Law and Natural Rights* (Oxford: Oxford University Press, 1980).

revolve around basic forms of good and their associated secondary goods, and this can be a useful way to identify these goods a posteriori.

The most important point here is understanding that the pursuit of these goods is what allows the intentional unification of human action, creating communities of action identified with their common goods. Or, in Augustinian terms, love and social friendship around goods constitute human communities. This would be the deepest root behind the formation of spheres and autonomous social fields.

The first and most important example of the basic forms of good, to which Finnis devotes an entire chapter in his book, is knowledge. He does so to illustrate his point about the self-evident nature of these goods. Without needing to reproduce his argument here in full, the important point is to notice the way in which these goods energize human social life, acting as catalysts or centers around which human beings come together. Scientific knowledge is a specialized and secondary form of this fundamental good, and this factor is what gives internal and fundamental coherence to the scientific field. Polanyi states this clearly:

> The coherence of science must be regarded as an expression of the common rootedness of scientists in the same spiritual reality. Then only can we properly understand that at every step, each is pursuing a common underlying purpose and that each can sufficiently judge – in general accordance with other scientific opinion – whether his contribution is valid or not. Only then are the conditions for the spontaneous co-ordination of scientists properly established.[30]

In this sense, we could speak of a "scientific fraternity." This fraternity has its conditions of emergence, common interest, cultivation, and protection of such fundamental and inexhaustible goods. The other more "external" aspects of science, such as places of power, means of financing, and technological capital, do not share the same inexhaustibility and universality that is possible with pure knowledge. The limited nature of these external aspects generates the possibility of conflicting relations, which subdue the intrinsic interests of the scientific field.

It is the task of the scientific community to meditate on the means of managing the cultivation, protection, and distribution of their internal goods, without neglecting the role of historical capitals and the porosity of

---

30. Michael Polanyi, "Foundations of Academic Freedom," in *Logic of Liberty*, 39.

the scientific field with the flow of other forms of human capital. It needs to maintain the preeminence of its internal goods, while working to make its internal distribution of goods fair and effectively common.

This internal work of promoting love for internal goods and their accessibility by all members of the scientific community, in order to obtain a fair and altruistic economy in science, is the search for the common good within the community. This search is fundamentally moral and depends on another type of capital: *moral capital*. The fact that moral capitals are relevant to scientific activity is another illustration of the porosity of scientific fields in relation to transversal dynamics.

Christian philosopher and historian Roel Kuiper described this ideal condition of inclusive articulation of human communities as "shalom."

> When fundamental moral attitudes are anchored in social and cultural practices, then the common good must be seen as the result of the interaction between all these different practices. The common good is the dynamic result of everyone's work to promote public welfare. It is the very fabric to which each one adds a bit of thread. This public well-being is much more of a state than a material "good." I set out to always use the word "shalom" for that state. . . . The common good, therefore, is the result of an interrelation of different practices and the good they generate. By sharing that particular good and including one another, the common good arises.[31]

The porosity of scientific fields also involves a moral dimension, and moral capital is necessary to maintain the internal ethos of science and its healthy relations with other fields. Finally, the scientific community as a whole can also contribute to the common good of the whole of society as the sphere of science adds new threads to the social fabric. This addition is not only through the promotion of knowledge, but also through the promotion of the love of knowledge and the virtues and practices necessary for the production of knowledge. These are virtues that are cultivated within the scientific field, which then reverberate throughout the social body.

---

31. Roel Kuiper, *Capital Moral: O Poder de Conexão da Sociedade* [Moral capital: The connecting power of society] (Brasília, DF.: Monergismo, 2009), 245–46.

## The Idea of a Bridge Community

The insights presented up to this point seek to outline an architectural understanding of the social structure of the dialogue between religion and science as we conceived it in Brazil. With a Christian and Augustinian theological understanding of good and human goods, and theologically motivated *principled pluralism*, both in Catholic social doctrine and in the Kuyperian idea of "spheres of sovereignty," we sought to reread some contributions from sociology and the philosophy of science with strategic eyes.

At the beginning of this essay, we talked about *incarnation and presence*, also mentioning James Davison Hunter's seminal concept of *faithful presence*. If, as we think, the scientific field has these concrete structures, and the relationship between spheres and fields obeys the logic of universality, autonomy, porosity, and vulnerability that we have described, then the best way to carry out our mission would be to "incarnate" it in a concrete community. The mediation between religion and science would then be done by *a transversalist intellectual community*.

From this perspective, our purpose, going beyond the issue of knowledge production, was to constitute a bridge community. Such a community would be a kind of *transversal subfield*, occupied with mediating languages and linking, in a fruitful way, internal goods taken from scientific and religious fields.

The key to such a bridge community is *love*. First of all, love of God, in such a way as to enhance a positive attitude toward every human good, according to the *imago Dei* view of human beings. This purpose must be pursued consistently, in a pastoral and therapeutic way, as the first pathology of differentiation is exactly the identity one. It is important that every member of the bridge community keeps his or her spiritual center, and retains an awareness of the mutual relativity and interdependence of each sphere and field of modern life.

Next, this community must cultivate love through *faith* and *knowledge*, searching for continuous contact with these fundamental forms of good, recognizing the cognitive dimension of faith and the faith-based dimension of knowledge. This love should be translated by an acute and interested discernment and respect for the internal goods which ground each social field, both to protect churches from scientism and to protect science from fideism. It is a matter of ethos and the very logic of proper transversality. Such love will redirect people to genuine concern for the common good. However, such concern, while sorely needed, appears to be on the decline in many societies. In the case considered here, love will redirect people to caring for the proper and empirical common good of the social fields at stake.

This love will also fight to defend science in a number of directions: defending it from pseudoscience coming from religious fundamentalism, just as much as defending it from efforts to bring so-called "social justice" to science in ways which overwhelm the core scientific goods, ethos, and capital by excesses from historical political-ideological capital.

In harmony with the classical view outlined above regarding common good, the sharing of this basic love for knowledge should create opportunities for social friendship and companionship among participants. This concern was translated into our effort to establish not only study groups, but relationship and fraternity, as the safe moral and social nest for the bridge-building effort. In these contexts of interpersonal relationships and friendships, we hope to promote appropriate moral and intellectual virtues to guarantee intellectual progress and the strengthening of cooperative ties between people working in fields on both sides of the "river."

Furthermore, the wider love for each community and field is important, in order to facilitate the respectful recognition of the internal sovereignty of each sphere and field. It is necessary to love science and churches. Thus, we teach a commitment to the rejection of predatory attitudes, either from scientism about common religious life, or from fideism which risks corrupting the forms proper to scientific experience.

We should not forget two more forms of love. One is social friendship in the broadest sense: love for society, so that attention to the broader common good helps us to carefully consider the effective impact that the dynamics of religion and the dynamics of science have on the direction of society. The other is love for the larger spiritual community – in our case, the Christian community called "church," whose universal mission calls for the proclamation of the gospel and service to all people everywhere.

## Concluding Remarks

This chapter has attempted to describe the social theology and philosophy required to ground and orientate efforts to enhance differentiation and integration in modern society, specifically at the frontiers of faith communities and scientific fields. It sketches a proposed *theory of faithful presence in science*, explaining why the science-faith rapprochement should be done by bridge communities, embassies of meaning, incarnated and present within both contexts. It has both a sociological structural theory and a moral view of such structures, which could contribute to a social-theological ethics for science-and-religion dialogue.

## References

Augustine of Hippo. *The City of God*. Translated by Marcus Dods. Edinburgh, T&T Clark, 1913.

Hunter, James Davison. *To Change the World: The Irony, Tragedy, and Possibility of Christianity in the Late Modern World*. Oxford: Oxford University Press, 2010.

Illouz, Eva. *Consuming the Romantic Utopia: Love and the Cultural Contradictions of Capitalism*. Berkeley: University of California Press, 1997.

Merton, Robert K. "The Normative Structure of Science." In *The Sociology of Science: Theoretical and Empirical Investigations*, edited by Robert K. Merton and Norman W. Storer, 228–80. Chicago: University of Chicago Press, 1979.

O'Donovan, Oliver. *Common Objects of Love: Moral Reflection and the Shaping of Community; The 2001 Stob Lectures*. Grand Rapids: Eerdmans, 2002.

Paiva, Geraldo José de. "Itinerários Religiosos de Acadêmicos: Um Enfoque Psicológico." Diss., University of São Paulo, 1993.

Polanyi, Michael. *Personal Knowledge: Towards a Post-critical Philosophy*. Abingdon: Routledge, 1962.

Ribeiro, Darcy. "Prólogo." *Carta': Falas, Reflexões, Memórias: 1961–1995: A Invenção Da Universidade de Brasília* [1961–1995: The invention of the University of Brasilia] 14 (April 1995): 7–11.

Shinn, Terry, and Pascal Ragouet. *Controvérsias Sobre a Ciência: Por uma Sociologia Transversalista da Atividade Científica* [Controversies about science: Toward a transversalist sociology of scientific activity]. São Paulo: Editora 34 / Associação Filosófica Scientiae Studia, 2008.

Straw, Brad D., and Warren S. Brown. *Enhancing Christian Life: How Extended Cognition Augments Religious Community*. Downers Grove: IVP Academic, 2020.

Svensson, Manfred. "Subsidiariedad y Ordopluralismo." In *Subsidiariedad: Más Allá del Estado y del Mercado*, edited by Pablo Ortúzar and Santiago Ortúzar, 77–94. Santiago: Instituto de estudios de la sociedad, 2015.

Taylor, Charles. *Sources of the Self: The Making of the Modern Identity*. Cambridge: Harvard University Press, 1989.

Torrance, Thomas F. "The Framework of Belief." In *Belief in Science and in Christian Life: The Relevance of Michael Polanyi's Thought for Christian Faith and Life*, edited by Thomas F. Torrance, 1–27. Edinburgh: Handsel, 1980.

Yeager, D. M. "Taylor and Polanyi on Moral Sources and Social Systems." In *Michael Polanyi and the Critique of Modernity: Pluralist and Emergentist Directions*, edited by Charles W. Lowney II, 189–214. Cham: Palgrave Macmillan, 2017.

## Further Reading

Key themes and ideas on which this chapter draws and builds are outlined in the following works:

Bourdieu, Pierre. *Os Usos Sociais da Ciência: Por uma Sociologia Clínica do Campo Científico* [The social uses of science: A clinical sociology of the scientific field]. São Paulo: Unesp, 2003. Originally in French: *Les Usages sociaux de la science: pour une sociologie clinique du champ scientifique*. Paris: Éditions Quæ, 1997.

Dooyeweerd, Herman. "The Criteria of Progressive and Reactionary Tendencies in History." In *Christian Philosophy and the Meaning of History*, 47–66. Vol. 1, series B of *Collected Works of Herman Dooyeweerd*. Lewiston: Edwin Mellen, 1996.

Finnis, John. *Natural Law and Natural Rights*. Oxford: Oxford University Press, 1980.

Kuiper, Roel. *Capital Moral: O Poder de Conexão da Sociedade* [Moral capital: The connecting power of society]. Brasília, DF: Monergismo, 2009.

Polanyi, Michael. *The Logic of Liberty: Reflections and Rejoinders*. Oxford: Routledge, 1951.

Walzer, Michael. *Spheres of Justice: A Defense of Pluralism and Equality*. New York: Basic, 1983.

A collected survey of engagement with a variety of issues in science and religion, viewed from Latin American perspectives, can be found in the following:

Silva, Ignacio, ed. *Latin American Perspectives on Science and Religion*. London: Routledge, 2014.

Vanney, Claudia E., Juan F. Franck, and Ignacio Silva, eds. *Diccionario Interdisciplinar Austral* [Austral interdisciplinary dictionary]. Buenos Aires: Universidad Austral, 2015.

Book series on science and religion in Portuguese and Spanish:

*Coleção Fé, ciência e cultura* [Faith, science, and culture collection]. São Paulo: Thomas Nelson Brazil.

*Serie Ciencia y religión* [Science and religion series]. Bilbao: Grupo de Comunicación Loyola.

# 5

# Darwin's Dragons: 150 Years of Greek Orthodox Apologetics and the Challenge of Darwinism

Kostas Tampakis, National Hellenic Research Foundation, Greece
Efthymios Nicolaidis, National Hellenic Research Foundation, Greece

## Abstract

Darwin and Darwinism have acted as the historiographical lightning rod for science-and-religion discussions for over a century now. It is thus noteworthy that there is a relative poverty of historical studies on how Darwinism has been discussed and perceived in Orthodox Christian circles. The relative few that do exist usually focus on specific key events, such as the "first appearance" of an article on Darwinism or the first condemnation of the theory by conservative circles. This chapter adopts a different perspective: the negotiation of Darwinism in Greece provides an opportunity to discuss the rise of Orthodox Christian apologetics, from its first appearance in the nineteenth century to its more recent incarnation as a form of neo-Orthodox creationism.

## Introduction: The Draconic Features of Darwinism

> We are as ignorant of the meaning of the dragon as we are of the meaning of the universe, but there is something in the dragon's image that appeals to the human imagination, and so we find the dragon in quite distinct places and times. It is, so to speak, a

necessary monster, not an ephemeral or accidental one, such as the three-headed chimera or the catoblepas.[1]

Thus says J. L. Borges of the dragon, in the preface to his 1957 *Book of Imaginary Beings*. This image of inescapability may feel familiar to scholars interested in the field of science and religion. Surely, if there is a Borgesian dragon to be found in science and religion, then it is Charles Darwin. Studying how Darwinism and Darwinian evolution emerged, and how it was accepted, negotiated, confronted, or lamented in scientific discourse or generally in the public sphere, has been a staple of historical literature for decades. We will not attempt here to try to summarize the extensive case studies focusing on places as different as Japan, Egypt, Russia, or the USA.[2] There is, however, a basic narrative that seems to emerge time and again: Men of science – and it is always inevitably men – learn of Darwin's theory, either by correspondence, direct study of his books, or usually through French and German translations. Some of them start to teach and write about the new theory, enraging conservative and religious circles, which respond in tones ranging from indignant outrage to thoughtful critical discussion. In the meantime, revolutionary minded men of letters, or even political activists, embrace Darwinism for their own political and philosophical ends. In the end, after an intellectual generation or two, Darwinian evolution follows the rest of the natural sciences in their path toward academic autonomy and respectability and becomes another subject to be taught in the novel biological departments that appear in the 1950s and 1960s all over the world. Usually, the effort for inclusion in secondary education curricula all over the world is far more perilous and remains contested for far longer.

The narrative above, familiar as it may be, is not the one this chapter will explore. It is true that the history of evolution and its problematic encounter with Orthodox Christian states and populations is one that has not yet been written, though there have been some attempts for spaces such as Imperial Russia and the USSR, and to a lesser degree for Greece. Nevertheless, our aim is not to provide yet another account of "Darwin in . . . ," with the blank filled in with "Greece." Instead, our focus will be on the actors that are usually considered to be on the other side of the historical fence: theologians, members

---

1. Jorge L. Borges, *The Book of Imaginary Beings* (Harmondsworth: Penguin, 1969), 12.

2. Though we point the reader interested in such diverse stories to the following works: David N. Livingstone, *Dealing with Darwin: Place, Politics, and Rhetoric in Religious Engagements with Evolution* (Baltimore: Johns Hopkins University Press, 2014); Marwa Elshakry, *Reading Darwin in Arabic, 1860-1950* (Chicago: University of Chicago Press, 2019); and Peter Bowler, *Darwin Deleted: Imagining a World without Darwin* (Chicago: University of Chicago Press, 2013).

of the clergy, religious-minded scholars, but also to a lesser extent writers, poets, and political activists. We want to explore the complex relationships and contexts that facilitated or necessitated these responses, if we consider the fact that Greece has a culturally, socially, and politically very powerful autocephalous Orthodox Church, which has been recognized as the official state religion since the beginning of the Greek state.

## The Necessary Contextualization

In order to discuss Greek Orthodox apologetics, however, a brief historical contextualization is necessary. The history of the modern Greek state is, after all, not widely known. In 1821, a revolution against the Ottoman Empire by mostly Greek-speaking, Orthodox populations across the Balkans led to the establishment of Modern Greece in 1832. This became possible after the decisive interference of Russia, France, and Great Britain in 1827, which continued to play a central role in Greek politics for almost a century onward. The original state was half its current size and did not include many of the populations in Epirus, Macedonia, Thessaly, or the Aegean and Ionian islands. The underaged Bavarian prince Otto, second son of King Ludwig of Bavaria, was chosen to be the king of Greece and he became the monarch of the nascent state in 1832. He was accompanied by three vice-regents who ruled in Otto's name until he came of age. The Bavarian administration was determined to establish a centralized state apparatus on the model of Bavaria, thus creating tensions with local powerholders. Nevertheless, the Bavarian vice-regency founded a series of institutions such as the University of Athens, the Polytechnic School of Athens, an observatory, and a botanical garden, as well as a three-tier public education system. They also upheld the military schools that had been created before their time. These institutions, especially the University of Athens and, later, the Polytechnic School, acted as the loci for scientific practice in Greece. Being modeled on Bavarian archetypes, the university notably included a School of Theology, but not an autonomous school for the natural sciences. Chairs in the natural sciences belonged to the School of Philosophy and continued to do so as late as 1904. Meanwhile, King Otto had been deposed in 1862, and had been replaced by the Danish prince William of Schleswig-Holstein-Sonderburg-Glücksburg (1845–1913), who reigned as George I until his assassination in 1913.[3]

---

3. For a discussion of the relationship between science and education in Greece, see Konstantinos Tampakis, "Science Education and the Emergence of the Specialized Scientist

The aforementioned School of Theology, despite being autonomous, had a complex relationship with the Orthodox Church. Members of the clergy often distrusted the university in general and the School of Theology specifically. Over the school's history, many of its chairs were indeed held by archimandrites and bishops, but that did not deter conservative priests and monks from believing that the university was a veiled Protestant, foreign interference to Greek religiosity. Greek professors of theology had more often than not studied in German universities and were seen as attempting to inject foreign dogma into what was one of the pillars of Hellenism and national identity, Orthodox Christianity. Another notable development was that, during the reign of Otto, the Greek Orthodox Church became autocephalous. Orthodox Christianity consists of a fellowship of patriarchates, archbishoprics, and metropolises, in which the Ecumenical Patriarchate of Constantinople is considered first among equals, followed by the other three Ancient Patriarchates of Alexandria, Antioch, and Jerusalem. Matters of dogma can be discussed only by Church councils, but, other than that, each patriarchate and archbishopric is self-governing, albeit in communion with all others. Until 1833, the Greek Church was under the auspices of the Patriarchate of Constantinople. The Bavarian regency feared the political power that such a relationship gave the Ottoman Empire, and thus followed the advice of several notable Greek theologians and clergymen, unilaterally declaring the Church of Greece to be an autocephalous archbishopric in 1833. After a series of tense negotiations and two decades of strained relations, the Ecumenical Patriarchate of Constantinople recognized the new status of the Church of Greece in 1850. Since then, the Greek state and the Greek Church have developed a symbiotic relationship. The Greek Church wields considerable political and cultural power within Greece, with the help of the state, and, vice versa, the Greek state has often forcibly intervened in Church politics.[4]

Thus, Greece in the 1860s, when Darwin's ideas were published and quickly got translated across Europe, was a state with a powerful Orthodox Church, but also with a university in operation for less than thirty years which was nevertheless the first of its kind in the Balkans. It was also a state whose intellectual and cultural life was dominated by a multitude of journals and

---

in Nineteenth Century Greece," *Science & Education* 22 (2013): 789–805. For a more general overview, see Efthymios Nicolaidis, *Science and Eastern Orthodoxy: From the Greek Fathers to the Age of Globalization* (Baltimore: Johns Hopkins University Press, 2011), 169–92.

4. A more detailed discussion of this can be found in Kostas Tampakis, "High Science and Natural Sciences: Greek Theologians and the Science and Religion Interactions (1832–1910)," *Zygon* 54 (2019): 1067–86.

newspapers, and which underwent frequent political upheavals. It is in this milieu that Darwinian theories first appear in Greek space.[5]

## The Familiar Narrative

It was in these turbulent ideological, political, and intellectual times that the ideas of Darwin appeared in Greece: first privately and only afterward in public. Theodor von Heldreich (1822–1902) was one of the many experts who came to Greece with the Bavarian regency, but he had become Greek in all but name by the time he died. Having studied botany in Freiburg, Montpellier, and Geneva, Heldreich came to Athens in 1843. He published numerous works on Greek flora and, from 1851 onward, became the director of the botanical garden. Heldreich corresponded with Darwin in the 1870s and was one of his first adherents, but he published very little on Darwinian theories. The first public mention of Darwin in Greek intellectual circles was instead in an 1871 lecture given in the elite intellectual club Parnassos, based in Athens, but it did not seem to generate lasting impressions. In 1873, Leandros Dosios (1847–83), the reader in chemistry in the University of Athens, gave another lecture on Darwinian evolution in the same venue. Then a translation of Darwin's "Biographical Sketch of an Infant" appeared in the newspaper *Estia* in 1877. The author was Spiridon Miliarakis (1852–1919), at the time a medical doctor studying botany in the University of Würzburg on a state scholarship and later the professor of botany in the University of Athens. Inaugurating a tradition that would last for many decades, Miliarakis learned about Darwin's work through German translations and sources, and in fact his translation was based on an article in German first printed in *Kosmos*. In Greece, proponents and adversaries of Darwin and Darwinism would argue based not on the work of Darwin himself as it appeared in English, but rather on the secondhand appropriation and translation by German and French thinkers. In any case, Miliarakis would go on to write on Darwin sporadically until his death.

Just a year earlier, in 1876, the first, and in many ways the foundational, response to Darwinism appeared in Greece, from the lecturer in theology Spyros Soungras (1850–1906). His 260-page book called *The Newest Phase of Materialism, Darwinism, and Its Lack of Substantiation* was the first to deal exclusively with Darwinism, setting the tone and providing the

---

5. For a more typological history of the relations between science and Orthodox Christianity in Greece, see Kostas Tampakis, "Orthodoxy and Science in the Greek State, 1830–1939," *Almagest* 8, no. 2 (2017): 137–57.

argumentation for Orthodox polemics for half a century. Future Greek theologians and clergymen tacitly used this book as a source, to the point of reproducing the typographical errors of the original in their own work. Moreover, Soungras's book was the first which explicitly tied the Orthodox critique against Darwinism with the intellectual struggle against materialism, which would be the leitmotiv of most future Orthodox critique. Soungras used German and French sources for his book, and states in the introduction that he considers evolution a serious threat to social coherence. He goes on to discuss evolution in three axes: physiological, anthropological, and moral. On the purely scientific front, Soungras marshals arguments from Agassiz, Spencer, Bischoff, Virchow, and Humboldt, among others, and references recent articles, mostly in German. His work is remarkably erudite, but clearly polemical, and, at the time of its publication, made a concise attempt at bringing together the various critiques of Darwinism. Ultimately, however, Soungras has no intention of being evenhanded or fair, and he often misses the complexity of Darwinian arguments, or conflates Lamarckian with Darwinian and Haeckelian ideas. In his later, more philosophically minded book *Short Comments on Faith and Science*, in 1885, Soungras once again briefly mentions Virchow and du Bois-Reymond but also Pasteur and Liebig to conclude that it is only when scientists try to create "new religions" based on spurious hypotheses that science seems to combat faith.

In the years 1875 to 1895, the discussions and debates on Darwinism in Greece were at their most heated. In the aftermath of the Crimean War and the Don Pacifico Affair of 1849–50, when French and British troops had blockaded the harbor of Piraeus and incidentally caused an outbreak of plague, Greek public opinion had slowly turned against the Guardian Powers of 1821. Many intellectuals came to believe that foreign cultural influences were suspect and could pollute what they saw as the Greek national soul. Darwinian evolution was seen as one more ploy of Western materialism, which could further such alienation. At the same time, a new generation of intellectuals and people of science would see in Darwinian thought, filtered as it appeared in Greece through French and German lenses, a way to free themselves of mystical Orthodox misconceptions. The professor of physiology in the University of Athens, Ioannis Zohios (1840–1912), discussed evolution in his lectures in 1880, in a class that soon became wildly popular. More conservative-minded students, as well as several professors from the Faculty of Theology, accused Zohios of being disrespectful toward Orthodox Christianity, but cooler heads prevailed and Zohios pledged not to overstep the bounds of his expertise by talking about religion. The Faculty of Theology, for its part, refused to file a complaint that would seem to dictate what a fellow professor should or should not teach. In the end, the matter was resolved amicably in the University Senate. Some of the students were less easily appeased, however, with one of them, Ilias Liakopoulos, publishing a pamphlet in 1880 which accused Zohios of providing "spiritual gunpowder" to students barely mature enough to comprehend what they were hearing. Another turning point was the appearance in 1886 of the journal *Anaplassis*, published by the religious organization of the same name, which had as one of its main goals to battle the prevalent materialism and atheism of its era. The editors of the journal became embroiled in a very public battle against another neophyte journal, *Prometheus*, one of the first scientific journals in Greece, whose editor was the respected professor of geology Konstantinos Mitsopoulos (1846–1911) and to which several younger intellectuals and men of science contributed. *Prometheus* published some of the first translated articles about Haeckel and for Haeckel, and many of its contributors were enthusiastic about evolution. *Anaplassis* took up the gauntlet and a series of heated polemical articles ensued. It is in *Anaplassis* that the second pioneer of Greek apologetical writing appeared, Ioannis Skaltsounis (1821–1905). A lawyer by training who had studied in Pisa, Skaltsounis was a prolific writer who published four books and many dozens of articles on the subject of the natural sciences vis-à-vis Orthodox Christianity. Alongside those of Soungras, Skaltsounis's arguments – an eclectic but well-informed collection of scientific refutations, ethical exhortations, and Orthodox reasoning – became the basis of much of the anti-Darwinian rhetoric of Greek conservatives until the 1940s. Michael Galanos (1862–1948), a lawyer, politician, and founding member of *Anaplassis*, also wrote extensively on the subject through a number of articles, but his attacks focused rather on materialism and thus by extension on Darwinism. Nevertheless, his writings are indicative of the general consensus among conservative writers, namely that Darwinism was a stepping stone toward materialism and Haeckelian monism, and thus to be fought at all costs.

A special case was that of Apostolos Makrakis (1831–1905), a charismatic, religious, and popular scholar who was initially welcomed by the Greek Orthodox Church but later condemned as a heretic. Makrakis wrote more than forty books and ended up going against what he saw as a corrupted church and a nation that was being seduced by Western, non-Greek, and non-Christian ideas. From his journal *Logos* he published extensively in 1891 against the ideas of Haeckel, at least as he was being presented in *Prometheus*. Makrakis's polemic does not really try to engage with the scientific evolutionary ideas and is instead based on biblical sources. Makrakis's writings were part of a reactionary push toward a nationalistic definition of Greekness that would shy away from Western ideas and influences.

## Intellectuals and Activists

Darwinism, even negotiated through German and French writing, had a small but significant influence on Greek poets and literary men and women, and, later on, to leftist intellectuals. Emmanuel Rhoides (1836–1904), a powerful iconoclastic writer and journalist, wrote in 1871 about how in 1863 he got "immersed in the theories of the Darwinian school," and how the theories of Vogt, Büchner, Darwin, and Lamarck had become his "inseparable companions." Rhoides cites the revelation that natural history could explain mechanistically the descent of humankind as a powerful factor turning him away from Orthodox Christianity and toward a critical, at times materialistic, viewpoint. Rhoides was not alone in this journey. In fact, many of the most famous Greek novelists and poets at times mentioned or implicitly referenced Darwinism as the crucial factor turning them away from "naïve Christianity" and usually toward Nietzsche and often, later on, to an idealistic spiritualism. Kostas Palamas (1859–1943), by far the most influential Greek poet of his time and an intellectual mentor to several younger men of letters, also flirted with Darwinism before turning to Nietzsche. Nikos Kazantzakis (1883–1957), of *Zorba the Greek* and *The Last Temptation of Christ* international fame and three-time nominee for a Nobel Prize, had a somewhat similar intellectual trajectory. Kazantzakis was in fact the translator of the first Greek edition of Darwin's *Origin of Species* in 1915.[6]

From 1890 to 1910, there was also a partial appropriation of Darwinism by Greek reformers and intellectuals. From the 1880s onward, the questions around proper Greek language had become dominant. Greece had adopted as its official language the so-called *katharevoussa*, an artificial language based on the grammar of Ancient Greek and a vocabulary purged of all Turkish and Slavic words. However, *katharevoussa* was far removed from the *demotiki*, the vernacular, everyday language used by most of the Greek population, and soon became a linguistic barrier that separated the educated from the uneducated. A fierce debate, driven by nationalistic feeling and rhetoric, had been raging

---

6. The most detailed history of Darwinism in Greece is Kostas Krimbas, Ο δαρβινισμός στην Ελλάδα [Darwinism in Greece] (Athens: Institute of Historical Research / National Hellenic Research Foundation, 2017). The reception and cultural impact of Darwin is discussed in Maria Zarimis, *Darwin's Footprint: Cultural Perspectives on Evolution in Greece (1880–1930s)* (Budapest: Central European University Press, 2015).

for decades about which language could express the essential Greekness of the nation. Those who favored the vernacular were often the same people who supported social reforms. Alexandros Delmouzos (1880–1956) was a pioneering educator who tried to reform Greek education during the first decades of the twentieth century. Delmouzos was in favor of the vernacular language and was actually involved in several high-profile trials concerning his language beliefs, as well as his reputed atheism and the fact that he supported Darwinism. Delmouzos had come into contact with Haeckelian ideas during his studies in Jena. A notable event was the Volos school trial, or the *Atheika*, as it soon came to be called. The case, one of the very few examples where the Greek Church took an official and active part in a science-related debate, began with the introduction by Delmouzos of new teaching methods in the Greek schools. In 1908 Delmouzos was appointed director of the girls' school in Volos, where he encouraged critical thinking among the students. These novel ideas disturbed conservatives, who tried to get rid of what they considered dangerous anarchists by organizing demonstrations. These became so heated that the cavalry was forced to intervene to defend the school and Delmouzos's house. The municipal council of Volos eventually decided to close the school in 1911 and prosecute Delmouzos and his collaborators. The trial took place in the town of Nafplion, with the prosecutors accusing Delmouzos and his collaborators of advocating for atheism. The theory of evolution was cited:

> In various periods, from September 1908 until the end of March 1911, in Volos and in Larissa, principally at the Workers' Foundation and the School for Girls in Volos, they [the accused] teaching out loud or with the aid of printed brochures, tried to proselytize in favor of so-called religious dogma, i.e. atheism. These actions are incompatible with the preservation of the political order, for they teach that God does not exist. . . . , that man was created from monkeys, that God is a cucumber, etc.[7]

The Holy Synod of the Church of Greece was directly implicated in the trial, but the accused were acquitted for lack of proof some years later.[8] An intellectual contemporary of Delmouzos, George Constantinidis (1878–1919),

---

7. The quote is from the published transcripts of the trial, Η δίκη του Ναυπλίου *(16–28 Απριλίου 1914)*, Στενογραφημένα πρακτικά [The Trial of Nafplio (April 16–28, 1914), Abridged Minutes] (Athens: Vasilleiou, 1915), 3.

8. The incident is discussed in Vasilios Makrides, "Secularization and the Greek Orthodox Church in the Reign of King George I," in *Greek Society in the Making, 1863–1913: Realities, Symbols and Visions*, ed. Phillip Carabot (London: Routledge, 2018), 179–96.

who worked under the pseudonym George Skliros, was one of the first Greek socialist intellectuals. He was the first to try to analyze Greek society using Marxist tools, and also used Darwinian ideas. We can observe a similar trajectory of Darwinian encounters with Dimitris Glinos (1882–1943), an educational reformer and close associate of Delmouzos; and with Constantinos Hatzopoulos (1871–1920) and Alexandros Papanastasiou (1876–1936), who were leaders of the Greek social movement. From the 1910s onward, Darwinism would add "association with Marxism" to its many intellectual sins in the eyes of conservative and reactionary Greek intellectuals.

The emergence of a socialist and communist movement in Greece led to a renewed discussion of Darwinism, this time as an intellectual component of Marxism. Despite the actual ambivalence of Marx vis-à-vis Darwin and vice versa, Greek apologists and conservative intellectuals were firm in the associating and jointly condemning the two theories. Some of the most prominent religious and conservative scholars, such as the so-called "Lion of Orthodoxy," Panagiotis Trempelas (1866–1977), and the professor of theology in the University of Athens, Gregorios Papamichael (1875–1966), wrote treatises denouncing historical materialism and, in passing, Darwinism. Most of their arguments were against the association of early Christian practices of communal life with the socialism of Marx and his followers, but Darwinism was a secondary but omnipresent theme. On another track, conservative scientists such as Thrassivoulos Vlissidis (1886–1964), the first professor of biology in the University of Athens in 1939, wrote books and articles defending Darwinism by arguing that, in fact, the Darwinian struggle for life disproves Marxism. Interestingly enough, and despite the protestations of conservatives, actual Greek Communists were more ambivalent regarding the use of Darwinism for revolutionary thought. Athena Gaitanou-Gianniou (1880–1952), a pioneer Greek feminist and socialist, wrote *Lamarck-Darwin-Marx: The Descent of Man and His Evolution in Society* in 1916 with the explicit goal of teaching Communists about evolution. Nevertheless, she writes that "Greek socialists should know that our opponents often try to turn Darwinism against us, and we should be able to respond,"[9] and also that "Haeckel, Ernst is a bourgeois philosopher who tried to turn Darwinism against socialism."[10] Not only was Darwinism a two-edged sword, as Vlissidis would go on to argue twenty years later, but Haeckel was no friend of Communists either.

---

9. Athena Gaitanou-Gianniou, Η καταγωγή του ανθρώπου και η εξέλιξη στην κοινωνία [The Origin of Man and Evolution in Society] (Athens: Socialist pages, 1910), 33.

10. Athena Gaitanou-Gianniou, Η καταγωγή του ανθρώπου, 45.

In 1937, the Christian Union of Scientists (CUS) was founded, under the aegis of the powerful religious organization Zoe (Life). From that point on, the Christian Union of Scientists and its journal *Aktines* (Rays), first published in 1938 and still in print, was at the forefront of anti-evolutionary and more generally anti-Communist discussions in Greece. In their manifesto – published in 1946: just after the end of World War II and at the beginning of the Greek Civil War of 1946–49 – the CUS saw the neglect of Orthodox Christian religion as the root of all recent national evils. The manifesto also proclaimed the harmony between Christianity and modern science. The manifesto itself was signed by most of the Greek professors of the natural sciences of the time; nevertheless, the apologetics developed by *Aktines* soon reappropriated the outdated rhetoric of Soungras and Trempelas.

Although written in the political context of anti-communism, the Christian Union of Scientists' manifesto did not expressly condemn communism, or dialectical materialism. The manifesto took up the values of spirituality and work, and denounced materialism, monism, and Freud. Unlike the values of the Orthodox traditionalists, the CUS's manifesto emphasized the importance of science for society: "Science is discouraged everywhere and the scientist has long ceased to be a leader in society or be honored as such," declared the manifesto.[11] According to the CUS, the spiritual decadence of humanity in general, and specifically of the Greeks, stemmed from the negation of spiritual values in general and of Christianity especially. Christianity was "the foundation of our modern society" and it was thus a tragedy that atheism was not "a singular deviation but the foundation of civilization." The CUS aimed to reconcile science and religion by citing recent discoveries that were not in contradiction with Christianity. In particular, CUS's manifesto declared that physics did not contradict the creation of the world by a pre-existing, eternal Supreme Being. Nor did physics contradict the existence of a spiritual world that does not obey the laws of matter.

Concerning evolution, the CUS's manifesto did not condemn Darwin himself but his epigones, and especially Ernst Haeckel. The manifesto declared,[12]

> We should at first notice that Darwin's theory in its pure and original aspect did not have any of the meaning that was later attributed to it, meaning the automatic creation by chance of

---

11. Christian Union of Scientists, Δια κάθε Έλληνα- Διακήρυξις της Χριστιανικής Ενώσεως Επιστημόνων [For every Greek – The Manifesto of the Christian Union of Scientists] (Athens, 1946). Translations are by the authors.

12. Christian Union of Scientists, Διακήρυξις, 33–40.

the world and especially of man, with no divine creative force. [Darwin,] as a scientist, knew how to limit his imagination. Nevertheless, others like Huxley in England and Vogt and Haeckel in Germany, who did not actually do scientific work but propagandized through popular editions, utilized this theory for their own purposes. At this time, the effort at atheist propaganda in the name of science was at its height.

The goal of the manifesto was to show that science refuted evolution by arguing that the transformative evolution of Lamarck was not corroborated by the paleontological findings, since intermediate types had not been found, and that Darwin's natural selection could explain the disappearance or conservation of species, but not their creation. Concerning the origin of humankind specifically, the CUS's manifesto made a distinction between Darwin and the popularization of his work by the "atheists" who used the existence of *Pithecanthropus* as proof of the filiation of human beings to the apes. Arguing against the existence of this so-called *Pithecanthropus*, it supported the idea that paleontological findings point only to degenerate human races. The Swedish geneticist Nils Heribert-Nilsson, who doubted evolution, was abundantly cited.

It is clear that the manifesto, although it made no direct allusion to communism, was a political response by Orthodox Christians to the materialist ideas propagated by the Communist Party camp, which at the time was embroiled in the Greek Civil War. The civil war and the strong-arm republic that followed would dig a chasm between the "left" and "right" camps that would last for almost thirty years. The fact that the manifesto was signed by committed evolutionists such as the professor at the Agricultural University of Athens Vasos Krimbas (1889–1965) shows how deep and powerful the political division of the era was. In 1950 Krimbas was accused by the Orthodox fundamentalist Avgoustinos Kantiotis (1907–2010) of being an enemy of Orthodoxy and was depicted with a tail and pointed ears signing the CUS's manifesto. Krimbas was elected a member of the Academy of Athens in 1960, and Kantiotis became metropolitan of Florina in 1967.

The manifesto had no effect on the teaching of evolution in the faculties of science and, in 1961, Kostas Krimbas (1932–2021), son of Vasos Krimbas and collaborator of the renowned geneticist Theodosius Grigorovich Dobzhansky, was elected professor of genetics at the Agricultural University of Athens and director of the university's Genetics Laboratory, becoming, at the age of only twenty-nine, one of the youngest ever professors in Greece. Nevertheless, the

Faculty of Theology continued to insist on an anti-evolutionist line. In 1969, during the dictatorship of the colonels after the coup d'état of 1967, Dobzhansky was invited to a conference of the Greek Anthropological Society. This Russian-born geneticist was taken aback by the attacks of Greek theologians, including university professors, who protested against the idea that humankind might descend from beasts because that would be in contradiction with the book of Genesis. Dobzhansky protested as a scientist, as well as a member of the Eastern Orthodox Church, that he was supporting humankind being created in the image of God – *via* the process of evolution.

## Schoolbooks and the Greek Church

The plurality of institutions and movements, which is a characteristic of the Orthodox Church and a result of not having a centralized international authority, translated into many and contradictory positions regarding creationism. For the Greek Orthodox Church, the highest governing body is the Holy Synod of the Greek Church, which is constituted by the metropolites, or bishops. It takes major decisions and elects the archbishop. Within the Holy Synod, a whole range of ideas are represented, from fundamentalists who believe in a six-day creation to those who would accept evolution under certain conditions. Nevertheless, the Holy Synod so far has avoided making official statements on subjects related to science, including evolution. Various religious fraternities are backing some of the groups within the synod. Members of the synod often express their own views publicly, ignoring the declarations of the archbishop on the subject, as happened recently in connection with his call for vaccination against COVID-19.

The fact that the Greek Ministry of Education is also in charge of the Church, and that all clerics are public servants, as well as the fact that the Church possesses extensive real estate, are strong arguments for avoiding conflict with those in political power. This is the main reason why the Church has avoided taking an official position when a problem has arisen with science, including discussion about creation and evolution, and instead put forward its friends and supporters, or its most combative metropolites.

In 1977, the geneticist Kostas Krimbas coauthored with his collaborator Giannis Kalopisis a secondary-education biology textbook which presented evolution. When the book was published, the Ministry of Education received many telegrams condemning the fact that "young Greeks were taught that they descend from beasts."[13] Some years later, in 1984, during the first Greek socialist government of Andreas Papandreou, the Ministry of Education and Ecclesiastical Affairs introduced to secondary education the book *The History of the Human Race*, written by the Greek-Canadian historian Lefteris Stavrianos (1913–2004). It presented humans as a result of the evolutionary process. The book was soon attacked in the press by a very wide range of people. Departing from its cautious attitude toward the state, the Holy Synod asked officially that the book be removed from schools. Questions were raised to the minister from political parties on both the left and the right, and protests were organized by the official Church and associations closely affiliated with it. One of the leaders of the protest was the metropolitan of Florina, Avgoustinos Kantiotis, who fought ferociously for the book's retraction. Facing such hard protests, the ministry was forced to react. In its reply, the ministry carefully balanced support for scientific evidence and concern for its constituency by noting that there have been previous mentions of the topic in other textbooks, and that any textual confusions will be clarified in subsequent editions.

The book was eventually withdrawn in 1990, under the right-wing government of Konstantinos Mitsotakis.

## The Metropolitans of Piraeus: Natural Selection or Holy Providence?

The teaching of evolution in schools and especially Stavrianos's book – which was not a biology book but a book about global history – was also fiercely attacked by another influential metropolitan, Kallinikos of Piraeus (1926–2020). In 1973, during the Colonels' regime, the future archbishop of Greece Christodoulos (1937–2008) founded with Kallinikos the Christian fraternity Chrysopigi. This fraternity fought against the teaching of evolution and materialism, and especially against Marxism. (During the Cold War the majority within the Greek Church feared that if Marxists prevailed, they would abolish Church structures and support atheism.)

In his book *Man from Monkey? Reply to the Materialist Thesis*, Kallinikos presents the fraternity's views on creation, evolution, and materialism; relates evolution to Marxism; and attacks Stavrianos's book.

> Marxism is not only an economic, social, and political system, it is a materialist and atheistic theory; its basis is in historical

---

13. The episode was recounted by Prof. Krimpas in an interview about science and religion hosted by Project SOW: "Κώστας Κριμπάς: Επιστήμη και Θρησκεία," (Kostas Krimbas: Science and Religion) 2 August 2019, YouTube, https://www.youtube.com/watch?v=WQwyBCI_NR8/.

materialism and that is why it is contrary to the Christian idea of life.... Now, the materialists strike mercilessly at anything that is related to God and the Church. And they forge myths, like that of the origin of man from the monkey, which they propagate by any means possible.... Defenseless children are poisoned by [Stavrianos's] book. They learn to disrespect the teaching of the Holy Scripture which says that man is a special creation of God, that he is the coronation of the Creation of God, that he belongs to two worlds, the celestial and that of this earth, that he has been fashioned in God's image.... Duane Gish, Doctor of Biochemistry of the University of Berkeley of California, says: "The theory of evolution has not a greater prestige than that of the biblical explanation as far as it concerns the origin of species. If we compare the events of the versions (of Bible and Darwin) we can verify that the discourse of the Holy Bible has greater validity."[14]

Kallinikos went on to found the Piraeus Association of Scientists in 1993, dedicated to fostering nationalist and anti-evolutionary ideas. Christodoulos was appointed archbishop in 1998 and, owing to his strong personality combined with powerful rhetorical talents, he enjoyed great popular success. Backed by Chrysopigi, Christodoulos continued to promote conservative ideas. As an archbishop, he protested publicly and strongly when Greek identity cards were reissued to not mention religious affiliations. He soon found himself at odds with the Ministry of National Education and Ecclesiastical Affairs, but also with the socialist government, something that previous archbishops had tried to avoid. His premature death in 2008 and succession by the moderate Ieronymos II marked the end of this particular Church-state controversy. Ieronymos II, like most of his predecessors, has avoided interfering in any open way in matters of education and the sciences.[15]

Seraphim (originally named Christos Mentzelopoulos), born in 1956, has been metropolitan of Piraeus since the retirement of Kallinikos in 2006. An active propagator of anti-homosexual and anti-Semitic opinions, Seraphim published in 2012 the book *The World: Evolution or Creation? Chance or*

---

14. Kallinikos, *Man from Monkey? Reply to the Materialist Thesis* (Athens: Chrysopigi, 1987), 5.

15. Another aspect of vehement reaction against Darwinism in modern Greece can be seen in Efthymios Nicolaidis, "Creationism in Today's Orthodox Community," *Almagest* 12 (2021): 208–26.

*Incomprehensible Aim? Natural Selection or Inconceivable Holy Providence?* We read on the website of the Metropolis of Piraeus:

> His holiness Metropolitan of Piraeus Seraphim wishes to contribute to the countering of the atheist propaganda which uses without any shame the science which is a gift of God.... [For this] he publishes on the web and also in print for free the collection of themes and conceptions that overthrow the atheist propaganda of the media.[16]

The book has a dedication to the "ecumenical father Basil" for his sermons on the *hexaemeron* (the six days of creation), and its first chapter is about ideas of evolution before Christianity. Seraphim laments that "unfortunately, some of our ancestors the Ancient Greeks believed in evolution," but fortunately "the best among them, such as Pythagoras, Socrates, Plato, and Aristotle did not believe in this foolish theory."[17] The second chapter presents ideas about evolution from the rise of Christianity until the end of the Middle Ages, and Seraphim is all too happy to announce to the reader that faith in the Christian worldview led to the eradication of belief in evolution from almost all the known world. Following that faithful period, from Paracelsus to Darwin and up to our day, the theory of evolution was revived. However, he says, great savants from all scientific fields, from the period of Lamarck and Darwin and since then, have overwhelmingly demonstrated with unbeatable arguments that this theory is absolutely unfounded. Seraphim lists two and a half pages of names of such scientists, most of them dating from around the end of the nineteenth and the beginning of the twentieth century, together with numerous citations. Despite this almost unanimous condemnation of evolution, and although people in many countries lament the catastrophes this theory has caused ("psychological and social, because historical materialism is the fruit of evolution theory"), this theory is propagated in "this glorious country [Greece], the motherland of true philosophy and science."[18] But the fact that humans have a spiritual soul demonstrates the unfounded nature of the theory of evolution. This spiritual soul is the means to control sexuality, which is strong in the construction of the human body. Having demonstrated that evolution is unproven and unfounded, Seraphim discusses in the last chapters of the book

---

16. "Ανακοινωθέν" (Announcement), 20th September 2012, Metropolitan of Piraeus, https://www.impantokratoros.gr/9C8C00CA.el.aspx.

17. Seraphim, *The World: Evolution or Creation? Chance or Incomprehensible Aim? Natural Selection or Inconceivable Holy Providence?* (Piraeus, 2012), 8.

18. Seraphim, *The World*, 42.

the unfounded belief that chance led to the appearance of life on earth. For him, science has demonstrated that the appearance of life is impossible without a holy design. The same is also valid for the human body, which is perfectly designed by God. Seraphim describes in detail all the parts of the body and he is impressed by the perfection of their conception. The book concludes with a presentation of the harmony of the material cosmos, in which reigns an unbelievable mathematical order but also necessity.

Seraphim founds his assertions on science, citing scientists and philosophers from Plato to Max Planck. His sources are mainly articles of science popularization in journals and outdated books such as *Dieu et Science* (Paris, 1912) by the Russian-French physiologist Elie de Cyon or *Nuclear Reactor Engineering* by the British physicist Samuel Glasstone (1897–1986). He also abundantly cites the book *Freemasonry and Theosophy* by the well-known Greek theologian Panagiotis Trempelas, who was active in the first half of the twentieth century.

Although they may have some influence on the traditional Greek flock, the ideas of Seraphim are not shared by the majority of Greek theologians. Unfortunately, there are no recent reliable polls for Greece concerning science-and-religion beliefs, such as evolution. The most recent one dates from 2005; in that poll 25 percent of the sample claimed to believe in creationism.

## Epilogue

In discussing the Western dragon specifically, J. L. Borges says,

> A tall-standing, heavy serpent with claws and wings is perhaps the description that best fits the Dragon. It may be black, but it is essential that it also be shining; equally essential is that it belch forth fire and smoke. The above description refers, of course, to its present image; the Greeks seem to have applied the name Dragon to any considerable reptile.[19]

Once more, the description seems eerily familiar. Greek scientists, scholars and intellectuals, revolutionaries, reactionaries or conservatives, proponents or opponents, seem to have applied the name "Darwinism" to any considerable evolutionary theory. Haeckel and later Büchner were considered at one time to be more Darwinian than Darwin, but later socialists cast them outside while religious scholars continued to rally against them. Lamarck was seen as

---

19. Jorge L. Borges, *The Book of Imaginary Beings*, 152.

a preferable precursor to Darwin, but was then also forgotten. Finally, issues of language and national identity quickly became paramount in discussing Darwinism, not only for poets and novelists, but also for members of the clergy, Communist revolutionaries, and cautious men of science. For all of the above, Darwin did indeed "belch forth fire and smoke," but even in their most heated debates they rarely agreed on what that fire and smoke signified, why, or how. The official Greek Orthodox Church, with all its cultural might and social gravitas, rarely – if ever – condemned Darwinism specifically. In fact, most of the discussions and debates were taken up by religious organizations and parachurch groups, and usually by theologians, not members of the clergy. We are thus forced to conclude that, as far as Orthodox Christian apologetics are concerned, Darwinism has been a moving target, but one that is being moved mostly by the apologists themselves.

## References

"Ανακοινωθέν" (Announcement). 20th September 2012. Metropolitan of Piraeus. https://www.impantokratoros.gr/9C8C00CA.el.aspx.

Bowler, Peter. *Darwin Deleted: Imagining a World without Darwin*. Chicago: University of Chicago Press, 2013.

Elshakry, Marwa. *Reading Darwin in Arabic, 1860–1950*. Chicago: University of Chicago Press, 2019.

Kallinikos, *Man from Monkey? Reply to the Materialist Thesis*. Athens: Chrysopigi, 1987.

"Κώστας Κριμπάς: Επιστήμη και Θρησκεία." Interview with Prof. Krimpas about science and religion hosted by Project SOW. 2 August 2019, YouTube. https://www.youtube.com/watch?v=WQwyBCI_NR8/.

Livingstone, David N. *Dealing with Darwin: Place, Politics, and Rhetoric in Religious Engagements with Evolution*. Baltimore: Johns Hopkins University Press, 2014.

Makrides, Vasilios. "Secularization and the Greek Orthodox Church in the reign of King George I." In *Greek Society in the Making, 1863–1913: Realities, Symbols and Visions*, edited by Phillip Carabot, 179–96. London: Routledge, 2018.

Nicolaidis, Efthymios. "Creationism in Today's Orthodox Community." *Almagest* 12 (2021): 208–26.

Seraphim, *The World: Evolution or Creation? Chance or Incomprehensible Aim? Natural Selection or Inconceivable Holy Providence?* Piraeus, 2012.

Tampakis, Kostas. "Orthodoxy and Science in the Greek State, 1830–1939." *Almagest* 8, no. 2 (2017): 137–57.

———. "Science Education and the Emergence of the Specialized Scientist in Nineteenth Century Greece." *Science & Education* 22 (2013): 789–805.

## Further Reading

The historical relations between Orthodox Christianity and the natural sciences is a field that has only recently been examined coherently. The most concise description can be found in the following book:

Nicolaidis, Efthymios. *Science and Eastern Orthodoxy: From the Greek Fathers to the Age of Globalization*. Baltimore: Johns Hopkins University Press, 2011.

An overview with a slightly different focus can be found in the following:

Nicolaidis, Efthymios, Delli Eudoxie, Livanos Nikolaos, Tampakis Kostas, and Vlahakis George. "Science and Orthodox Christianity: An Overview." *Isis* 107, no. 3 (2016): 542–66.

For discussion of how Greek theologians approached the natural sciences in the nineteenth century, see:

Tampakis, Kostas. "High Science and Natural Sciences: Greek Theologians and the Science and Religion Interactions (1832–1910)." *Zygon* 54 (2019): 1067–86.

Specifically for the negotiation of Darwinism in Greece, there is the excellent book by the pioneer evolutionary biologist and historian of Darwinism Kostas Krimbas, which unfortunately at present exists only in Greek:

Krimbas, Kostas. Ο δαρβινισμός στην Ελλάδα [Darwinism in Greece]. Athens: Institute of Historical Research / National Hellenic Research Foundation, 2017.

For Darwin's literary and cultural impact, see:

Zarimis, Maria. *Darwin's Footprint: Cultural Perspectives on Evolution in Greece (1880–1930s)*. Budapest: Central European University Press, 2015.

Finally, an abundance of scholarship on Orthodox Christianity and science has emerged from the Science & Orthodoxy around the World project (http://project-sow.org/), which has been operating since 2012 under the aegis of the Institute for Historical Research of the National Hellenic Research Foundation.

# 6

# Of Science, Religion, and Culture: An African Reflection

Bernard Boyo, Daystar University, Kenya
Samuel M. Karenga, Mount Kenya University, Kenya
Peter G. Kirira, Mount Kenya University, Kenya

## Abstract

The interaction between science and religion takes place within the prism of a cultural grid that differs from context to context. Diverse African contexts place high value on culture that defines and shapes life and living. In Africa, every aspect of life, beliefs, and practices, as well as natural and supernatural realms, is all-inclusive. Religion is thus embedded within the core of African societal existence. Africans are generally pragmatic regarding the sustenance of the whole community, meaning that science is practiced with the aim of contributing to communal well-being. This chapter will discuss the significance of the wholeness of human life for the African person, hinging on the perspective of the integration of science, religion, and culture.

## Preamble

As a continent Africa comprises diverse people groups whose beliefs, mannerisms, and cultural practices are distinct and different. Through family ties and bonds of socialization from generation to generation, traditional values have been passed on and have helped shape psychosocial and religious beliefs, as well as societal perceptions and practices. Despite such cultural variances, these groups hold in common a holistic view of life where the physical (visible) and the spiritual (invisible) arenas of life, while distinguishable, cannot be separated.

This view of life implies that there is no gulf between what is considered sacred and what is considered secular, since all aspects of life, in their entirety, are intrinsically intertwined.

> The "sacred" or spiritual presents one of the predominant ways many Africans think about and/or shape their world. Traditional religion(s) were often oriented around the divine, or sacred, and permeated all facets of life. They focused on how the spiritual affects such "mundane" realities as agricultural cycles, birth, death, and developments within the community.[1]

The African holistic view of life is embedded within the African philosophy of life. A clear manifestation of this perspective is the conceptualization of an individual's identity which is intricately connected with the whole community. In this sense, an individual's identity is not just associated with, but finds meaning and value in relation to, the whole community. It is through the link with the whole that an individual person (*mtu*) manifests personhood (*utu*), which gives one acceptance and honor, or disdain. Essentially, then, the saying "mtu ni watu" (a person is people) is akin to the *ubuntu* philosophy of life, which John Mbiti explains as "I am because we are and because we are therefore I am."[2]

It is also worth noting that pragmatism, rather than theory, characterizes African life in general. This is clearly seen in the context of poverty and sustenance of life, when the search for that which works to address current situations of need is of such significance. But underlying this is the fact that life is viewed as a whole, with every aspect being interrelated. This can be seen in the way in which the question of God is not primarily an academic venture but a practical one.

Belief in God is embedded in society, and therefore a high sense of the reality of the spiritual realm and its interaction with the human sphere is common. Among the Kikuyu people of Kenya, for instance,

> belief in God (*Ngai*) and in the ancestral and departed spirits was the fundamental basis of life as a Kikuyu. Any person who lost his faith in the religious beliefs of the Kikuyu ceased to be a

---

1. Gregg A. Okesson, "Sacred and Secular Currents for Theological Education," *Africa Journal of Evangelical Theology* 26, no. 1 (2007): 40.

2. John Mbiti, *African Religions and Philosophy* (New York: Frederick A. Praeger, 1969), 141.

Kikuyu to all intents and purposes, and became an outcast. Law and order depended more upon religious beliefs than upon the police activities of the *njama* (warrior's council), or the judicial authority of the *kīama* Council of elders.[3]

These threads of intertwined ideas – which, even when distinct, remain inseparable – still run throughout African thought today: the visible and the invisible, the sacred and the secular, the individual and the community, religion and the practical functioning of society. Some scholars write about indigenous African worldviews in the past, as if this is no longer the dominant view in Africa. However, to this day, these worldviews provide the context in which we find people living and seeking to make sense of all aspects of life, with the joy and sorrow that it brings.

## Definitions of Terms

Before we embark on discussing the relationship between science, religion, and African culture, it is important to give some operating definitions of terms for this chapter.

### Science

The term "science" relates to the process in which people acquire knowledge of the natural world through empirical means. This entails a sustained observation and analysis of phenomena, of mega and minute components of nature and of life.

Science was practiced in traditional Africa, although there was no specific term for it as we have it today. The traditional practice of science was done through observation of events and phenomena over a period of time in an attempt to describe, understand, predict, and control nature. It typically adopted an inductive approach that involved long periods of observing patterns, experimentation, and generalizations.

Different African communities had their own ways and means of acquiring and applying knowledge. Some communities engaged natural processes such as fermentation for preparation of foodstuffs and brewing; others used designated animals to predict seasons; still others utilized skills in arts and

---

3. Richard Leakey, *The Southern Kikuyu before 1903*, vol. 1 (Nairobi: Intra-Lab Services, 2007), 16–17.

crafts for construction and production of objects and tools of trade. There were those who were skilled in medical-related knowledge of natural means that included healing practices. This indigenous knowledge was transmitted orally, experientially, and undocumented across generations.

A common feature of all such endeavors in the traditional African context is that they were geared toward the enhancement of life and the well-being of the community, as well as addressing the challenges that the community encountered.

## *Religion*

In a general sense, "religion" is understood to be human social and cultural activity involving veneration of certain natural or supernatural entities as objects of reverence or worship. It is an ontological phenomenon that relates to the debate on being, discerned in terms of beliefs, ceremonies, rituals, artifacts, and practices. In traditional Africa, religion was communal, embracing all individuals. It permeates all arenas of life, encompassing "people's hearts or spirits, minds, oral history, rituals, and religious personages such as priests, rainmakers, officiating elders, and kings."[4]

## *African Culture*

African cultures, like any other human cultures, involve many aspects of the people's existence. These include actions, mannerisms, behaviors, and beliefs, as well as physical and intellectual feats. Culture is manifested through art and literature, artifacts, dance and music, clothing, drama, styles in building houses, social organizations, political systems, values and ethics, religion, customs, morals and philosophies, institutions, and laws, along with economic life.

The diversity of African peoples implies that there are many varied and distinct cultures manifested among Africans across the continent. While each people group may reflect commonalities in the way they share values and beliefs, they still retain their individual uniqueness. The sharing of values helps create bonds of unity for each of the cultural units in a way that differs from one group to another. In this sense, then, we cannot talk of common African values, much as these may be positive. Indeed, in considering religious expression, culture is often driven by the diversity found across Africa, rather than by the unity of African cultures. This may explain why there is no sense of

---

4. Mbiti, *African Religions*, 5.

"Africanism" that might be compared to, for example, American identity, where people are defined more by their Americanness than by their relationship to their individual state. Despite such diversity, there is nonetheless a distinctive characteristic across African cultures, which is the holistic nondichotomization of all the dimensions of life and living.

It is vital to underscore the fact that African culture has evolved through time. A brief historical overview is important at this juncture to illuminate the trajectory of African culture, especially in view of the influence of Western culture through colonialism.

## Historical Overview
### Precolonial Africa

As already noted, life in Africa is holistic. From time immemorial religion, culture, and science have been inseparable. The precolonial period gives us a view of a continent that was characterized by diverse ethnic ties which were fluid and flexible: where individuals or whole communities could be assimilated into other ethnic groups; adopt and adapt their practices, beliefs, and values; and easily blend in and become amalgamated.

While each group of people living in specific African regions had different socioeconomic systems of survival and sustenance based on their locality and environment, African tribes were generally subsistence farmers, hunters, or gatherers. A number of those who were pastoralists moved from one region to another in search of pasture and safe havens. The land was expansive, and population flow and migration from one region to another was common. Hodgson notes, for example, that the early Maasai-speaking tribes practiced small-scale agricultural farming and raised livestock. A later pastoralist group emerged and took advantage of "material, political, cultural, social, and ecological changes."[5] In this context, the need for survival was a driving force that caused occasional interethnic conflicts.

Regarding religion, Africans generally believed in a supreme being who transcended the natural world and who was in control of all forces of nature. This supreme being was identified variously among the different African peoples, based on their perception of his interaction with them, particularly his providential works of benevolence. The names given to the supreme being were descriptive of his work of creation. For instance, the supreme being is

---

5. Dorothy Louise Hodgson, *The Church of Women: Gendered Encounters between Maasai and Missionaries* (Bloomington: Indiana University Press, 2005), 7.

called *Mawu*, meaning "creator," in the West African Ewe language of Ghana; *Oludumare*, "the one entrusted with creation," in the Yoruba language of Nigeria; *Qamatha*, a name given to the Creator God in the Xhosa language of South Africa; and *Ngai*, meaning "the divider" or "one who divides" with reference to creation, in the Kikuyu language of Kenya. Humans – indeed all creatures – were perceived to have derived from the creative work of the supreme being.

There was also cultural engagement with the downward side of life: suffering, sickness, and death. In most traditional African cultures, for example, sickness was not seen as incidental, but believed to be brought about by the negative forces of life, which included witchcraft, sorcery, curses, and spells.

In an attempt to address these negative forces, different cultures utilized diverse healing practices depending on the nature of the sickness. In West Africa, for instance, bonesetting – which may correspond to modern-day chiropractic, osteopathy, and physical therapy – was practiced by many tribes such as the Akan, Mano, and Yoruba. Inoculation against such diseases as smallpox was well known among the Akan of West Africa, while immunization against diverse diseases was common across all African communities. The Bunyoro of Uganda had traditional surgeons who treated lung inflammation and pleurisy by piercing holes in the chest until air flowed freely. Before modern medicine and surgery, trephining was done, and depressed fractures were elevated. Serious wounds resulting from wars were treated and surgical procedures were successfully performed.

Many other scientific skills used today, though now modern and more sophisticated, were utilized during precolonial times. Food preservation techniques involving salt, honey, and smoking the food were commonly practiced and continue today across African cultures. Africans also had traditional wineries for brewing liquor through fermentation.

Many technological discoveries and practices that predate modern science were also alive in precolonial Africa. Fishing was common in several African communities. Boat-making and the building of canoes and small reed-based vessels was widespread. Moreover, it was the Egyptians who developed the first 365-day, twelve-month calendar through studying the stars.

These examples indicate that, while there may not have been specific African expressions by which science was defined, it would be misleading for us to assume that science never existed in its functionality and operatives. Some scientific discoveries were almost incidental and based on, for example, deductive reasoning, observation of patterns, and individual creativity. Such practice of scientific knowledge was found among African peoples in diverse contexts, even where intercommunication for transfer of knowledge was limited or absent. All these precolonial endeavors that characterize African traditional values were geared toward making life easy and focused on communal welfare rather than individual gratification or aggrandizement.

## *Colonial and Postcolonial Africa*

The influx of Western imperialism and the European domination of Africa, along with the Western missionary enterprise, had an immense impact on Africa. Notably, though, the influence of Western Christianity did not abate the worship of the supreme being in Africa. Africans who converted to Christianity amalgamated their newfound faith with local concepts and the traditional nomenclature of their deity. Religion was, and always has been, the fulcrum around which every activity revolves in Africa. Over the years, and since the introduction of missionary Christianity, religion has influenced culture while science has made inroads into cultural and religious beliefs and practices. This has created tensions, although Africans in general still hold to the holistic view of life where religion can never be separated from science and culture.

Modern scientific knowledge has, however, influenced some traditional beliefs and practices. For instance, the causes of diseases are now attributed to pathogens, natural causes such as exposure to radiation, certain foods, weather changes, and such things as lack of sleep. Nonetheless, there is also still the belief that sickness may result from broken relationships with one's kinship and family or even the ancestors. It is therefore not uncommon to find people going beyond the biological causative agents of diseases to cultural and religious factors in search of a cure for sickness and disease.

## *Contemporary Issues*

The discussion about whether – and how – science, religion, and culture can coexist harmoniously has gained currency lately. It has been accentuated by various conflicts in thinking, such as regarding tetanus and polio vaccinations and, most recently, in connection with COVID-19.

In 2003, the polio immunization drive in Northern Nigeria was halted as religious and political leaders addressed fears that the vaccines were deliberately laced with antifertility agents and the HIV virus. The tetanus boycott of 2014, led by the Catholic Church of Kenya, started when Catholic bishops campaigned against the tetanus vaccine administered to women of reproductive age, claiming that it was laced with contraceptives in the form of human chorionic gonadotropin (hCG). The government ordered an independent analysis before the controversy eventually fizzled out. In 2015, the Kenyan Catholic bishops were once again up in arms against the polio vaccine campaigns and demanded that the vaccines be tested first. The government gave in and postponed the program for a couple of months to allow for further discussion and testing. Similar forms of resistance have been experienced in other parts of Africa.

The COVID-19 pandemic prompted major efforts to look for preventative as well as curative healing. In Madagascar, for instance, the government promoted and distributed a herbal tonic, Covid-Organics, which President Andry Rajoelina claimed could prevent and cure the disease.

The establishment of associations like the Christian & Scientific Association of Kenya (CSAK) has played an important role in creating forums that allow the debate on synergy or conflict between science and Christianity to go on outside the purview of emotive controversies.

## Healing in Africa

Among the major challenges facing Africans today are poverty, limited access to education, and sickness. Sickness is a perennial problem that causes untold suffering due to lack of access to proper treatment. Consequently, many people employ diverse healing methods, involving witchcraft, traditional medicine and healers, and modern and Western healing, as well as seeking divine intervention through prayer and ecclesiastical practices. In many African communities, as people seek solutions not only to the effects but also to the causes of illness, biomedical (Western) and traditional medicine are not seen as being in conflict, but rather as going hand in hand. As Leakey notes from a historical perspective,

> Among the Kikuyu, ill health and diseases of many kinds were attributed to a variety of causes, some medical and some magical. Thus, treatment depended not only on the physical diagnosis, but on which power was thought to be the agent of the illness. Six principal causes of ill health were recognized: infectious epidemic diseases, infectious non-epidemic diseases, natural causes, influence of angry departed spirits, witchcraft (*ūrogi*), and the breaking of taboos.[6]

---

6. Richard Leakey, *The Southern Kikuyu before 1903*, vol. 2 (Nairobi: Intra-Lab Services, 2007), 888.

As a matter of fact, "by no means were all of the diseases that European science would class as epidemics regarded as *mūrimū* by the Kikuyu . . . due to the fact that the Kikuyu and European conceptions of disease differed greatly."[7] Among the diseases classified as infectious epidemic were *Mūtūng'ū* (smallpox), *Mūthandūkū* (chicken pox), *Mūthūūkū* or *Githūūkū* (measles), and *Mūngai* (mumps). For each of these, there was a clearly defined method and process of identification and treatment which necessitated skill and expertise.

While the decision to use either a Western or a traditional healing system differs from person to person, the influences of culture, history, personal attitudes, and philosophy are significant. It should however be observed that an appropriate "integration of biomedicine, Traditional healing, Western medicine (integrative approach) can yield extensive results in healing the physical body and psychological illnesses if applied in a knowledgeable manner."[8]

The use of traditional medicine is enhanced by the exposure and expertise of many African peoples in their knowledge of curative herbs, leaves, roots, bark, grasses, and bulbs. Such knowledge pertains to the value and benefits of different types of medicinal plants for various ailments and how they are administered without the use of modern technology. Herbal drugs are taken in different forms, such as ground to a powder, chewed, or boiled and the solution smeared on the body. While physical means are often used, healing is not limited to physical symptoms. In African traditional healing,

> the healer deals with the complete person and provides treatment for physical, psychological, spiritual, and social symptoms. Traditional healers do not separate the natural from the supernatural, or the physical from the spiritual. This will cause them to address health issues from two major perspectives – spiritual and physical.[9]

This knowledge of healing practices, as noted by Gunda among the Shona people,[10] was passed on from father to son, while others received their

---

7. Leakey, *Southern Kikuyu*, vol 2, 888.

8. Edward Shizha and John Charema, "Health and Wellness in Southern Africa: Incorporating Indigenous and Western Healing Practices," *International Journal of Psychology and Counselling* 3, no. 9 (2011): 167–75.

9. Peter White, "The Concept of Diseases and Health Care in African Traditional Religion in Ghana," *HTS Teologiese Studies/Theological Studies* 71, no. 3 (2015): Art. #2762, 3.

10. Masiiwa Ragies Gunda, "Christianity, Traditional Religion, and Healing in Zimbabwe: Exploring the Dimensions and Dynamics of Healing among the Shona," *Swedish Missiological Themes* 95, no. 3 (2007): 229–46.

knowledge from their ancestral spirits through dreams and visions. As such, there is no formalized knowledge of traditional medicine in many societies, as

> it largely remains in the non-codified folk knowledge form. Diversity, collective ownership guided by customary laws, adaptability to changing contexts and oral transmission are some of the prominent characteristics of this knowledge. Unlike common understanding, it is highly dynamic thus contemporary and not pertaining to a period in time. While knowledge generation and transmission might vary with cultures, there are several similarities in the value systems and modes of transmission of knowledge among communities.[11]

## Religion and Healing

Given the holistic nature of African thought, it should be no surprise that religion and healing are intertwined. Many aspects of this relationship are positive, leading to close positive connections in African culture between religion and healing practices. However, the interrelations also lead to clashes where religious concerns or objections can be raised against medical practices, of both Western medicine and traditional medicine.

### Religion and Healing Go Hand in Hand

As we have seen, the holistic perspective of life in most African cultures means that the spiritual and physical arenas of life are intrinsically intertwined, and that all aspects of life are inescapably connected to religion. Professor John Mbiti insisted that "Africans are notoriously religious,"[12] a much-noted and variously interpreted assertion. As such, the use and efficacy of traditional medicine is not just for physical purposes but has far-reaching spiritual implications.

There is great debate about the nature of the diversity of religious expressions among African communities. According to David Barrett, for instance, Africa's religious heritage rapidly succumbed to the missionary advances of Christianity and Islam. In 1982 he postulated that, by the end of the twentieth century, Africa would be divided more or less evenly between adherents of

---

11. Unnikrishnan Payyappallimana, "Role of Traditional Medicine in Primary Health Care: An Overview of Perspectives and Challenges," *Yokohama Journal of Social Sciences* 14, no. 6 (2009): 59.

12. Mbiti, *African Religions*, 1.

Christianity and adherents of Islam.[13] In retrospect, this postulation seems to have been accurate, as is demonstrated by the current religious divide between Christianity and Islam in Africa. Whether in indigenous traditional or exotic religions, Africa is portrayed as one of the most religious continents in the world. This religiosity has contributed to the manner in which virtually all aspects of life – and especially health and wellness – are perceived. As observed by Leakey from a historical perspective,

> religion held each family together, united the inhabitants of every village, bound together the inhabitants of the various villages of a territorial unit, and gave them the cohesion that was essential to their mutual security. If the inhabitants of different villages in a territorial unit lost touch with each other and became too independent of one another, the wrath of God visited them and persisted in punishing them until they became united once more by joint acts of public worship and sacrifice.[14]

Most African communities believe that healing is a religious phenomenon encapsulating all spheres of life. Belief in magical or mystical powers has often played a major role in determining human existence, thus placing religion at the core of human wellness and healing.

An important aspect that characterizes the use of traditional medicine in Africa is the affinity to cultural beliefs and practices with the attached symbolism and spiritual value of traditional healing. This, as Robert Wyllie suggests, appears to "serve a legitimating function in a culture which, despite modernizing influences and changes, is still heavily infused with religious and magical values and perceptions."[15] For this reason, there needs to be an ongoing interaction between modern and scientific developments and traditional practices and beliefs in matters of health and healing. Provision of health care is not just a one-dimensional venture that focuses on mere physical health, since human well-being involves the totality of a person in all aspects – spiritual, social, psychological, mental, emotional, and so on.

---

13. David B. Barrett (ed.), *World Christian Encyclopedia: A Comparative Survey of Churches and Religions in the Modern World AD 1900–2000* (Nairobi: Oxford University Press, 1982), 789.

14. Leakey, *Southern Kikuyu*, vol. 1, 17.

15. Robert W. Wyllie, "Ghanaian Spiritual and Traditional Healers' Explanations of Illness: A Preliminary Survey," *Journal of Religion in Africa* 14, no. 1 (1983): 57.

## *Challenges of Engagement with Western Medicine*

As pointed out above, lack of easy access and affordability of medicine and treatment is a major determinant of the health practices and processes that people engage in. Although Western medicine is readily available, the cost is prohibitive for a majority of Africans, who resort to using alternative sources of healing.

Although biomedicine has been a great remedy for the sorry state of health in Africa, there remains a major gap in its effectiveness and acceptability, mainly due to social and emotional factors. Deeply rooted cultural beliefs and practices also continue to dominate the individual and communal lives of people. Those still entrenched in these practices consult traditional experts for healing in addition to conventional medical care and medicine.

The need for healing in Africa leads to an increase in the use of nonscientific modes of healing among certain communities in Africa, particularly the poor who are quite often taken advantage of by malevolent proponents of the prosperity gospel.

## *Challenges of Engagement with Traditional Medicine*

While modern development in science and advances in Western medicine are increasingly providing relief, both research and practice indicate that the majority of Africans revert to traditional cultural practices of healing. Studies on the use of herbal medicine indicate that

> although, over time, Traditional medicine had suffered a declining reputation, and some Christians altogether deprecate the use of any form of medicine, traditional or Western, at present, substantial transformations are taking place in Africa in the practice of traditional medicine and many educated Africans now supplement Western with Traditional medicine.[16]

Among Christians, there is a strong ambivalence regarding the use of nonbiomedical medicine. There are those who believe that it contravenes the tenets of Christianity. For example, Ayoola states that "Christian doctrines usually condemn alternative medicine as a means of curing ailment. The use of herbal medicine seems not to be encouraging to the Christian practice, due to the belief that it has attachment to occult powers . . . those who are

---

16. Olusayo Bosun Oladejo, "Herbalism, Healing and Health: Developing a Biblical Attitude," *Ogbomoso Journal of Theology* 18, no. 1 (2013): 165–66.

involved in it are never seen to be Christians."[17] Such concerns and objections notwithstanding, many Christians continue to use traditional medicine for healing purposes. Evidently, many Christians in contemporary Africa have not severed major ties to their ancestors or the spirit world in general. Though they are Christians, they persist in traditional healing rituals. These commonly involve the use of herbs, leaves, bark, or roots of trees, though some rituals may involve animal sacrifice. Acculturation: A Direct Effect of Modernization Acculturation is a process that is defined as cultural modification of an individual, group, or people by adapting to or borrowing traits from another culture. The coming of Europeans to Africa and the attendant occupation heralded "cultural infiltration, pollution as well as alteration."[18] The most fundamental change was the gradual breakdown of the African view of wholeness, in which culture incorporated religion and science, to viewing them as distinct. For example, the missionaries introduced the practice of weekly communal worship in churches for all. This departed from the traditional worship ceremonies that were done in special shrines by only a few revered elders. The places of worship became symbols of religiosity. In addition, schools were introduced that brought formal learning and introduced alien language, dress, and science. The indigenous communal and apprenticeship education system gradually lost currency. The introduction of hospitals that managed all health conditions with modern medicine departed from the African practice of associating diseases with both the natural and the supernatural.

The African philosophy of wholeness was therefore in collision with the Western form of thinking and practice. Gradually, Africans embraced some of the new cultural elements, and abandoned some long-held traditions. As Sibani observes, "either by design or accident, Africans have imbibed the Western culture and have appropriated it so much that it now becomes almost part and parcel of their lives."[19] From a cultural viewpoint, we view this transformation in the following ways:

---

17. Abiola A. Precious Ayoola, "Alternative Medicine and Healing from a Christian Perspective," *Ogbomoso Journal of Theology* 18, no. 3 (2013): 41.

18. Adegbite Tobalase, "Masculinity and Cultural Conflict in Chinua Achebe's *Things Fall Apart*," *International Journal of English and Literature* 7, no. 6 (2016): 81.

19. C. M. Sibani, "Impact of Western Culture on Traditional African Society: Problems and Prospects," *Journal of Religion and Human Relations* 10 (2018): 57.

## Cultural Alterations

Some of the new cultural elements that were embraced led to alterations in indigenous cultural practices. Examples include adoption of new languages, religious practices, dress, education systems, and naming practices (where the first name is now usually foreign).

## Cultural Persistence/Tolerance

In other cases, some African cultural practices withstood the onslaught of modernization and were tolerated within the new cultural dispensation. Examples include initiation rituals, customary marriage practices, and burial rituals.

## Cultural Alienation

Some of the African cultural practices were infiltrated and eroded by modernization. While some pockets of these practices may still be in existence, they are usually carried out discreetly and are generally frowned upon. Typical examples include female circumcision, human sacrifice, polygamy, wife inheritance, infanticide, and witchcraft.

While acculturation affects the detail of cultural practice, the process also takes place at the level of the grand structure of thought. The theme of the holism of African thought, of the intertwined nature of ideas, has run consistently through this chapter. However, despite traditional African thought having little time for a sacred-secular divide, the sacred-secular divide is now common, not only in Kenya, which is a predominantly Christian country, but also in other parts of the continent. The debate has elicited a variety of views with "serious questioning and rethinking . . . occurring both in the sacred and secular side of the divide."[20] The sacred-secular divide is primarily a Western construct whereby religion and family issues are relegated to the private realm.

There are, however, voices such as Stuart Kaufmann[21] who recommend a deep connection between the natural world and religion, as well as partnership between the realm of science and religious values. This indicts as unwarranted the simplistic and reductionist understanding of the division between the two.

---

20. David Kim, David McCalman, and Dan Fisher, "The Sacred/Secular Divide and the Christian Worldview," *Journal of Business Ethics* 109, no. 2 (2012): 204.

21. Stuart A. Kauffman, *Reinventing the Sacred: A New View of Science, Reason, and Religion* (New York: Basic, 2010).

This shows that acculturation can be resisted, and even when ideas change because of outside influence, those changes are not irreversible.

## Healthy Interactions of Science, Religion, and Culture

It is clear from the above observations that the area of health and healing provides opportunities for engagement at the nexus of science, religion, and culture. It is also clear that this engagement must be navigated carefully as the interactions are also potentially fraught with difficulties. In this section, we discuss how such interactions might be successfully navigated, and what must be taken into account in achieving this.

We have noted that a distinct characteristic of the African context is the diversity of its cultures, with resulting effects on African life and – more significantly – African political history. Each context has its own history and tradition, based on the culture the people have grown up in. This shapes every aspect of their way of life and their thinking patterns. For this reason, the link between religion and science in Africa must have an understanding of the context in which traditions and cultures and the various other aspects that define a people's existence emerged.

The different cultures that characterize African peoples have also contributed to the diversities in religious beliefs and the uptake of developments achieved by science. There are those, for instance, who shun scientific processes such as blood transfusions, genetically modified foods, immunization, or vaccinations because of their religiocultural beliefs. While it may be argued that these diverse cultures are the embodiment of the wealth of African traditions, it is important to note that they could also be the genesis of retrogression in other areas that pertain to sustainability in terms of human survival and well-being. An authentic theology of politics must be relevant to the culture and its dynamics of change and evolvement.

The diverse cultures cannot simply be ignored, or pressed too rapidly to change. Within African thought is an underlying belief that culture is God-given and cannot be abandoned without betraying one's heritage and divine destiny. Even with significant advances, care and sensitivity should be exercised in choosing what medicine to use. It is also important to note the impact of sin and the fact of living in a fallen world which may explain the genesis of sickness and death. As Oladejo postulates,

> Christians need to accept the fact that although God has power to heal all diseases and sicknesses, at any time He chooses, using

whatever method He wills, He works generally in consonance with His nature and revealed truth. Every form of the use of herbs that contradicts the Bible should be critically questioned.[22]

As with any other Christian practice, a clear exegetical analysis of scriptural passages should be used to ascertain the use or nonuse of traditional medicine. This indicates that common sense and God-given wisdom and knowledge should not act contrary to scriptural teaching, whether on the nature and character of God or the exercise of human freedom and liberty.

Healing extremism and cultural fundamentalism can be detrimental to both science and religion. Such detrimental positions can be avoided by finding ways in which science, religion, and culture can converge in discourse and in practice. The results of a survey on the use of traditional medicine, carried out among the Maasai tribe of Kenya, concluded that "the integration of science, religion, and culture is entrenched in a people's way of life."[23] The survey demonstrated that science and religion can be integrated. In particular, this can be achieved through practices that affirm the many people who, because of their inability to access medical facilities, opt for traditional cultural knowledge which uses readily available materials to remedy ailments. One example of this is where science, by utilizing plants to produce biomedical substances, can help ascertain the viability of ethnomedicine for Christians in the African context. In this sense, an appropriate dialogue between science, religion, and cultural practices in the African context can provide for holistic healing.

## Conclusion

African thought is holistic, in that one can make a distinction, but not a separation, between the sacred and the secular, the individual and the community, and religion and the practical functioning of society. Science, even if not by that name, has existed in Africa alongside religion from time immemorial, and has always been directed toward enhancing life and the well-being of the community.

In traditional African beliefs, God was placed at the center of everything. Every aspect of life, including the environment, seasons, calamities, and other events, could be interpreted with reference to God. Religious beliefs and practices were part and parcel of African culture. As such, they were part

---

22. Oladejo, "Herbalism," 165–66.

23. Bernard Boyo, *The Integration of Science and Religion in Traditional Healing (Ethno-Medicine) and Faith Based Healing* (St. Louis: Society for the Scientific Study of Religion, 2019).

and parcel of medicine and healing practices, in which science – whether in its modern or traditional African forms – plays a significant role.

When Christianity was introduced to Africa, it did not override such holistic views, but rather was fruitfully integrated with them. There is therefore a continuity of thought between modern Christianity in Africa, the traditional practice of science, traditional religious practices, and traditional healing practices. All these perspectives bring a richness and a complexity to the application of Western healing in African contexts.

Traditional medicine has much to offer in the African context, as does Western medicine. Christian engagement with these areas is inseparably intertwined with the cultural history of the continent as a whole, and with the specific cultural and political history of each place. It is necessary to understand this complexity, and, as we have argued in this chapter, doing so is both possible and fruitful.

## References

Ayoola, Abiola A. Precious. "Alternative Medicine and Healing from a Christian Perspective." *Ogbomoso Journal of Theology* 18, no. 3 (2013): 41–54.

Barrett, David B., ed. *World Christian Encyclopedia: A Comparative Survey of Churches and Religions in the Modern World AD 1900–2000*. Nairobi: Oxford University Press, 1982.

Boyo, Bernard. *The Integration of Science and Religion in Traditional Healing (Ethno-Medicine) and Faith Based Healing*. St. Louis: Society for the Scientific Study of Religion, 2019.

Gunda, Masiiwa Ragies. "Christianity, Traditional Religion, and Healing in Zimbabwe: Exploring the Dimensions and Dynamics of Healing among the Shona." *Swedish Missiological Themes* 95, no. 3 (2007): 229–46.

Hodgson, Dorothy Louise. *The Church of Women: Gendered Encounters between Maasai and Missionaries*. Bloomington: Indiana University Press, 2005.

Kauffman, Stuart A. *Reinventing the Sacred: A New View of Science, Reason, and Religion*. New York: Basic, 2010.

Kim, David, David McCalman, and Dan Fisher. "The Sacred/Secular Divide and the Christian Worldview." *Journal of Business Ethics* 109, no. 2 (2012): 203–8.

Leakey, Richard. *The Southern Kikuyu before 1903*. 2 vols. Nairobi: Intra-Lab Services, 2007.

Okesson, Gregg A. "Sacred and Secular Currents for Theological Education." *Africa Journal of Evangelical Theology* 26, no. 1 (2007): 39–64.

Oladejo, Olusayo Bosun. "Herbalism, Healing and Health: Developing a Biblical Attitude." *Ogbomoso Journal of Theology* 18, no. 1 (2013): 164–75.

Payyappallimana, Unnikrishnan. "Role of Traditional Medicine in Primary Health Care: An Overview of Perspectives and Challenges." *Yokohama Journal of Social Sciences* 14, no. 6 (2009): 57–77.

Shizha, Edward, and John Charema. "Health and Wellness in Southern Africa: Incorporating Indigenous and Western Healing Practices," *International Journal of Psychology and Counselling* 3, no. 9 (2011): 167–75.

Sibani, C. M. "Impact of Western Culture on Traditional African Society: Problems and Prospects." *Journal of Religion and Human Relations* 10, no. 2 (2018): 56–72.

Tobalase, Adegbite. "Masculinity and Cultural Conflict in Chinua Achebe's *Things Fall Apart*." *International Journal of English and Literature* 7, no. 6 (2016): 81–87.

White, Peter. "The Concept of Diseases and Health Care in African Traditional Religion in Ghana." *HTS Teologiese Studies/Theological Studies* 71, no. 3 (2015): Art. #2762. 7 pages.

Wyllie, Robert W. "Ghanaian Spiritual and Traditional Healers' Explanations of Illness: A Preliminary Survey." *Journal of Religion in Africa* 14, no. 1 (1983): 46–57.

## Further Reading

John Mbiti has written seminal texts which provide an introduction to and overview of African religious thought and practice:

Mbiti, John. *African Religions and Philosophy*. New York: Frederick A. Praeger, 1969.

———. *Introduction to African Religion*. London: Heinemann Educational, 1975.

Viewing and attempting to understand any culture from the outside is fraught with difficulties. Galina Lindquist and Simon Coleman provide an overview of anthropological writings on belief in cross-cultural contexts, and how this can be politically loaded:

Lindquist, Galina, and Simon Coleman. "Introduction: Against Belief?" *Social Analysis* 52, no. 1 (2008): 1–18.

Patrick Chabal and Jean-Pascal Daloz provide a systematic analysis of the role of culture in understanding politics:

Chabal, Patrick, and Jean-Pascal Daloz. *Culture Troubles: Politics and the Interpretation of Meaning*. Chicago: University of Chicago Press, 2006.

Klaas Bom and Benno van den Toren provide engagement with contextualization of issues in Francophone Africa:

Bom, Klaas, and Benno van den Toren. *Context and Catholicity in the Science and Religion Debate: Intercultural Contributions from French-Speaking Africa*. Leiden: Brill, 2020.

In addition to those provided in the footnotes and References section of this chapter, we highlight some noteworthy articles on traditional African scientific practices:

Davies, J. N. "The Development of Scientific Medicine in the African Kingdom of Bunyoro-Kitara." *Medical History* 3, no. 1 (1959): 47–57.

Oyebola, D. D. "Yoruba Traditional Bonesetters: The Practice of Orthopaedics in a Primitive Setting in Nigeria." *The Journal of Trauma* 20, no. 4 (1980): 312–22.

# 7

# Doing Science and Theology in a Secular, Siloed, Multicultural New Zealand Society

Nicola Hoggard Creegan, New Zealand Christians in Science/
Ngā Karaitiana Kimi Matū, Aotearoa New Zealand

## Abstract

Science and theology in the world's traditional Anglophone centers is done in departments of both theology and science, and is lent prestige by departments, publishing houses, universities, and well-known thinkers within the church. Creationism, where it exists, is more often on the sidelines of the conversation. One of the most pressing challenges facing New Zealand Christians in Science is the burgeoning of creationism among university students and university-based churches. This is related to New Zealand's distinctive issue of secularism: because the universities are all relatively young, and are state-owned and aggressively secular, there is no serious public theological conversation within university precincts outside of Otago, and to a lesser extent, Auckland. Theology is misunderstood and almost eclipsed from the public sphere, especially as it relates to science. Scientists who are Christian have little time to engage theology, and the complexities of the science/theology dialogue; the pressure of life in the university for students and staff leaves little time for the Big Questions of our existence. New and engaging topics gain some – but very little – traction and are done in liminal university-chaplaincy spaces. Cross-disciplinary engagements must reckon with the high status of secular science (and the money behind it) and also the deconstructive turn in the humanities in which faith and trust are no longer legitimate practices. Thus religion and faith are in danger of becoming silos within an aggressively secular New Zealand society which values science and pragmatics most highly. However, this secularism is all-pervasive in New Zealand, except for Māori, the indigenous people of Aotearoa. Māori provide a protected holistic alternative of parallel engagement with the world in which *karakia* (Māori word for prayer) is permissible if it is said in Te Reo, the language of the Māori. And Mātaraunga Māori (Māori ways of knowing) is rapidly – if controversially – gaining prominence and has been incorporated into the school science curriculum. This chapter discusses the history of science and faith in New Zealand, the current engagement in this distinctive context, and the impact of the increasing space given to Māoritanga (the traditions and culture of the indigenous New Zealanders) and Mātaraunga Māori under the legal protection of the Treaty of Waitangi, on the inclusion of the spiritual in New Zealand public discourse.

## Introduction

In this chapter, I first examine the ways in which global science and religion themes play themselves out in Aotearoa, New Zealand, both in the contours of the conversations and in the creationist presence. I then look at modifying factors which, on the one hand, tend to make the global situation worse in this very secular context and, on the other hand, open up new opportunities.

The first distinctive factor in New Zealand is the lack of mediating institutions and people by which creationist influence is moderated, as it is in the older parts of the world. I look at the history of science and theology in New Zealand and I argue that, although there has been a tradition of influential voices in the past, that past is now inaccessible to a radically secular society in which patterns of influence and authority have changed. The way in which authority works in the only large churches now functional, especially among the young, is upwards and local; voices and traditions from the past and well-known experts from overseas have very little traction. Similarly, high-profile academics carry very little weight. This is particularly true as New Zealand's demographics change and there is a rise in ethnic churches which are also authorities unto themselves. On the other hand, and on a more hopeful note, the radical secularism of the larger society is broken and interrupted by Māori spirituality. I examine the possibility that this can be a wedge, as partner, which can be explored in terms of opening up the conversation about nature and God to a wider public.

In New Zealand, we must admit that the old Christendom is gone – along with any form of triumphalist or popular Christianity. Christian leaders are no longer household names. But Christians in Science can explore and exploit the prophetic gaps that emerge in a society which remains spiritual, even while it is no longer church-attending.

## The Conflict Model

I returned to New Zealand in the year 2000, from studying and teaching in the US. I had had a lot of exposure to the world of science and theology, and been encouraged by Templeton grants and conferences in the US and UK. Back in New Zealand I spent fourteen years teaching systematic theology at a conservative theological school in Auckland. This was an institution which served the wider evangelical church. I was unprepared for the depth of creationist conviction in the students when I first arrived, and for the suspicion evolution engendered in many of the faculty. While I was on leave in 2012-13, I was told about a conversation that took place at a faculty meeting where it was said that evolution should not be taught openly or in public, but only discussed in private conversations among staff. Conflict often exists where people care deeply. Religions incite some of the most passionate emotions, and because we cannot judge or really view the inner person, propositions often stand instead. Most of my colleagues were not actively creationists, though I think some thought that the concept of evolution was morally unsavory, and should not be talked about. There seemed to be a general view that one was a better Christian if one avoided science altogether, and concentrated on biblical purity. And there was the ever-present "constituency" to be wary of offending. And indeed, many students did come to the institution as hard-line creationists, or as a softer kind where they assumed creationism was the status quo, even if not a litmus test for faith.

I am an Anglican. Anglicans on the whole do not participate in the conflict model of science and religion; rather, they are inclined to tell me that they "have no problem with science," as though to say, "What are you doing spending so much energy on an issue that had been resolved long ago, if you were a properly liberal-thinking person?" I always want to say to them – and sometimes do – that there is plenty to find in science that is in tension with faith if one digs a little deeper than the surface. And this is where all the more interesting conversations open up.

I am now based at a chapel associated with the University of Auckland, and I am codirecting New Zealand Christians in Science (with Dr. Graeme Finlay), though this chapter is not a reflection of the organization as a whole. On the Auckland University campus there are sixteen Christian groups, serving about

500–800 Christian students, out of a student roll of 40,000. From my experience of, and conversations with, students and student leaders from these groups over a period of four years, I would judge that the majority of the young Protestant Christians with commitment and energy are creationists to some degree. They also tend to be conservative about gender, and are attending relatively large nondenominational churches, or evangelical Baptist or Anglican churches in which these positions are taught or tolerated. Students, however, have not been surveyed since 1991, when only 20 percent of those attending a TSCF (Tertiary Students Christian Fellowship) conference were fully committed to evolution. (Follow-up surveys are planned.)

## Creationism and Mediating Institutions

In this sense, then, New Zealand is simply repeating a global pattern, and repeating global conversations and themes. And indeed, the influence of American creationism is significant, though the influence is on an ever-smaller segment of the overall society. What is different in New Zealand is that the mainstream church is very far progressed in its decline, and also that the fundamentalist churches have no mediating presences or institutions. Figures differ on degrees of secularism and church attendance between the UK and NZ. The largely Christian Polynesian population skews our figures, but there never was a state church in NZ, so the church receives almost no media attention except for sex abuse cases which represent a steady dribble of negative exposure.

I have noticed, in my frequent sojourns to the more established parts of the globe, that the conversation with creationism does not really touch the centers of powerful institutions where science and faith have most voice. Science and theology in the Old-World centers is done in departments of theology, and is lent prestige by departments, publishing houses, professors, scientists, universities, churches, journals, and well-known thinkers within the church. That ensures that a space is always there and is welcoming of those who wish to engage.

By mediating presences, I am referring to these renowned organizations and individuals which provide a model for another way of looking at the issues. For instance, in the USA theology is done in most of the big private universities, originally founded by Methodists, Reformed denominations, Congregationalists, or Roman Catholics. The oldest prestigious Ivy League universities were started as training schools for clergy, and still teach theology and train ministers. Academic standards at some of the more sectarian seminaries are also kept very high by accrediting boards. Moreover, there are other institutions beyond the universities. Francis Collins has established the BioLogos Foundation. The American Scientific Affiliation (ASA), and its affiliated journal, *Perspectives on Science and Christian Faith*, is now a renowned institution with a long history of Christian dialogue. Theology of a more scholarly type is done in many private colleges and universities, with science and religion being commonly a part of the curriculum. The situation is conflicted, then, as many things are in the USA, but there are ready models for students to follow. Authority in the USA is very bound to a theological tradition, but there are authorities enough to go around: there are those who are Methodist, liberal, Reformed, broadly evangelical, Pentecostal, Wesleyan, or Roman Catholic, who are leaders in their cross-disciplinary fields. Then there are the journals: *Zygon*; *Theology and Science* (Journal of the Center for Theology and the Natural Sciences); and *Philosophy, Theology and the Sciences*. All of these are mediating and culture-defining institutions.

In the UK, Alister McGrath, John Hedley Brooke, Tom McLeish, Keith Ward, Celia Deane-Drummond, Sarah Coakley, Arthur Peacocke, Christopher Southgate, and John Polkinghorne are among the many theologians, and scientists-turned-theologians, who inhabit (or inhabited) this mediating space. They are well known, widely read, and have produced a much larger reading public who understand these issues. Science and theology books are published by Oxford University Press, Cambridge University Press, and other prestigious publishing houses. Theology is still taught in many of the UK's universities. There are chairs and lectureships in science and religion at a number of UK universities. Chaplaincies are central to many of the universities in England and Scotland. They are not the more marginal institutions they are in New Zealand. The various Templeton foundations have now spent almost four decades pouring money into cross-disciplinary research and teaching in the USA, the UK, and mainland Europe.

In contrast, university theology in Aotearoa is done primarily in our oldest university, Otago. On the whole, this small department sticks to a theological core which it does exceptionally well. There is a Centre for Public Theology but it is involved mostly with political issues, and more lately with environmental theology. A private donor funded a School of Theology in Auckland fifteen years ago. Soon this was downgraded to a department and there is now just one professor as part of a wider area, with religion being emphasized over theology. Auckland University in particular is stridently secular. It is a space that encourages the siloing of faith and spirituality.

This problem, I realize, is not unique, even if it is mitigated to some extent in the big centers of science and theology. I was surprised in my brief visit to the Netherlands in 2018, to a conference on the "Metaphysics of Evolution," to find that creationism was on the agenda there too: there was evidently a huge problem with the teaching of creationism in some schools. The Netherlands perhaps shares a commonality with New Zealand in being a highly secular society. Additionally, the Dutch problem appears to be an unusual wedding of American thought to Dutch Neo-Calvinism. However, the Netherlands also has a long and more moderate theological tradition. The Dutch experience shows that however strong the tradition, it can be quickly lost and that populist churches emerge, which are ignorant of the past and the traditions.

## History of Science and Theology in New Zealand

All of this brings me back to the antecedents of science and theology in New Zealand. Prof. John Stenhouse from Otago University has published detailed work on the defenders of Darwin in the early colony. He gives the impression of overall equanimity. Indeed, he says, "New Zealanders responded to Darwin with more ease, greater enthusiasm, and less social division than the inhabitants of any other region in the English-speaking world."[1] In the nineteenth century, one of Darwin's great defenders made his way to Otago University and there, over a number of years, defended Darwin in Presbyterian Dunedin. This was F. W. Hutton, who wrote one of the first reviews of *On the Origin of Species*, which delighted Darwin. He was not alone. What is more, in this small university town he persuaded many of the clergy not to fear Darwinism. The same was true of scientists involved in government and industry in Anglican Christchurch. James Hector was a surgeon/geologist who became influential in New Zealand, and who was a lifelong Christian and a defender of Darwin. Before them, Samuel Butler arrived in New Zealand in 1860 and, as Stenhouse says, he came "with a Bible and *The Origin of Species* in his baggage, leaving behind an angry clergyman father and the Anglican Establishment."[2] Stenhouse does mention that early colonists on the whole had little time for deeply polarized positions, or for in-depth discussions on science, but that there were fewer of the public conflicts than were found in Europe or

---

1. John Stenhouse, "Darwinism in New Zealand 1859–1900," in *Disseminating Darwin: The Role of Place, Race, Religion and Gender*, eds. Ronald Numbers and John Stenhouse (Cambridge: Cambridge University Press, 1999), 72.

2. Stenhouse, "Darwinism in New Zealand," 61.

America. He says, "For diverse reasons, New Zealand's cultural mainstream absorbed Darwinism with both equanimity and enthusiasm."[3] It was after all a new idea, threatening and challenging much of the older authority, as was the young colony in its essence.

I have not discussed here the earlier and persisting use of nineteenth-century eugenics in the New Zealand context, where many early settlers including Samuel Marsden used phrenological and eugenic ideas casually to undergird systematic and private prejudice against the Māori as an inferior race. Indeed, Darwinism was misused by believers and agnostics, keen to denigrate the chances of Māori surviving, now that a "superior" race had come. That story is now emerging slowly from the shadows and is the content for another paper. In more academic arenas, however, there was a good beginning to the church acceptance of Darwin in New Zealand, but this was not a tradition that survived the further hardening of Darwinism in the twentieth century, with its liberating effect on many intellectuals, nor the eventual rise of American creationism.

## The Twentieth Century: Movements and People

Insight into the dynamics of academic and popular engagement with science and religion in New Zealand can be gained from a survey of some key individuals and organizations which have played significant roles in the developing story in the twentieth century.

Christine Berry tells the story of how, in the twentieth century, the Student Christian Movement (SCM) made a difference to the perception of Christianity in society. The groups under the banner of Inter-Varsity Fellowship (IVF) were also keen on integration of faith and learning, and both groups were active in integrating science and theology. The SCM was brought to Australasia in 1896 by John Mott, at a time when both New Zealand and Australia were still largely and homogeneously Christian, even though the universities were secular and often stridently so. This movement was the representation of Christianity on New Zealand campuses for at least twenty years. At one stage, 47 percent of the Otago University student body belonged to it. It was enthusiastic and open, taking on all areas of theology and public service, and training many students over the years, who then took a Christian mindset into secular areas of teaching, politics, medicine, law, and public service.

---

3. Stenhouse, 86.

However, in the late 1920s in New Zealand, mirroring the rest of the world, a breakaway group, the Evangelical Union (EU), formed in opposition to the SCM. The founders of the EU (under the umbrella of IVF) were worried that many students in SCM barely understood Christianity and were not concerned at all with matters of salvation.[4] Up until the 1970s, SCM and EU groups both flourished on campuses as rivals. In the period since then, IVF became the Tertiary Student Christian Fellowship, overseeing some of the smaller groups on campuses. SCM had died out by the end of the 1990s. In both Otago and Auckland, very small church groups are now attempting to revive the SCM because there is no other platform for a more liberal campus Christianity. In the last twenty years, individual Protestant/evangelical churches have sought to have their own representation on campus and this is what has finally split the Christian witness and fragmented it. What is important from our point of view is that the early cohesiveness of the Christian view of the world, one that was open and generous, quickly gave way to the more fragmented, more contentious, less ecumenical groups we have today.

There were two historic figures from the mid to late twentieth century who came as close as is possible in New Zealand to being science-and-religion experts. One was the flamboyant Prof. John Morton QSO (1923–2011), a widely read and widely respected professor of zoology at Auckland University in an era when the university system was still small and one professor could have enormous impact. He was also a public figure due to his very popular television programs. He influenced a whole generation of Christian and non-Christian life-science students who came and listened to his lectures on God and science. He would deliver his course of lectures on zoology for the semester and then ask students back to an optional extra lecture on the theological impact of all this science. His reputation was huge, as was his influence. And he wrote up his ideas, first in a book, *Man, Science and God*, and then later in another small book, *Redeeming Creation*, in which he not only took up issues at the interface of science and theology, including the fall, but also briefly dealt with the topic of the purpose and the end of humanity and the planet. As is often the case with expert scientists who openly profess faith, his very presence was reassuring to several generations of professing scientists entering school teaching, industry, and the university. He was also a well-known lay Anglican and respected in that world as well. But his tenure extended over the last period of time in which that kind of authority worked in New Zealand society.

---

4. Stenhouse, 81.

A less-well-known expert was the maverick Dr. Harold Turner (1911–2002). Turner was a theologian with an interest in new religious movements around the world. He spent most of his working life in the UK and Africa. But he returned to New Zealand to retire and spent a few decades attempting to talk about science and theology in a more positive way, teaching, for instance, popular courses in continuing education at the University of Auckland. His bête noire was Prof. Lloyd Geering, an atheist theologian who was always able to garner a sizeable audience. But Turner, who described himself as being on the "margins" and had started the Deep Sight Trust in New Zealand, had always studied and defended religious groups who were, or were thought to be, on the edges of Christian respectability – movements or congregations such as the Moonies, Mormons, and Rastafarians. Later in life Turner turned his attention to the roots of science in Western thought, and defended a thesis that Reformed Christianity, especially, had desacralized nature, opening the way for science to flourish. Thus, he presented a strong and powerful apologia for the unity of science and theology at a time when this was not widely accepted. As a corollary, he made much of the creator/creature distinction, but in a way that had no time for even the more orthodox conversations around the presence of God in nature. All forms of pantheism or panentheism were, in his mind, the enemies of both faith and science.

Turner was interesting, and influential for a time, but left no lasting legacy in any theological institution or in the church in New Zealand. Morton's legacy was seen in a generation of life scientists now in retirement who had some sort of voice in the science/faith arena in New Zealand. Both these men were operating from a perspective of "Christ transforming culture."[5] Interestingly, and significantly for our work today, Bill Ballantine said this of John Morton:

> Biologists consider that evolution happens fastest among small isolated populations on the fringes. Useful adaptations – like good ideas – can spread more rapidly through a small group. Human advancement is similar. Small isolated places like New Zealand often lead the world in implementing ideas – women's suffrage, the welfare state, introducing a nuclear ban, tariff removal, unsubsidized agriculture, etc. And within places like New Zealand it is a small group of free thinkers who goad the rest of us. Morton has been one of those, and notable because of the extraordinary breadth of his interests and expertise. There are not too many

---

5. See H. Richard Niebuhr, *Christ and Culture* (New York: Harper & Row, 2001).

shore ecologists who have saved forests, significantly advanced the cause of women's equality, articulated considered positions on the centrality of God in the cosmos and on free public transport, and who can write speeches in Latin.[6]

One wonders whether Bill Ballantine does not, in this brief paragraph, have clues to our future, and an explanation, also, of why Darwinian ideas got off to such a good start in the small early colony.

Also important for their general contribution to a holistic Christian integration of science and faith are Prof. Wilf Malcolm CBE and Prof. Duncan Roper. Malcom (1933–2018) was general secretary of IVF (1962–67), professor of mathematics at Victoria University in the 1970s, and then vice-chancellor of Waikato University. He never wrote directly on science and faith, though he did write more generally on the calling of the university, as mentioned below. He was openly Christian, and modeled a gracious integration and compassion. When he moved to Auckland in the 2000s he was a thoughtful contributor to every meeting of NZCIS or TANSA (Theology and the Natural Sciences in Aotearoa) until his death. Roper (1940–2016), also a mathematician, both before and after his sojourn in Australia gathered around him a community of people engaged in integration and dialogue of many multidisciplinary issues within the Reformed tradition. He published numerous articles on these topics.

Another voice, albeit one which reinforced secularism, was Prof. Lloyd Geering ONZ, CBE, GNM. He is notorious for having been tried in the Presbyterian Church for heresy in 1967 (he was acquitted), then joining Victoria University as professor of religion late in that decade. Geering is at the time of writing now 106 and is still much sought after as a speaker and commentator, especially at arts festivals, and around Christmas and Easter. He has also written a book, *From Big Bang to God*, which is an ecological call for action and which makes a plea for the scientific story of origins to be heard. In a recent book on public intellectuals in New Zealand, *Speaking Truth to Power*, Geering was prominent, and the only religionist.[7] Although he is a public voice, the fact that he is the *only* public theological voice says as much about the society as it does about Geering or any other possible contenders. His voice is relevant mostly only to the secular press and to very liberal sectors of the church. There is something about a theologian who does not believe in

---

6. Quoted in Simon Grant, "John Morton," *New Zealand Geographic* 69 (Sept. 2004), https://www.nzgeo.com/stories/john-morton/.

7. Laurence Simmons et al., eds., *Speaking Truth to Power: Public Intellectuals Rethink New Zealand* (Auckland: Auckland University Press, 2007), ch. 5.

God which is particularly attractive to secular New Zealand, but he has very little if any authority within the church itself.

## The Last Two Decades

When I returned to New Zealand in 2000, there was a small group of scientists associated with Auckland University who were meeting privately to discuss various science/faith issues. In 2001 this group sponsored a conference to honor both Morton and Turner in their last years. The papers were edited by Robert Mann and published as *Science and Christianity: Festschrift in Honour of Harold Turner and John Morton*. Other works written by this group include *How Blind Is the Watchmaker?* and *Life's X-Factor*, both by Prof. Neil Broom; and *The Gospel According to Dawkins* and *Human Evolution*, by Dr. Graeme Finlay. In another part of the country, Prof. Carolyn King – the New Zealand expert in introduced mustelid pests – was teaching a course in religion and science, and received a PhD in religion and science in addition to her doctorate in zoology. At Otago, several members of the anatomy department – Prof. Grant Gillett and Prof. Gareth Jones – spoke openly and engagingly in this area. Gillett is a neuroscientist/philosopher and Jones a bioethicist. There are also two historians in New Zealand working in the area of the history of science: Ruth Barton at the University of Auckland has published a book entitled *The X Club* about science and authority in nineteenth-century Britain, and John Stenhouse at Otago University has published numerous books on Darwin's reception in New Zealand and on secular society.

In 2007 I received a small grant from Metanexus and started a center, TANSA (Theology and the Natural Sciences in Aotearoa), within Laidlaw College, a theological training institution in Auckland. TANSA foundered when I left Laidlaw in 2014. The institutional presence of science and theology was revived, however, in 2017 when (now Dr.) Jacob Martin, a young chemistry PhD student, applied for and was successful in obtaining a grant from the Templeton World Charity Foundation to start a New Zealand Christians in Science (also known under its Māori name, Ngā Karaitiana Kimi Matū).

In 2020, Dr. Christa McKirland, an American trained in systematic theology at St. Andrews in Scotland, brought a Templeton grant with her to Carey Baptist College in Auckland. This grant was for science-engaged theology, and was focused in particular on theological anthropology and cognitive psychology, with a particular focus on women, and supporting women in PhD study. She has enthusiastically begun the work of integrating systematic themes around personhood with science in this traditional Baptist

Christian context. Her appointment marks a departure from business as usual for conservative Christianity in New Zealand.

## Status and Authority in Younger Generations

Present-day generations know nothing of the historic sources, neither the orthodox ones nor the heretical voices, and they would not count them as authorities if they did. Those authorities and traditions have been lost in the late twentieth and early twenty-first centuries. This must partly be because of the way status works among the young where, on the whole, peers, social media, and loose and temporary groupings are the major influences; and these peer and local groups, together with their nondenominational churches, confer influence and authority. The society, too, is now inherently siloed and fragmented (or diverse). This is not a problem only for New Zealand, but it definitely is more of a problem for a country in which there are no mediating institutions. Students who commit as Christians are largely to be found now in nondenominational and Pentecostal churches. These have grown in the late twentieth and early twenty-first centuries as mainline churches have declined steeply.

In his book *Losing Our Religion*, Kevin Ward examines this phenomenon, and suggests that the growth in these churches is misleading. On the whole, they are taking younger people from older denominations, and the children of believers. Very little radical conversion has been going on in New Zealand in recent memory. Instead, there is now a huge unchurched population who know nothing (or next to nothing) at all about the Christian church, about the Bible, or about church history, apart from the sex abuse cases (now being investigated by a Royal Commission), antagonism to gay issues, and Christian opposition to abortion, euthanasia, legal prostitution, and other "progressive" legislation. A good part of New Zealand society also "knows" that Christians are against science. The Wilberforce Foundation in New Zealand sponsored research into belief and religious practice in New Zealand. They found that at least 43 percent of New Zealanders who ticked "no religion" on the census said they were not religious because they preferred a more secular scientific approach to life. Seventeen percent thought religion was outdated, 14 percent thought it was a crutch for the weak, and 3 percent thought it was only for the uneducated.[8]

---

8. Mark McCrindle, *Faith and Belief in New Zealand: Report* (Wilberforce Foundation, 2018).

The churches with large youthful congregations, however, are almost all of a type that Ward describes as working from the local church up, rather than vice versa. Authority works that way as well. They would say that their authority lies in the Bible, and they would (on the whole) gloss over problems of interpretation. This model of church is adamantly "Christ against culture," deeply suspicious of those who embrace culture, especially in areas of evolution or gender equality.

Added to this, Ward shows that New Zealand's demographics have changed drastically in the last thirty years. In 1987 New Zealand started to expand its immigration policies, accepting huge populations from Asia and the Pacific. On the whole, new immigrant believers, as well as Polynesians, congregate in churches serving their own languages and/or culture. The Anglican Church, very controversially, divided into three tikanga (people groups), allowing Pākehā (New Zealanders who are non-Māori, but sometimes referring to Europeans), Māori, and Pacifica Anglicans to have a level of independence within the larger denomination. Only the Roman Catholic Church has managed to transform into multiethnic congregations. This means, again, that authority is very local and certainly churches do not act as "communities of memory" (to use Robert Bellah's term) in the culture at large. This is compounded by the fact that many Asian Christians adopt a stance of "Christ against culture," especially those coming from conservative Korean congregations back home.

Students may be coming to university to study STEM subjects in order to progress their own and their family's fortunes in New Zealand. They are not coming to study in order to integrate science and theology. Nor do they have the time. The golden era of expansive student formation – that in which SCM played such a huge role – is now past. Students in New Zealand, as in other countries, are typically working part-time or full-time alongside their (mostly full-time) studies. Moreover, they are in competitive fields, eager to get into graduate school or medicine. They have very little time to dedicate to leisurely discussion and deep thoughts about life. Faculty, too, are under great pressure to publish and to contribute to the university in an era when even academics are being purged; they have much less time for these nonobligatory activities in any reliable way.

## Universities as Conscience and Critic of Society

In spite of the early Otago and Christchurch intellectualism, and in spite of John Morton's success, New Zealand society is not in many ways the ideal soil on which big and integrative intellectual ideas can grow. First, there is a well-known and much-touted anti-intellectualism. I have spoken of the intense secularism of New Zealand tertiary education, but this has more recently been exacerbated by the trend toward commercialization in universities at every level. This is a worldwide phenomenon, but particularly afflicts New Zealand institutions because there are no private or well-endowed alternatives, although there are small specialized degree-granting institutions. But the ideal of a more impartial, more lofty value in university education remains latent. Much is made in New Zealand universities of their role as the "conscience and critic" of society. This idea was first mentioned in the book *Crisis of Identity* by Wilf Malcolm and Nicholas Tarling, which looked at the role of universities in society. It became enshrined in the Education Act in 1990.

Nevertheless, as the pressure to publish, win grant money, gain promotion, and please ever more students becomes ever more intense, the public voice becomes harder to execute. Moreover, the big ideas with which science and theology grapple are not in favor in a postcolonial environment. As Simmons argues, turning universities into marketable commodities undermines the larger intellectual function.[9] In New Zealand universities, as in much of the West, humanities faculties are using critical theory or positivist research methodologies which do promote vigorous and much-needed critiques of hidden power dynamics, exposing earlier understandings of the hegemony of knowledge, not least through feminist and postcolonial lenses. This enables people to call out racism and prejudice against LGBQT communities. Yet in a country where the science and theology discourse is imported from larger Western world centers, here is another reason why the university context is not very open to promoting a unified story of our origins, nor engaging in what is seen as too-universal an understanding of disciplines. There are aspects to postmodernity which encourage interdisciplinary work and also a more holistic take on the world, but the more critical voice is the one which dominates, especially when the subject matter is religion, and even more so when it is religion in dialogue with science.

Are we then a completely fragmented society? We are the country that worked together and put paid to the earlier versions of the COVID-19 virus. We are the country whose prime minister at the time (Jacinda Ardern) famously told Muslim communities after the 2019 Christchurch mosque massacre, "They are us." But Ardern's compassion, and our collective pragmatism which allows on the whole for any strategy which will have a decent chance of achieving a goal, belies the deeper tensions. We do have collective conversations, around

---

9. Simmons, *Speaking Truth to Power*, 244–48.

racial identity especially. The politics of our national day, Waitangi Day, provokes this conversation; but there is ample room in that dialogue for tension between Pākehā and Māori. Polynesians and Asian New Zealanders often feel left out. What does it mean to be Pākehā? What does it mean to be Māori? And what are you, if you are neither of European origins nor Māori? On the other hand, Māori is now heard fluently on radio and television. There has been a Māori renaissance. We are grasping toward some sort of national identity in this area, but it does not openly touch the deeper topics which are the concern of this chapter, even if the new emphasis on Māoritanga (the traditions and culture of Māori) may suggest a new way ahead.

## Religion Is Private, Except for Māori

Religion is meant to stay private in New Zealand society, as it is in many secular countries, even if it is not enshrined in law in the way that *laïcité* is in France. Māori, however, are an exception. Māori provide a protected holistic alternative, a parallel engagement with the world because of the renewed attention to New Zealand's founding document, the Treaty (Te Tiriti) of Waitangi. Māori have remained resolutely spiritual, and that spirituality extends to the idea of *kaitiakitanga*, or guardianship of nature. In the late nineteenth century, the gospel was for a while supremely successful in Māori tribes, and Māori have always maintained huge independence in their interpretation, appropriation, and spread of Christian faith. The success turned sour with increased immigration from the UK, casual racism in early policymakers and educators, pressure on land, and eventually land wars. These days, many tribes still fear the imperialism they associate with Christianity. Māori have continued their own indigenous forms of spirituality, blended to an extent with Christian input in some areas, and recognizing historical prophetic figures such as Rātana. Because of the revival of the Treaty, first signed with missionaries in 1846, Māori spirituality is allowed in secular New Zealand spaces. Māori, and even Pākehā, are allowed *karakia* (prayer) in every public setting in New Zealand. Where (Christian) prayer is not permissible or appropriate, *karakia* and *waiata* (song) are. Moreover, Māori spirituality was, and always has been, nature-centered and holistic. Māori voices critique, very often, the objectivity of Western epistemology, especially in science, and they bring a contemporary critical voice to all matters of life in New Zealand. New Zealanders have abandoned church, but we are all engaged at some level in the discussions around Māoritanga and the Treaty of Waitangi, and these are spiritual matters.

Māori may yet be the key to a return to a spirituality which combines nature/science, God, and community, and which critiques scientific imperialism.

An example of this is *Huia Come Home* by Jay Ruka. This book begins with typical Māori independence, with a dream – his American wife's dream – about a hen the size of a pohutukawa tree, and the word "huia." Huia is the sacred bird of the Māori, which guards the entry to the highest heaven, but is now extinct. After much contemplation and the study of New Zealand church history on Ruka's part, he interpreted this to mean that Western Christianity has imperialized Māori – the hen increasing to the size of the tree – and has brought with it an objectified nonholistic approach to life. He sees links between the Hebrew and Māori worldviews, with their common love of intuition and holism. Ruka describes how Māori embraced Christianity in the early nineteenth century. The early missionaries on the whole had no desire for colonization, and the gospel had been preceded by an indigenous prophecy that there would come a God called "Son-who-was-killed." Ruka would see the return of the gospel in Aotearoa being led by Māori and by this more holistic nature-centered interpretation.

Recently, an even more science-oriented conversation and controversy has arisen in this space. Mātauranga Māori stands for Māori ways of knowing or understanding the world, and has been understood as referring in a way to Māori science. Some scientists have embraced the idea, and it is now to be a part of the New Zealand science curriculum. Others have rejected Māori claims to inclusion of indigenous knowledge and instead argue that science is universal. Roberts and Wills argue that we can all learn from Mātauranga Māori, in its inclusion of *mauri* (or spirit in nature), and its insistence on all knowledge being located in *whakapapa* (or genealogy). To quote them in more detail:

> This conception of the whole of reality as a continuous unfolding of vital generative processes, rather than as mechanical occurrences within inert material substance, is irreconcilable with most of modern science. However, the Maori worldview contains the seeds of a more sustainable relationship between humanity and the world that science studies. Assimilation of conceptions like *whakapapa* and *mauri* into science would make it no longer possible, especially in biology, to separate questions of science and ethics. The continuity of relationships and processes that constitute *whakapapa* carry intrinsic obligations, manifest not only in tribal society as mores of kinship, but in the responsibilities of humans

to all other living and non-living descendants of Papatuanuku. However, if the rigorous reduction of all experience to descriptions in terms of events within the material world were regarded as a limitation of science, rather than as a necessary precondition for reliable knowledge, we believe science would have much to gain.[10]

Christians will recognize that, and the issues around integration and kinds of evidence and knowledge are common to both faith and Māori.

Universities which are on the whole very secular places technically embrace the idea of *whanau* (or wider family) and connection to the land. All universities have a *marae* (traditional building and a place set aside for Māori) on their campus as a part of their commitment to the Treaty of Waitangi.

Māori spirituality is, therefore, a possible conversation partner; it provides a wedge which might yet break open New Zealand society into deeper realms of spirituality and conversation around spirit-and-nature, and nature-and-science; it provides a starting point from which science and religion might enter into new and distinct domains of thought and integration in Aotearoa, forged out of the messy conversations between two peoples, two outlooks, two traditions.

## The Way Ahead

Older Christians sometimes look back with nostalgia and longing. Surely, they think, it cannot be too hard to get back the crowds and thinking spaces of the past, to reclaim the cultural ground which has been lost. Some younger academics also had grand visions for NZCIS, envisioning it as making a splash in New Zealand society. Arguably, that has never been realistic, or even desirable, in the current climate. A close analysis shows that those spaces of the past have been lost forever. As the arguments of Kevin Ward discussed above have shown, Christian churches are now recirculating congregants. Some of the young are still at large centers, but there is almost no new blood entering the church arena. The one redeeming feature of this siloed situation is that spirituality, by all accounts, is not dead in New Zealand. Faith is not dead. It has shifted to the "believing but not belonging" mode, to small fresh expressions, to home groups and Bible studies, and simply to the home. Out of death it is always possible to find new life, but it will not be the kind of life we had before.

---

10. Roma Mere Roberts and Peter R. Wills, "Understanding Maori Epistemology: A Scientific Perspective," in *Tribal Epistemologies: Essays in the Philosophy of Anthropology*, ed. Helmut Wautscher (Aldershot: Ashgate, 1998), 67.

In this space, a group like NZCIS can be a prophetic voice, partnering with churches, modeling engagement, and being flexible and nimble enough to take up opportunities where they arise. In this sense, we have kept alive a web presence, including Facebook and Instagram, and we will dedicate more work to this in the future. We will partner with churches that are open to this engagement. We have already partnered with A Rocha (a Christian environmental group) and also with Otago Theology Department. In that respect, we have now three times taught a (hybrid) course in Christian Theology and Science at Otago. The last teaching stint drew ninety students. These are on the whole not drawn from the usual ranks of students in conflict with evolution. Instead, they seem to be a diverse group: theology students who have never really encountered the dialogue with science before, Christians in science who do not belong to the conservative Christian groups or have left them behind, as well as a good number of students who have never had any encounter with religion at all. Students include a young Tongan woman leading a youth group in a Tongan Assemblies of God church, a pastor of a large Polynesian church in South Auckland, a school teacher in a Catholic school in Auckland, a theology PhD student who now looks back on her creationist upbringing with embarrassment, and a Hindu student who welcomed the chance to have a "confessional" conversation in an academic setting. All of these students will pass on their new skills in integration to a much wider public who might never come to an NZCIS event. We have also begun a year-long mentoring program for young theologians and scientists who wish to begin the journey of integration.

We hope in coming years to make the partnership with Māori more programmatic and, in this way, to lean into the spiritual wedge which does exist in New Zealand society, as well as forging links which will provide mutual support, and nurturing a distinctively New Zealand integration of science and faith. It is helpful to bear in mind, as Bill Ballantine reminds us above, that smallness can result in fast evolution of ideas and the emergence of intellectual landscapes which are unique, as well as reflecting the larger, more global patterns.[11] At the same time, the future will bring a balance of deliberate partnership and openness to opportunities as they arise.

---

11. Quoted in Simon Grant article above, fn 6.

## References

Grant, Simon. "John Morton." *New Zealand Geographic* 69 (Sept. 2004).
McCrindle, Mark. *Faith and Belief in New Zealand: Report*. Wilberforce Foundation, 2018.
Niebuhr, H. Richard. *Christ and Culture*. New York: Harper & Row, 2001.
Simmons, Laurence, et al., eds. *Speaking Truth to Power: Public Intellectuals Rethink New Zealand*. Auckland: Auckland University Press, 2007.

## Further Reading

Books by current New Zealand scientists and historians in the area of science and theology or history:
Barton, Ruth. *The X Club: Power and Authority in Victorian Science*. Chicago: University of Chicago Press, 2018.
Broom, Neil. *How Blind Is the Watchmaker? Nature's Design and the Limits of Naturalistic Science*. Downers Grove: IVP, 2001.
———. *Life's X-Factor*. Wellington: Steele Roberts, 2010.
Finlay, Graeme. *Evolution and Eschatology: Genetic Science and the Goodness of God*. Eugene: Wipf & Stock, 2021.
———. *The Gospel According to Dawkins*. London: Austin MacAuley, 2017.
———. *Human Evolution*. Cambridge: Cambridge University Press, 2013.
Mann, L. R. B., ed. *Science and Christianity: Festschrift in Honour of Harold Turner and John Morton*. Auckland University: Centre for Continuing Education, 2001.

These books relate to early New Zealand history and reception of Darwin. Berry documents the early history of the SCM in New Zealand.
Berry, Christine. *New Zealand Student Christian Movement 1896–1996: A Centennial History*. Christchurch: SCM of Aotearoa, 1996.
Stenhouse, John. "Darwinism in New Zealand 1859–1900." In *Disseminating Darwin: The Role of Place, Race, Religion and Gender*, edited by Ronald Numbers and John Stenhouse, 61–90. Cambridge: Cambridge University Press, 1999.

Books by John Morton, Harold Turner, and Lloyd Geering:
Morton, John. *Man, Science and God*. London: Collins, 1972.
———. *Redeeming Creation*. Auckland: Zealandia, 1984.
Turner, Harold. *The Laughter of Providence: Stories from a life on the Margins*. Auckland: DeepSight Trust, 2001.
Geering, Lloyd. *From Big Bang to God: Our Awe-Inspiring Journey of Evolution*. Wellington: Steele Roberts, 2013.

Books on New Zealand universities, and religion and society:

Malcolm, Wilf, and Nicholas Tarling. *Crisis of Identity? The Mission and Management of Universities in New Zealand.* Wellington: Dunmore, 2007.

Ward, Kevin. *Losing Our Religion? Changing Patterns of Believing and Belonging in Secular Western Societies.* Eugene: Wipf & Stock, 2013.

Books engaging a Māori worldview:

Morrison, Hugh, et al., eds. *Mana Maori and Christianity.* Wellington: Huia, 2012.

Roberts, Roma Mere, and Peter R. Wills. "Understanding Maori Epistemology: A Scientific Perspective." In *Tribal Epistemologies: Essays in the Philosophy of Anthropology*, edited by Helmut Wautscher, 43–71. Aldershot: Ashgate, 1998.

Ruka, Jay. *Huia Come Home.* Oati, 2017.

Theology and science – theological books and theses:

Beattie, Sarah. "From Eden to Interstellar Space: Thomas Nagel, Biblical Hermeneutics and the Search for 'The True Extent of Reality.'" PhD diss., Melbourne University of Divinity, 2022.

Hoggard Creegan, Nicola. *Animal Suffering and the Problem of Evil.* Oxford: Oxford University Press, 2013.

Hoggard Creegan, Nicola, and Andrew Shepherd, eds. *Taking Rational Trouble over the Mysteries: Reactions to Atheism.* Eugene: Wipf & Stock, 2013.

# 8

# Canadian Perspectives on Christianity and Creation Care

Henry Brouwer, Redeemer University, Canada
Edward Berkelaar, Redeemer University, Canada
John Wood, The King's University, Canada
David Clements, Trinity Western University, Canada

## Abstract

Canada is known both as a nation rich in natural resources (forests, fossil fuels, minerals, fisheries, and vast agricultural lands) and as a multicultural society. The utilization of natural riches leads inevitably to challenges of caring for creation, with Christian groups expressing a wide range of opinions and responses to the environment: these range from complete separation of faith and the world around them, to humble and grateful acknowledgment that we are stewards of God's creation. There are few easy answers to the pressing environmental problems of our day. But there is hope for fresh ways to imagine our relationships under God's care, as reflected in a growing creation-care. As Christian scholars, our goal is to relay this all-encompassing theology of creation to our students and anyone else who will listen. Together we have been privileged to teach many students, exploring with them the rich stories of Canadians who care for the earth. This chapter tells the story of six individuals speaking prophetically to Canadian culture, instructing and inspiring us all.

## Introduction

> Where, oh where is dear little Nellie?
> . . .
> Way down yonder in the pawpaw patch.
> Pickin' up pawpaws, puttin' 'em in your pocket
> . . .
> Way down yonder in the pawpaw patch.

How many of us sang this American folk song in childhood and, to this day, have no idea what we were singing about? What is a pawpaw, and why would you put it in your pocket? Why is it worth saving?

Pawpaw (*Asimina triloba*) is a fruit tree native to eastern North America; its range includes parts of southern Ontario. It is a species that few people outside of this region are familiar with, but it has a number of interesting characteristics. It produces the largest native North American fruit, which has a hard-to-describe taste. It can sprout multiple shoots from its roots, so after time, a single original tree will spread and grow into a patch. Although a temperate species, it is in the family *Annonaceae*; its closest plant relatives (which include cherimoya and custard apple) are tropical fruit trees.

The tree may have medicinal properties; laboratory studies suggest that some compounds called acetogenins in its leaves may be toxic to cancer cells. As a native tree, it is resistant to most local pests and can be grown without the use of insecticides, making it a good candidate for a beautiful landscaping tree that diversifies your yard without a heavy demand of care. To grow its unique, tropical-tasting fruit, two trees are needed as flowers need to be cross-pollinated to set fruit. In its home range, pawpaws provide habitat for the zebra swallowtail butterfly, while its leaves are the sole food for this striking migratory insect that occasionally delights the eye of a watchful Ontarian gardener.

Why open a chapter about environmental stewardship in Canada by talking about pawpaws? Because doing something as simple as growing a pawpaw tree – or any fruit tree or edible plant, for that matter – can better connect you with your local place than almost any other action. The experience of our students is predominantly urban living. Many arrive in the post-secondary classroom more familiar with the charismatic wildlife of Africa or Asia, as seen on TV, than the plant and animal species of their own hometowns. Awe and wonder for our own backyard can be learned. With a skillful guide one can literally learn to "grasp the nettle" and eat it, too!

We are all educators, scholars, people of the book and the mind. Yet caring for creation is about action. Simple practices by ordinary people like "pickin' up pawpaws, puttin' 'em in your" garden, especially if done in multiples, will help reduce some of the pressures currently straining the creation.

The creation, God's good earth, is a beautiful and complex system that supports an amazing diversity of life. But it suffers from the demands placed on it, particularly since World War II. Rapid population growth, increasing affluence, resource consumption, and waste generation have placed strains on numerous environmental processes. Yet we know that with care both humans and the rest of creation can flourish; that restoration and renewal are possible and within our purview.[1]

As science educators at Christian universities, we strive to help students see the creation they study not only with a sense of wonder, but also with a thirst for wisdom, to see where the human interchange within the more-than-human community is broken. Many of these issues go beyond science – they impact all aspects of life: health, economics, politics, justice, to name but a few. Every Canadian is a user of resources to a varying degree, so each one of us is responsible for what is happening in the vast farms of the prairies, oil sands of Alberta and Saskatchewan, fisheries of the east and west coasts, mines in northern Ontario and Quebec, and forests of British Columbia.

The list of environmental concerns seems endless. These "wicked problems"[2] (which are difficult to solve because of incomplete or contradictory information) are complicated and require interdisciplinary solutions. Major issues include climate change, ocean acidification, ozone depletion, chemical pollution, atmospheric aerosols, freshwater use, land-system change, biodiversity loss, and biogeochemical flows which result in excessive nutrient runoff into aquatic and marine environments. Integrative models can help organize our thinking. Researchers at the Stockholm Resilience Centre in Sweden, for instance, have created a planetary-boundary model that is useful for understanding the global environmental issues of our day.[3]

---

1. One of the earliest expressions of this hope is found in Francis Schaeffer's *Pollution and the Death of Man: The Christian View of Ecology* (Carol Stream: Tyndale House, 1970). For a contemporary contextualization of his thought, see John R. Wood, "Biophilia and the Gospel: Loving Nature or Worshipping God?," ch. 8 in *Living in the Lamblight: Christianity and Contemporary Challenges to the Gospel*, ed. H. Boersma (Vancouver: Regent, 2001), 153–76.

2. For an example of one type of "wicked problem" in global food security, see Heather Looy and John R. Wood, "Imagination, Hospitality, and Affection: The Unique Legacy of Food Insects?," *Animal Frontiers* 5, no. 2 (2015): 8–13.

3. J. Rockström, W. Steffen, K. Noone, et al., "A Safe Operating Space for Humanity," *Nature* 461 (2009): 472–75; Will Steffen, Katherine Richardson, Johan Rockström, et al., "Planetary Boundaries: Guiding Human Development on a Changing Planet," *Science* 347, no. 6223 (2015): 1259855.

The raising of the environmental crisis to global status, while helping to organize and prioritize concerns on a massive scale, might seem to remove it from the purview of the local. But this impression ought to be resisted. For example, local biodiversity loss can be alleviated by restoring a particular stream, while excessive nutrient runoff might be monitored in a particular urban watershed. Anthropogenic climate change may be addressed by adding solar panels to the roofs of homes, churches, and our university buildings, and by making these buildings more energy efficient.

As faculty members at Christian universities in Canada, it has been our privilege to interact with individuals from local and national organizations, institutions, and movements devoted to addressing the human-caused brokenness in creation. In this chapter, we describe six Canadians who are committed to addressing planetary boundary concerns in their own unique and gifted ways. We begin with three public intellectuals and end with three alumni, each speaking to the environment from a faith perspective. It is our hope that these stories may offer hope, encouragement, and inspiration to all.

## Preston Manning: Mixing Red, Blue and Green – A Canadian Conservative Politician

Preston Manning has always eschewed the conventional approach. This is evident in the fact he was instrumental in forming not one, but three new official political parties in Canada. His political career indirectly followed that of his father, Ernest Manning. The senior Manning, a "Red Tory," served as premier of Alberta from 1943 to 1968 and sat in the Canadian Senate from 1970 to 1983.

Preston Manning did not immediately follow in his father's footsteps in politics, as he first pursued a career in research and then as a management consultant for the Alberta energy sector. But in 1987, he helped organize and then served as the first and only leader of the Reform Party of Canada, which became the Canadian Conservative Alliance party in 2000, uniting the conservatives under one banner. After one more reorganization in 2003, Stephen Harper, a key member of Manning's Reform Party, led the new Conservative Party of Canada to power in 2006 and served as prime minister for nearly a decade.

Publicly, Manning has been recognized as a leading proponent of a greener approach to the environment; a *National Post* article in 2015 proclaimed,

"Twenty years after Kyoto, Manning has become Canadian conservatives' most prominent green advocate."[4] As Manning himself says,

> There is no inherent reason why conservatives should be ambivalent on the environment, since conservation and conservatism come from the same root, since living within our means ecologically is a logical extension of living within our means fiscally, and since markets (in which conservatives strongly believe) can be effectively harnessed to environmental conservation.[5]

How did Manning arrive at such a pro-environmental position? His views are rooted in his Christian faith and reinforced by the influence of his family. Integrating faith and politics is an art that Manning inherited partly from his father Ernest, who taught him to think deeply on how to be "wise as serpents and harmless as doves" (Matt 10:16 NKJV).[6] Family influences on Manning's views on creation stewardship include not only his father but also his children and wife Sandra. *Maclean's* magazine once referred to the "Sandra factor" in Canadian politics, and as a long-serving member of the A Rocha Canada board of directors, Sandra has caught the vision of this Christian conservation organization for a holistic, uncompromising approach. Sandra did not encounter creation care theology in the church in which she grew up. In a 2010 *Christian Week* interview, she said it was while she pursued a degree at Regent College (a graduate-level Christian college affiliated with the University of British Columbia) that she discovered creation care was in the Bible all along. She explained, "It's as if we've taken scissors to the Bible and cut out the passages on creation."[7]

Furthermore, Manning's eldest son, Nathan, had been exposed to Wendell Berry's infectious rhetoric on a more ethical approach to raising food and living in harmony with the land. Nathan was taking a program in environmental literature when he discovered Wendell Berry. To make it real, he convinced

---

4. Tristin Hopper, "Twenty Years after Kyoto, Preston Manning Has Become Canadian Conservatives' Most Prominent Green Advocate," *National Post*, 2 January 2015, https://nationalpost.com/news/politics/twenty-years-after-kyoto-preston-manning-has-become-canadian-conservatives-most-prominent-green-advocate/.

5. Preston Manning, "The Blueing and Greening of the Political Centre," *The Globe and Mail*, 16 March 2010, https://www.theglobeandmail.com/opinion/the-blueing-and-greening-of-the-political-centre/article1210070/.

6. Preston Manning, "Navigating the Faith/Political Interface," *C2C Journal*, 19 June 2009, https://c2cjournal.ca/2009/06/navigating-the-faithpolitical-interface/.

7. Josiah Neufeld, "Manning Preaches Three-Cornered Gospel," *Christian Week*, 2 November 2010, https://www.christianweek.org/manning-preaches-three-cornered-gospel/.

his parents to support him in a prairie farming venture. Now at the Manning Alberta farm, several generations of Mannings raise "shaggy-haired Galloway cattle on [a] piece of Alberta grassland that's never felt the tooth of a plough." Speaking about the experience of investing in both the farm and the farming lifestyle, Sandra Manning said, "I think this is the best thing that has ever happened to us. What it has produced in us is a great desire to be stewards of God's creation."[8]

Preston Manning urges a "three-cornered gospel" that involves humanity's reconciliation not only with God and with each other, but also with the oft-neglected relationship to the created world, seeing the traditional focus on the human-God relationship as too narrow. He points to Jesus's values of spiritual wealth over physical wealth, in perhaps another departure from many of his conservative colleagues obsessed with generating financial wealth.

As Manning strives to preach a green vision to reluctant fellow conservatives, he has simultaneously received favorable attention from an unlikely source, namely world-renowned Canadian author Margaret Atwood. Although Atwood has referred to herself as a small-c conservative or "Red Tory," one might not expect the novelist who penned *The Handmaid's Tale*, a highly acclaimed dystopian novel that critiques fundamentalism, to offer public support to a conservative Christian politician. Atwood's writings indeed advocate for many environmental and social issues, which will be discussed in the next section. First, though, we will highlight an editorial she wrote for the *National Post* in 2015 entitled "Preston Manning, Man of the Future."[9]

To launch her defense of such an epithet for Manning, she points to A Rocha as a Christian environmental-stewardship organization, carefully attending to the nuances of its mission before setting the scene of a 2015 A Rocha event featuring atmospheric scientist Katharine Hayhoe speaking on climate change and Christianity. Hayhoe's talk was followed by a panel discussion, as Atwood reports, with conservationist Peter Robinson (chief executive of the David Suzuki Foundation), theologian Jeffrey Greenman (president of Regent College), and the man of interest himself, Preston Manning. Most Canadians reading the editorial would have thought, "Well,

---

8. Neufeld, "Manning Preaches."

9. Margaret Atwood, "Preston Manning, Man of the Future," *National Post*, 28 August 2015, https://nationalpost.com/opinion/margaret-atwood-preston-manning-man-of-the-future/.

that must have been awkward." But if you watch the online video of the event, it is clear that Manning fit right in,[10] as Atwood goes on to observe.

Manning, as a panelist, said, "Economics have to be brought to bear," and that "for every economic activity there are negative environmental consequences, so we should determine what the costs are and incorporate them into the price of the product."[11] As Atwood points out, for statements like these, "some oil-worshipping commentators" from Manning's Alberta base have "accused Mr. Manning of going over to the Dark Side."

This is where Atwood gets to the "future" bit, as she explains why Manning's ideas are badly needed:[12]

> We're now in a period of global transition. Our planet is changing, and so is our energy culture. It's happening a lot faster than predicted even a few years ago, and it's going to be a hair-raising high-wire act for us humans. We have to move from $CO_2$-heavy to $CO_2$-lite – if we don't, we perish – and we have to find ways and means that don't wreck the economy and drive us into anarchy in the process.
>
> Who can best guide us through the big transition? Wild-eyed denouncers on either extreme? Vilifiers who label environmentalists as terrorists? Short-term profit-makers? Foot-draggers in denial? Or grownups of the quality of Mr. Manning, who's rolled up his sleeves, joined with his one-time polar opposites, and begun working with them towards viable plans? Because without viable plans, we humans won't actually have much of a future.

A willingness to roll up his sleeves, join his polar opposites, say "sorry" when needed, and be willing to compromise: all embody Manning's political philosophy. In his 2017 book *Faith, Leadership and Public Life: Leadership Lessons from Moses to Jesus*, Manning describes his strategy for faith-based political campaigns to be "wise as serpents and harmless as doves," based on Jesus's instructions to his disciples heading out on a mission in Matthew 10:16 (NKJV).[13] Manning writes that "campaigns [are] to awaken and mobilize faith-

---

10. A Rocha Canada, "Panel Response (Earthkeeping: A Climate for Change)," YouTube, 19 May 2015, https://www.youtube.com/watch?v=eMXfkTRa6wA.

11. A Rocha Canada, "Panel Response."

12. Atwood, "Preston Manning."

13. Preston Manning, *Faith, Leadership and Public Life: Leadership Lessons from Moses to Jesus* (Paris: Castle Quay, 2017), 362.

oriented citizens to the challenges of creation care, environmental stewardship, and the voluntary constraint of consumerism as spiritual responsibilities."[14] He later goes on to nudge the reader to be part of such an awakening, asking,

> Could it be that for you as a Christian believer an increasing consciousness of and concern for environmental degradation constitutes providential leading – a providential call for you as a believer to act; to constrain your own demands for goods and services in the spirit of Christian self-sacrifice; to rediscover environmental stewardship and creation care as a spiritual obligation to our Creator and his creation . . . ?[15]

What lesson does this story of a conservative politician gone green have for Canada, and for the world? Although retired from his public political career, Manning continues to speak into Canadian politics. He continues to urge conservatives to take environmental issues seriously; in the 2019 Canadian election, it was clear that most Canadians placed environmental improvement (especially climate change) high on their list of concerns, leading to the conservative defeat. The fact that Manning's convictions come out of influences such as the green theology his spouse soaked up from Regent College, and a care for the land proclaimed by the modern-day prophet Wendell Berry, is instructive. His vision for merging an uncompromising stance on environmental protection with full-cost accounting to ensure both human and environmental flourishing provides a promising model for Canada's future.

## Margaret Atwood: Meets God's Gardeners and Friendship Blooms

Calling again on the celebrated storyteller Margaret Atwood, we turn to an interview conducted by *Sojourners* magazine to learn about her relationship with A Rocha Canada:[16]

> I met Markku and Leah Kostamo of A Rocha, an international Christian environmental organization, on the set of a television show in Toronto. The show was *Context*, hosted by the welcoming

---

14. Manning, *Faith, Leadership and Public Life*, 111.
15. Manning, 290.
16. Margaret Atwood, "Saving What We Love: A Hopeful Encounter with Real-Life 'God's Gardeners,'" *Sojourners*, February 2014, https://sojo.net/magazine/february-2014/saving-what-we-love/.

Lorna Dueck. This show explores the stories behind the news from a frankly Christian viewpoint.

I had been invited to talk with Dueck about my MaddAddam future-time book trilogy, and in particular about characters in the second book, *The Year of the Flood*, called the "God's Gardeners," a green religious group that raises vegetables and bees on flat rooftops in slums. It is headed by a man called Adam One and includes a number of ex-scientists and ex-doctors who have withdrawn from a too powerful, greedy corporate world in which they can no longer function ethically. The God's Gardeners group represents the position – probably true – that if the physical world is going to remain possible for human life, religious movements of many kinds will be an important element. We don't save what we don't love, and we don't make sacrifices unless "called" in some way to make them by what AA refers to as "a higher authority."

Dueck and I talked a little about that, and then – surprise – right before me were two people who closely resembled the God's Gardeners of my fiction. Leah and Markku Kostamo are walking the God's Gardeners' walk – through A Rocha, a hands-on creation-care organization. A Rocha's origins go back to the Christian Bird Observatory (cf. St. Francis) founded on the coast of Portugal by Peter and Miranda Harris in 1983. Leah met the Harrises in 1996 when she took a class they were teaching at Regent College in Vancouver, British Columbia, and A Rocha Canada was born. It was soon augmented by Markku, an environmental scientist. A Rocha is now running 20 projects around the globe, engaged in everything from habitat restoration to organic community farming.

The story did not end there – far from it! Later in 2014, Atwood accepted an invitation to join Leah Kostamo at a Green Gala, a fundraising event for A Rocha Canada, where the two women swapped stories and laughs. Leah is a writer herself, having penned *Planted*, which chronicles the story of the first twelve years of Markku and Leah's adventures with A Rocha Canada with humor and insight.[17] As well as endorsing the book, Atwood has supported the

---

17. Leah Kostamo, *Planted: A Story of Creation, Calling, and Community* (Eugene: Wipf & Stock, 2013).

cause. In early 2020, Atwood challenged others to donate to A Rocha Canada, promising to match up to $10,000 in donations.

Although her works are well known in many countries, in certain parts of the world one might still ask, "Who is Margaret Atwood?" Here in Canada, she is a household name, largely thanks to her 1985 book *The Handmaid's Tale*.[18] This dystopian tale, updated in 2015 (and also made into a movie and TV series), along with her recent sequel, *The Testaments*,[19] has made her famous. She has been recognized through numerous awards – six times nominated for the Booker Prize, winning in 2000 for *The Blind Assassin* and again in 2019 for *The Testaments*. Beyond her artistic contributions, Atwood's activism on behalf of the environment and women's rights is also widely heralded.

Although Atwood refers to herself as an agnostic, she writes and speaks warmly about God's Gardeners. Atwood is no easy friend of religious fundamentalists, but rather she is against fundamentalism of all kinds. Yet for Atwood, A Rocha, which is largely evangelical Christian, obviously has an appeal. There is a winsomeness about its approach that is not lost on her. A Rocha provides a bridge between some environmentalists who often think Christians are concerned only about saving souls and those Christians who do not understand the biblical call for creation care and are ambivalent about environmental issues. Through its approach, A Rocha Canada has quietly won converts from both sides since its formation in the late 1990s.

What is the A Rocha secret to engaging with diverse communities? In a word, it is *incarnational*. Everything about the work of A Rocha is embodied in the whole community of creation – human and nonhuman alike. When A Rocha Canada was established, there was no field site. The fledgling group awkwardly began operating by staging field trips and outdoor educational events. After purchasing the first field studies center in South Surrey near Vancouver (with no money in the bank to pay for it), and beginning with ecological restoration activities on the site, the mantra became "come and see." Visitors to the beautiful site, complete with a heritage home, wetlands, fields, and forests, instantly understood the vision. Unlike traditional environmental organizations that center operations out of offices, this group of dedicated people lived together on the site, in community. They were there for the long haul. The goal was to pursue stewardship of the Little Campbell River Watershed, working within the watershed itself. A key pursuit initiated then, and continued to this day, was the gardening that Atwood speaks fondly of –

---

18. Margaret Atwood, *The Handmaid's Tale* (Toronto: McClelland & Stewart, 1985).
19. Margaret Atwood, *The Testaments* (New York: Vintage, 2019).

undertaken with core principles including sustainable agriculture, organic methods, long-term soil health, and the belief that the Lord himself provides wisdom to unleash the potential of the land.

Deborah Bowen, professor of English at Redeemer University in Ontario, did an analysis of Atwood's MaddAddam trilogy in relation to ecology and eschatology.[20] In the process, she highlighted Atwood's recent connection with A Rocha Canada and how this real-life relationship dovetailed with what Atwood is trying to say in her works of dystopian fiction. As Bowen notes, although dystopian in nature, the stories told in the MaddAddam trilogy do contain seeds of hope. Bowen points to the current vision for creation care within Christian theology, and lived out by groups such as A Rocha, as the beginning of a movement against Christian dogma adhered to in some quarters that promotes separation between humanity and creation.

Atwood's vision for the potential end of things is dark and apocalyptic, and yet it is the Gardeners who bring hope even when they themselves face near eradication in *The Year of the Flood* as they sing:

> Give up your anger and your spite,
> And imitate the Deer, the Tree;
> In sweet Forgiveness find your joy,
> For it alone can set you free.[21]

## Katharine Hayhoe: Climate-Change Communicator

We now move our focus into the realm of climate-change science. Katharine Hayhoe, an atmospheric scientist and professor of political science, grew up in a family of faith. She was born in Toronto, where she spent her first nine years, until her missionary parents moved the family to Colombia. Thus, many of her formative years spent outside North America sparked her imagination and empathy for others. Hayhoe makes no apology for her faith. In an editorial for *Science*, one of the premier science publications in the world, she wrote, "I'm a Christian – but I'm also a scientist."[22] Hayhoe has earned the respect of colleagues across the spectrum of science and faith communities for her forthright approach to the science and policy of climate change. This move

---

20. Deborah C. Bowen, "Ecological Endings and Eschatology: Margaret Atwood's Post-Apocalyptic Fiction," *Christianity & Literature* 66, no. 4 (2017): 691–705.

21. Margaret Atwood, *The Year of the Flood: A Novel* (Toronto: McClelland & Stewart, 2009), 427.

22. Katharine Hayhoe, "When Facts Are Not Enough," *Science* 360, no. 6392 (2018): 943.

to transparency is, she says, "the most important step I've taken to make my science communication more effective." And it has nothing to do with science, but everything to do with relationships and connecting "climate directly to what's already meaningful in one's life."

Today, *Global Weirding*, as her short video series with PBS is called, is her signature venue. Interestingly, one of the most popular episodes in this series is entitled "The Bible Doesn't Talk about Climate Change, Right?" It is filled with clever and informative cartoons that grab your attention. As a climate communicator, she is leading us all into a new way of thinking about this planetary system, and also about ourselves.

Hayhoe did her undergraduate degree in astronomy and physics at the University of Toronto, intent on becoming an astronomer. But, needing one more science course in her final year, she decided to take the newly developed climate science course. Through it, a new intellectual world opened up, and she was hooked on the science of climate change. Here was a discipline based on the same science she learned for astronomy. She soon realized that climate change cannot be limited to an "environmental" issue; rather, it is a threat multiplier, making the most challenging humanitarian issues of the day – things like access to clean water, food security, poverty, and transnational refugee migration – much worse. She asks, "How could I not do everything I could to help fix this huge global challenge?"[23]

Her journey to policy specialist and public intellectual involved graduate degrees in policy-relevant science and in methods for translating global models into regional and local projections. Today, some 125 publications later, she has well-established international scientific credentials. Her public influence in climate change discussions has taken numerous forms, including writing books, taking up speaking engagements, giving a TED talk, and founding ATMOS Research, a group bridging the gap between stakeholders and the science community. Now based in the Department of Political Science at Texas Tech University, Hayhoe is a director of the Climate Center, where she holds the Political Science Endowed Professorship in Public Policy and Public Law.

Hayhoe's role as spokesperson for action on climate change has led to numerous awards and honors. In 2019 she was named United Nations Environment Programme Champion of the Earth. That same year she was also named Chatelaine Woman of the Year in Canada "for being a relentless (and reasonable!) voice on climate change." The international media has also

---

23. Katharine Hayhoe, "Katharine Hayhoe: Climate Scientist," 2016, http://www.katharinehayhoe.com/wp2016/biography/.

been paying attention. Catchy phrases, such as "A thermometer is not liberal or conservative," dot her public discourse. The realities of a warming earth, such as forest fires occurring inside the Arctic Circle in 2018, make their way into her research. Her awards bring greater opportunity to communicate the need for action now.

The projections for Canada, of increasingly record high temperatures and killer heat waves – like those already seen in Canada in the past few years – are what our future holds. How does one communicate the immensity of climate change to the public? Here is where Hayhoe shines; she has noticed something that many have missed. Facts do not change people's minds; relationships and respect do. Her insights into changing minds came in the most personal of ways – with her husband, Andrew. The young couple talked about many things while dating but, while it seems remarkable in hindsight, climate change never came up. Katharine had never met anyone who thought that climate change was not real, and Andrew had never met a Christian who thought that it was. Imagine the mutual incredulity they then had to navigate together. So what held them together when the topic surfaced? It was their relationship that allowed for conversation. Their love was the glue that created the opportunity to look at the facts, to consider the alternatives. Could it be that in the debates today we have forgotten to love one another? It was said of the early Christian church, "See how they love one another." Could it be that Katharine Hayhoe has found a pathway that can lead us forward, together?

## Cindy Verbeek: Streamkeeper

When Cindy Verbeek arrived at The King's University in Edmonton, Alberta, it was evident that she and her four new study friends had a passion and determination for environmental issues, becoming leaders not only within the university community, but also in their respective communities beyond the university. Verbeek lives in Houston, BC, where she is the spokesperson for the Upper Bulkley River Streamkeepers, and the A Rocha Canada Northern BC Community mobilizer and representative.

Houston is a logging and mining town located on the highly modified delta flats of Buck Creek. Cindy and her husband Dennis have raised three children in this valley community of about three thousand people. Historically, the rivers and valleys of the Central Interior produced prodigious runs of Pacific salmon in a rich ecosystem supporting the First Nations peoples (broadly, the Wet'suwet'en Nation). However, because of unsustainable resource-extraction practices, this stretch of river is now one of the most endangered in the Skeena watershed. Today, after a decades-long journey of planning, advocacy, and fundraising, a community-based salmon hatchery and separate educational interpretive center are serving this community. The Buck Creek Streamkeeper/Canfor hatchery project has raised over $250,000 in grants, gifts, and volunteer hours to build these new solar-powered facilities. Verbeek knows that the key to community transformation is tapping into the passion of people. She says she discovered that

> fish are the language of our community. Whether you are the clerk in a grocery store or a CEO of a big company, as soon as you start talking about salmon their eyes light up. They get all excited and have stories to tell. There is much brokenness in our watershed, both relationally between people and between people and the land.[24]

Salmon enhancement through small-scale grassroots community-led stewardship projects is vital, not only to a sustainable BC salmon fishery, but to a redemptive community in this wilderness landscape.

Verbeek's journey from capable undergraduate to community leader in the Bulkley Valley has deep institutional roots in faith-based environmental programs. In the spring of 1994, she enrolled at the Au Sable Institute of Environmental Studies, located in Michigan between the Great Lakes of Michigan and Huron. This institute specializes in intensive field-based undergraduate-level education, drawing students from across North America. Its faculty are not just subject experts, but also experienced at building a faith-based community of active learners. Weekly integrative discussions and field trips shape the unique pedagogical approach. On her way to earning a Naturalist certificate Verbeek was daily immersed in learning within the context of field and forest, an approach to creation care pioneered by Au Sable.[25] Prayer, reflective walks, field trips, journaling, and volleyball, swimming, and long hikes are all part of an Au Sable day.

Buildings on any campus are central to what David Orr called the hidden curriculum, but especially so at the institute.[26] Designed to blend into the

---

24. Personal communication with the author.

25. The source of this term ("Creation Care," "Caring for Creation," or "the Care of Creation") in the North American evangelical context can be traced to the community at the Au Sable Institute of Environmental Studies, Michigan. It is detailed in the first edition of Calvin B. DeWitt's *Earth-Wise: A Biblical Response to Environmental Issues* (Grand Rapids: CRC, 1994).

26. David Orr, "What Is Education For?," ch. 1 in *Earth in Mind: On Education, Environment, and the Human Condition* (Washington: Island, 1994), 9–15.

forest, the half-buried Earth Hall has a forest meadow for its roof. Looking around the 270-degree views from the dining hall windows at the antics of chipmunks, nuthatches, jays, and the occasional raccoon is a regular treat for guests. Communal meals provide moments to linger for in-depth conversations with students, faculty, and their families. After lunch one day in conversation with Au Sable's founder and director, Dr. Calvin DeWitt, Verbeek asked, "You call this an environmental institute, but what is so environmentally friendly about it?" An hour and a half later, after a campus walkabout with "Cal," as he is affectionately known, she had the answers. There, hiding in plain sight, were fifty or more features reducing the ecological footprint of the institute. Today at each new-class orientation Verbeek's list of energy, water, food, waste, and other innovations as taught by DeWitt are in the "Welcome" pack.

Verbeek's journey from capable undergraduate to community leader, author, and innovator in a small British Columbia community is exemplary. It shows the possibility that personal qualities can have, such as perseverance and imagination combined with a deep love of people and all of God's other creatures, especially when shaped by innovative educational programs. As David Orr has said, "the crisis we face is first and foremost one of mind, perception, and values."[27] We need a new generation like Verbeek. When she sees a need she imagines a change, and then rallies friends and communities into focused action. She is a builder. She has a founder's vision, and an earthkeeper's heart. The challenge, then, is to create educational opportunities that will continue to shape minds, perceptions, and values to prepare the next generation of environmental stewards.

## Rick Faw: Earthkeeping Missionary

Unlike Verbeek, Rick Faw did not intend to pursue his undergraduate education with creation care in mind. Although he grew up in the fertile Fraser Valley Bible Belt in lower BC, creation care was not a message he ever heard clearly – not at home, nor in church, nor at Canada's largest Christian liberal arts university, Trinity Western University (TWU). (As an aside, one of the authors of this chapter is a faculty member at TWU. Since Faw graduated, creation care has become more widespread at TWU. Now it would be hard to obtain a degree at TWU without hearing the message of creation care.)

As he pursued his chemistry major, Faw had a vague plan of becoming a chemical engineer. Unlike Verbeek, Faw went to the Au Sable Institute of

---

27. Orr, *Earth in Mind*, 27.

Environmental Studies for a summer adventure and to pick up a few more course credits – nothing more. He describes the eight-week period at the field-station site in Michigan as one of the most emotionally turbulent periods of his life. He would never see the world the same way again.

What he learned from Christian faculty teaching at Au Sable, and the whole Au Sable milieu, was that creation care was not simply an add-on. As he testifies, "Every aspect of life has some impact on creation and, thus, the Spirit aims to transform *every* aspect of my life. I remember thinking, 'This changes everything!'"[28]

Faw may be described as mild-mannered, but his evangelical fervor, especially after his summer at Au Sable, has the burnished edge of righteous anger. Again and again he asked his mentors in the faith, "Why did you never tell me?" And if they did not seem aware of the creation care element, "Why have you not heard?" Faw's father, Harold, a psychology professor at Trinity Western University, listened intently to his son's passionate message and eventually became an evangelist for creation care, too.

In 2004, Faw joined the A Rocha Canada team after completing a master's in Christian studies at Regent College, giving him the opportunity to advocate for earthkeeping as a full-time career. To this day he is a key leader at A Rocha, as vice president of programming. Joining A Rocha is not like joining a corporation, where your salary is defined. Most of the A Rocha team members fundraise for their positions, going to their communities and beyond. An A Rocha staffer is an *earthkeeping missionary* – a very fitting title for Faw.

Rick and his wife Crista raised their two kids, Jared and Zoë, at A Rocha. The family loves living in community with like-minded souls. When A Rocha was gifted a larger property to serve as the new center in the BC Lower Mainland, the previous property, acquired "on a wing and a prayer" but never fully paid for, went up for sale using a bid system where the potential buyers had to demonstrate their stewardship commitment. Faw's family, along with other A Rocha families, put in the winning bid, and thus Kingfisher Farm, as it is known, became part of the A Rocha work in the Little Campbell watershed. Being part of A Rocha means an active community life, sharing devotions, meals, outdoor activities, growing and harvesting food, as well as hosting interns and visitors.

Faw is involved in many aspects of the public face of A Rocha, hosting events, both large and small, and staging many creation-care conferences in British Columbia and across Canada, often as the "behind the scenes guy." He

---

28. From personal communication.

is also a very effective communicator, speaking at churches or to various groups that come to the A Rocha Brooksdale Environmental Centre.

Faw's core message is always the same, true to his life-changing and life-giving experience at Au Sable. At Regent, when a professor asked him about his goals as a Christian, he answered, "I want to help Christ followers better understand the creation-wide implications of the gospel." As he says, "We are invited to join the Spirit in cultivating shalom in our relationships with God, each other, and creation." If this earthkeeping missionary was sitting across from you, the reader, right now, he would likewise invite you into this deeper experience of the Christian life, if you are not yet there.

A Rocha's incarnational work does involve Faw and other A Rocha staff engaging in deep conversation with many souls. For example, every year A Rocha Canada hosts interns from around the world, and seldom do they return home unchanged. After spending the summer of 2020 at A Rocha's Brooksdale Environmental Centre, intern Laura Naftel reflected:

> At A Rocha I have found myself dwelling in a place where hope is founded, delight is genuine, and rest is a given. This is not some naïve escape from the harshness of life. If anything, it exists as a direct response to the surrounding predicament in which the world is found.
>
> Throughout my time here, I have acquired no simple conclusions to any of my questions, hurts, and dreams. This I appreciate; I possess no patience for such things. However, I am learning to hope, learning to rest, maybe, even learning to live. Being blessed into loving the land – and to do this alongside others – has done wonders to my being.
>
> I have seen abundant harvests cultivated from this hallowed land. I have tasted radical generosity in the form of grace, understanding, and blueberries. I have felt pieces of my being made whole while listening to children fall in love with creation care. I have been held captive by the aroma of this community, a resilient and committed community. This is no fairy-tale, it is a very real piece of a very different sort of kingdom.[29]

---

29. Used with permission.

## Elizabeth Zwamborn: Whale Whisperer

Elizabeth Zwamborn grew up in the A Rocha Canada milieu. Her mother's donation of their family's beautiful estate to A Rocha became the Brooksdale Environmental Centre, an eighteen-acre property with historic Tudor-style buildings, fields, and woodlands, and a significant section of the Little Campbell River for salmon spawning. Zwamborn's sights were always set further downstream, however, as the Little Campbell River empties into the Salish Sea, where the leviathans frolic.

Her unique love for marine life began with special childhood experiences. At age five she visited the Newport Aquarium in Kentucky where she saw the killer whale star of *Free Willy* being rehabilitated before his release off Iceland. Her first encounter with wild killer whales came at age eleven on a whale watching boat. As she describes it, "I'll never forget the moment A33 (Nimpkish), a mature bull northern resident killer whale with the textbook perfect six-foot tall dorsal fin, broke through the waters coming out of the fog. Around him, the rest of his family surfaced to breathe. This was another formative moment in my childhood. A precious moment where I felt one with creation, beyond just being a silent witness to the wonder of nature around me."[30]

When Zwamborn entered her undergraduate program at Trinity Western University in 2009, she already had a passion for marine biology and soon found a niche where she could flourish. As she relates,

> For the first time in my life I found a collection of like-minded people, who were passionate about conservation and stewardship of creation from both a scientific and personal approach. I took courses that taught me not only about the diversity of nature, but the application of restoration as well as the joy of science beyond experimentation and the simple asking of questions. It was here that I learned about being an advocate for both the applications of my scientific research and current environmental crises that I was connected to.

The highlights, though, of her undergraduate experience took place off campus. She enrolled in field courses offered by Trinity Western on Salt Spring Island and on Hawaii, which allowed each student a chance to truly explore his or her connection with creation in a unique way. Her grasp of the spirit of

---

30. All quotes from Zwamborn in this section are taken from personal communications with her from November 2020.

these courses equipped her to be a teaching assistant for the Salt Spring Course and even to fill in as an instructor.

Likewise, her enrollment in the Au Sable Institute of Environmental Studies field courses on Whidbey Island was transformative: "These classes introduced me to the endangered Southern Resident killer whales, as well as other beautiful marine mammals that call these urban waterways home." Once again, the student became the teacher, becoming one of Au Sable's youngest faculty members ever, teaching the Au Sable marine mammals course in 2016 and 2017, while still in the midst of her graduate studies. In 2016 she was truly a whale whisperer, as whenever Zwamborn took the class on a field trip, a marine mammal or two showed up; the class saw not only these amazing creations, but also the unabashed excitement of their young professor.

At the time of writing Zwamborn has nearly completed her PhD research on long-finned pilot whales at Dalhousie University in Nova Scotia. As she reflects on her budding academic career that has already taken her around the world chasing whales (including the west and east coasts of North America, the Galapagos, and the Caribbean), Zwamborn has the following advice:

> The more you know about the plight of creation, the easier it is to despair about all the destruction, and the more you will have to search for hope. Surround yourself with people who won't give up, not those who are complacent. Never give up on advocating for the protection of the natural world, because one person can make a significant difference for the better in how we steward the earth.

## Redeemer University: Water Monitoring Project

In 2012, professor of chemistry Dr. Darren Brouwer began to rethink how to teach analytical chemistry to second- and third-year students at Redeemer University in Ancaster, Ontario. When talking with local stakeholders, he learned that the Chedoke Creek Watershed, an urban watershed very close to Redeemer's campus, was suspected of being contaminated with sewage. No one was closely monitoring this stream that drains into Cootes Paradise, an ecologically significant wetland at the western edge of Lake Ontario. Brouwer incorporated standard water quality tests into the laboratory portion of the course. Then he invited local stakeholders from the community to hear the students present their results.

Monitoring has continued, involving senior students in a summer research program and expansion of the project through external research grants. In partnership with local environmental NGOs and City of Hamilton staff, Redeemer University has hosted public events informing the community of the issues, and steps are being taken toward improving water quality. Project-based learning can be chaotic and requires detailed planning and faculty guidance. Yet this community-engaged research is a rich learning experience that typically accomplishes more than classroom-based learning would. Students work with the local community, connecting their academic knowledge and skills with local needs or issues. The community benefits too, as people gain a deeper understanding of the local ecological context. This is another concrete way in which educators can help to restore creation, serving others and practicing what we preach.

## Hope That Endures

Our beautiful world faces numerous significant environmental challenges. Yet there are many wonderful stories of people committed to using their gifts and talents to restore God's good earth, including politicians, authors, scientists, earthkeeping missionaries, streamkeepers, educators, and whale whisperers. All are faithfully striving to bless and keep God's world and inspire others to not give up hope.

Pawpaw trees reflect a deep history and richness of the earth. Planting a tree, knowing our local flora and fauna, loving the place where we're planted – if not putting it in our pocket, but putting it in our minds and hearts – is a way to access those riches. By enhancing native diversity (planting pawpaws!), restoring habitats, protecting whales, monitoring water quality, serving in NGOs, effectively communicating the urgency of climate change, and striving to faithfully educate a new generation of graduates in Christian institutions, we demonstrate our love of creation and can all help address planetary boundaries one small step at a time. We trust that these lessons from Canada will find fertile ground and germinate in hope that will endure throughout God's good earth.

The authors are most grateful for an extremely helpful review of the manuscript by Katharine Bubel. We also thank Markku and Leah Kostamo for providing insights on many of the characters we have portrayed.

## References

A Rocha Canada. "Panel Response (Earthkeeping: A Climate for Change)." YouTube. 19 May 2015. https://www.youtube.com/watch?v=eMXfkTRa6wA.

Atwood, Margaret. *The Handmaid's Tale*. Toronto: McClelland & Stewart, 1985.

———. "Preston Manning, Man of the Future." *National Post*, 28 August 2015. https://nationalpost.com/opinion/margaret-atwood-preston-manning-man-of-the-future/.

———. "Saving What We Love: A Hopeful Encounter with Real-Life 'God's Gardeners.'" *Sojourners*, February 2014. https://sojo.net/magazine/february-2014/saving-what-we-love/.

———. *The Testaments*. New York: Vintage, 2019.

———. *The Year of the Flood: A Novel*. Toronto: McClelland & Stewart, 2009.

Bowen, Deborah C. "Ecological Endings and Eschatology: Margaret Atwood's Post-Apocalyptic Fiction." *Christianity & Literature* 66, no. 4 (2017): 691–705.

DeWitt, Calvin B. *Earth-Wise: A Biblical Response to Environmental Issues*. Grand Rapids: CRC, 1994.

Hayhoe, Katharine. "Katharine Hayhoe: Climate Scientist." 2016. http://www.katharinehayhoe.com/wp2016/biography/.

———. "When Facts Are Not Enough." *Science* 360, no. 6392 (2018): 943.

Hopper, Tristin. "Twenty Years after Kyoto, Preston Manning Has Become Canadian Conservatives' Most Prominent Green Advocate." *National Post*, 2 January 2015. https://nationalpost.com/news/politics/twenty-years-after-kyoto-preston-manning-has-become-canadian-conservatives-most-prominent-green-advocate/.

Kostamo, Leah. *Planted: A Story of Creation, Calling, and Community*. Eugene: Wipf & Stock, 2013.

Looy, Heather, and John R. Wood. "Imagination, Hospitality, and Affection: The Unique Legacy of Food Insects?" *Animal Frontiers* 5, no. 2 (2015): 8–13.

Manning, Preston. "The Blueing and Greening of the Political Centre." *The Globe and Mail*, 16 March 2010. https://www.theglobeandmail.com/opinion/the-blueing-and-greening-of-the-political-centre/article1210070/.

———. "Navigating the Faith/Political Interface." *C2C Journal*, 19 June 2009. https://c2cjournal.ca/2009/06/navigating-the-faithpolitical-interface/.

Neufeld, Josiah. "Manning Preaches Three-Cornered Gospel." *Christian Week*, 2 November 2010. https://www.christianweek.org/manning-preaches-three-cornered-gospel/.

Orr, David. "What Is Education For?" In *Earth in Mind: On Education, Environment, and the Human Condition*, 9–15. Washington: Island, 1994.

Rockström, J., W. Steffen, K. Noone, et al. "A Safe Operating Space for Humanity." *Nature* 461 (2009): 472–75.

Schaeffer, Francis. *Pollution and the Death of Man: The Christian View of Ecology*. Carol Stream: Tyndale House, 1970.

Steffen, Will, Katherine Richardson, Johan Rockström, et al. "Planetary Boundaries: Guiding Human Development on a Changing Planet." *Science* 347, no. 6223 (2015): 1259855.

Wood, John R. "Biophilia and the Gospel: Loving Nature or Worshipping God?" In *Living in the Lamblight: Christianity and Contemporary Challenges to the Gospel*, edited by H. Boersma, 153–76. Vancouver: Regent, 2001.

## Further Reading

Suggested readings related to the individuals featured in this chapter, and their work:

Preston Manning
Manning, Preston. *Faith, Leadership and Public Life: Leadership Lessons from Moses to Jesus*. Paris: Castle Quay, 2017.

Margaret Atwood
Bowen, Deborah C. "Ecological Endings and Eschatology: Margaret Atwood's Post-Apocalyptic Fiction." *Christianity & Literature* 66, no. 4 (2017): 691–705.

Katharine Hayhoe
Hayhoe, Katharine. *Saving Us: A Climate Scientist's Case for Hope and Healing in a Divided World*. New York: Simon and Schuster, 2021.
Karelas, Andreas, and Katharine Hayhoe. *Climate Courage: How Tackling Climate Change Can Build Community, Transform the Economy, and Bridge the Political Divide in America*. Boston: Beacon, 2020.

Cindy Verbeek
Moyer, Joanne. "Faith-Based Environmental Work in Canada: A Profile." *Western Geographer* 23 (2018): 60–85.
Moyer, Joanne M., and Stephen Bede Scharper. "The Fabric of Faith-Based Environmentalism in Canada." *Worldviews* 23 (2019): 33–38.

For a seminal treatment of community-based ENGOs (environmental nongovernmental organizations), and especially faith-based ones, see:
Hawken, Paul. *Blessed Unrest: How the Largest Movement in the World Came into Being and Why No One Saw It Coming*. New York: Viking, 2007.

Rick Faw
Bliss, Lowell. *Environmental Missions: Planting Churches and Trees*. Pasadena: William Carey Library, 2013.
DeWitt, C. B., and G. T. Prance, eds. *Missionary Earthkeeping*. Macon: Mercer University Press, 1992.

Regent College and A Rocha, both of which featured prominently in this chapter, have had a close and fruitful working relationship over the years. For details see:

Harris, Peter. *Kingfisher's Fire: A Story of Hope for God's Earth*. Grand Rapids: Monarch, 2008.

Wilkinson, Loren, ed. *Earthkeeping in the Nineties: Stewardship of Creation*. Eugene: Wipf & Stock, 2003.

# 9

# Christian Engagement with Artificial Intelligence across the Continents

Ah Chung Tsoi, University of Macau
Martin Ester, Simon Fraser University, Canada

**Abstract**

Artificial intelligence (AI) has recently achieved spectacular breakthroughs which have caused a great deal of optimism and even hype. On one hand, AI has great potential benefits in bringing economic prosperity, improving human health, and protecting the environment. To this end many countries, are heavily investing in AI research and development. On the other hand, the risks of AI-powered decision-making, such as bias, lack of explainability, and lack of accountability, are receiving more – and more critical – attention in the public discourse. In this chapter, we discuss the commonalities and differences of this discourse in China, the USA, and Europe. At a more philosophical level, proponents of "strong" AI promise human beings to attain unprecedented intellectual capacity and to achieve superhuman intelligence. This raises ultimate questions about the nature of consciousness and of humans, in particular the question whether body and mind are distinct entities. We engage this debate from a Christian point of view, which suggests the existence of a distinct mind and soul. We show that the utopian hope of achieving superhuman intelligence is misplaced, as it usurps the sovereignty of God and places our trust on the created.

## Introduction

The term "artificial intelligence" (AI) was coined in a 1956 summer school of Dartmouth College by John McCarthy who defined it as "the science and engineering of making intelligent machines."[1] AI research has a long history and has gone through phases of exciting progress as well as great disappointments and funding cuts. It has seen the so-called AI winter in the late 1980s and early 1990s, as well as its recent advances and resurgence. The first generation of AI systems was knowledge-based, relying on symbolic knowledge representations and deductive reasoning. Knowledge was represented by facts and rules that had to be coded by human domain experts, which meant that these systems did not scale and could not adapt to dynamic environments. To avoid these limitations, more recent generations of AI systems rely on machine-learning algorithm to automatically generate a predictive model from given training data. There is a general notion among researchers that the more training data there is, the better will be the predictive capabilities of the machine-learning models.

Powered by machine learning, AI research has achieved impressive breakthroughs over the past decades, and has entered an industrial age, being deployed by industries and commerce, the sciences, and governments. Prominent AI systems include AlphaGo, which can beat the best human Go players; autonomous driving systems, which exhibit driving abilities comparable to those of human drivers; virtual assistants such as Alexa and Siri, which communicate using natural language; DALL.E, which can generate original high-resolution images that match a given caption; GPT-3, which can generate sensible and readable prose from initial prompting texts; and AlphaFold, which can predict the 3D structure of proteins with human-expert-level performance. Less-well-known AI systems work in the background to classify images on the internet, translate texts between languages, and power customer financial-credit-rating systems in financial institutions. The successes of AI systems in solving complex practical problems, and apparently achieving human-level intelligence, has led people to ponder the question: Has AI already developed to such an extent that one might consider some of these AI systems as being conscious?

Some national governments have adopted the idea of Big Data in their IT systems. India, for example, has launched a national-identity program for all its citizens. China has created a social-credit system to score citizens' honesty,

---

1. James Moor, "The Dartmouth College Artificial Intelligence Conference: The Next Fifty Years," *AI Magazine* 27, no. 4 (2006): 87–91.

# Christian Engagement with Artificial Intelligence across the Continents    177

sincerity, and integrity, with the score being used to determine crucial aspects of individuals' lives, such as where they can live, whether they can purchase a plane ticket, or whether they are being given preferential treatment by hospitals, universities, or government services. Additionally, China's strategies to enforce their zero COVID-19 policy were based on database systems which recorded the test status of each citizen, with a QR code which was normally green but turned red if the person tested positive. That person was then not allowed to travel outside his or her place of residence. Someone living in an area which had known occurrences of COVID-19 cases needed to be tested daily, and would not be allowed to travel until the QR code turned green. These Chinese systems made heavy use of AI technology to determine the identity of persons on surveillance camera images, and to detect suspicious patterns of behavior in their large databases.

Given that AI is affecting, impacting, and permeating all aspects of human society, interesting questions arise: What are the perspectives of governments, companies, and individuals on the challenges and opportunities offered by AI? How do these perspectives differ in different cultural contexts? Moreover, how do Christians across diverse continents engage with the development and deployment of AI?

In this chapter, we will first introduce AI more thoroughly, briefly present its goals and methods, and discuss its relationships to concepts such as consciousness. We will then discuss the different perspectives on AI from three different continents: Europe, America, and Asia. Finally, we will sketch a Christian perspective on AI, which shares aspects with the secular perspectives across the continents but also has important distinctives.

## What Is AI?

Artificial intelligence has been defined as intelligence demonstrated by machines, as opposed to the natural intelligence displayed by animals or humans. AI research explores computer systems that perceive their environment and take actions that maximize the chance of achieving specified goals. Such research aims to create computer programs that can solve tasks that have been generally considered to require intelligence, and the following subareas of AI have been distinguished: computer vision, natural language processing, robotics, reasoning, planning, and learning. As mentioned in the introduction to this chapter, modern AI systems are typically based on machine-learning methods that learn to perform a certain task from large collections of training examples. AlphaGo, for example, has been trained from millions of Go games that a computer played against itself, and image-classification algorithms have been trained from similar numbers of images that were labeled by humans as belonging to a class such as "tiger," "cat," or "dog."

## *Neural Networks*

Among machine-learning methods, neural networks – and, more specifically, deep neural networks – have become especially prominent due to their outstanding learning capacity and high generalization accuracy of the resulting models when tested with samples which were not used to train the model. Neural networks consist of nodes (neurons) that are connected to each other through edges (synapses), which are associated with learnable weights. Input nodes receive the input data, such as an image. Output nodes produce the output predictions, such as the class of the image. The input and output nodes are connected to each other via various layers of inner (hidden) nodes, which generate latent representations of the input during the training process. The weights associated with the edges/links between nodes of the neural network are trained such that they optimize an objective function, for example minimizing the difference between the predicted class and the true class on the training data.

Once the objective function is optimized, the model is said to be trained, and this trained model may be applied to predict the class of samples which were not used in the training process. Well-designed neural-network architectures (e.g. a deep neural network consisting of a number of hidden layers), when trained with a large volume of labeled data, can produce high generalization accuracy for previously unseen samples. The results are often much more accurate than those of other methods, including classification performed by humans.

Even when the AI can surpass humans' classification, it is not the case that humans are removed from the process. With respect to input, human experts are required to design the architecture of the neural network and its objective function, and humans are needed to provide suitable training data. The computer then automatically learns the best weights of the neural network. Humans are also intimately involved as the data is being processed, not least because the data being processed is often about humans. Making heavy use of sensitive personal data, AI systems raise privacy concerns. For example, it has been demonstrated that the training data share information through the class information. If the input data contain personal information, such personal information could be shared unwittingly by the fact that two examples share the same class. Finally, with respect to output, human experts are required to interpret how the results should be understood. The AI model discussed here is a black-box model, as it cannot explain in a human-understandable way how and why a certain prediction is produced as output. The lack of explainability would create a major problem if one were to apply a deep-learning model to problems which require some accountability of the model, for example self-driving cars, or systems for medical decision-making.

## *Weak and Strong AI*

Two different paradigms of AI have emerged: weak and strong. Weak AI attempts to build systems which perform certain tasks that are generally assumed to require intelligence, and which function at a skill level comparable to that of humans. However, with weak AI, the computer's method of solution can be completely different from the human's solution method. Strong AI sets the much more ambitious goal of not only solving tasks so that the results are similar to those of humans, but solving them in a way that emulates the human art of cognition and reasoning. This is seen as a way to potentially create AI systems with consciousness, and ultimately even to create "superhumans," as the next step in the evolution of our species. It is worth noting that these two paradigms sometimes mix. For example, deep neural networks were originally inspired by scientific insights into the structure and function of human brains (which is aligned to the strong paradigm), but their subsequent development has been driven mainly by computational approaches to improve their robustness, efficiency, and interpretability (as per the interests of weak AI).

Technology throughout human history has served humans to accomplish the tasks at hand by enhancing their natural abilities, initially mainly their physical abilities, and more recently also their mental abilities. According to Ming-Hui Huang and Roland Rust, there are four levels of AI intelligence: mechanical, analytical, intuitive, and empathic.[2] Mechanical intelligence is mostly algorithmic, often repetitive, requiring consistency and accuracy. Analytic intelligence is analytical, rule-based, and for tasks which require logical thinking and decision-making. Intuitive intelligence involves creative thinking for problem-solving. Lastly, empathic intelligence requires social communication and relationship-building. Mechanical and analytic intelligence are in the domain of weak AI, while intuitive and empathic intelligence are

---

2. Ming-Hui Huang and Roland Rust, "Artificial Intelligence in Service," *Journal of Service Research* 2, no. 2 (2018): 155–72.

considered to be in the domain of strong AI. According to Hadi Esmaeilzadeh and Reza Vaezi, a machine can be said to be conscious if it is able to accomplish intuitive or empathic intelligence.[3]

Esmaeilzadeh and Vaezi argue that "consciousness is an emergent phenomenon when two machines co-create their own language through which they can communicate their internal state of time-varying symbol manipulation, especially when these co-created symbols do not correspond to external objects and represent shared metaconcepts."[4] In other words, two conscious machines are able to communicate their internal states with one another through a language of their own creation through collaboration, and such a language is different from that used by the humans who created those two machines in the first place.

To dig more deeply into this idea, let us do a thought experiment. Consider an artificially intelligent machine running GPT-4, a state-of-the-art AI text-generation system which can converse with humans in a natural language such as English. The user enters an input text prompt, and the GPT-4 system will generate an output text as a response. We select this system for our thought experiment, as it seems to some people to be "intelligent" or even "conscious" because it is able to create an output text which gives a well-reasoned and nuanced response to the input text. The GPT-4 model works by being pretrained on a large text corpus – for example, crawled from the internet – and is fine-tuned based on examples of human feedback to avoid undesirable responses. A fully trained model can then be applied to any input text (called the prompt) to produce a corresponding output text (called the response). This is sufficient detail for the present discussion, though we provide a more detailed description of GPT-4 and GPT technology later in this chapter.

Now imagine having two such machines, with each being able to provide input text to the other, which can respond by providing an output text. The two machines can continue to converse back and forth in such a manner for as long as they want. To see if these machines become "conscious" (in Esmaeilzadeh and Vaezi's sense), one would need to examine a continuous dialogue between them. The two machines would need to slowly change their natural language into a language which they co-create and both understand and use to communicate with each other.

---

3. Hadi Esmaeilzadeh and Reza Vaezi, "Conscious Empathic AI in Service," *Journal of Service Research* 25, no. 4 (June 2022): 549–64, DOI: 10.1177/10946705221103531.

4. Esmaeilzadeh and Vaezi, "Conscious Empathic AI."

Let us call these two machines M1 and M2. M1 issues an initial text, T1. Upon receiving T1 as prompt, M2 will apply its GPT-4 model to produce a response text, T2. Note that there is no learning taking place by M2 from the content of T1. M2 is simply taking the input T1 and applying its GPT-4 model, which has been pretrained and fine-tuned prior to the dialogue. The text T2 then becomes an input to M1, and M1 will apply its GPT-4 model to T2 to produce a response, T3. Again, there is no learning or training involved. In addition, the vocabulary of a GPT-4 model is fixed after training, which means that the model cannot "invent" new words at the time of application. In conclusion, we argue that the two machines M1 and M2 will not be able to develop a new language between themselves and would fail the Esmaeilzadeh and Vaezi test of being "conscious."

What if we allow a human into the loop – say, a human attached to M2 – to examine the output T2 which resulted from the input prompt T1 from M1? The human could then evaluate whether T2 is a good response to T1 and adjust it, if necessary. As an example, let us assume that T1 is inquiring about a manuscript called *Jesus Messiah Sutra*, a Chinese manuscript which is attributed by some scholars to first Jingjiao/Nestorian missionaries to China ca. AD 635 and considered by others as a 1930s' "fake" manuscript which emerged from an antique market in Beijing. Knowing that this information was probably not contained in the internet corpus as of mid 2021, the corpus on which GPT-4 was trained, the human attached to M2 will be able to modify the response T2 to be more truthful and nuanced. However, in this case, the model is no longer autonomous, and thus it again cannot be called "conscious."

From this simple thought experiment, we conclude that a state-of-the-art machine like GPT-4 is unlikely to meet the criterion of consciousness, as set down by Esmaeilzadeh and Vaezi. Unsurprisingly, Esmaeilzadeh and Vaezi in their paper indicate that it would require a paradigm shift to be able to conclude that a machine has emergent consciousness, that is, being self-aware of its environments, and being able to communicate its internal states to another machine. While this example considers AI art based on prompt sentences, it can readily be seen that the limitations it highlights are general across diverse AI applications.

Note that the above analysis does not diminish the tremendous advances in machine learning or weak AI. It merely cautions that we, as human beings, are prone to take a word from the human domain, for example "create," and transfer it to the machine and technology in describing its activities; for example, "this algorithm, called generative adversarial network, is capable of creating a new image which is indistinguishable from a given set of images."

Problematically, we then forget that this is a transfer or borrowing. This is what Raymond Tallis called "the tendency to think by transferred epithet."[5] In this case, the word "conscious" might belong to this category.

To test whether an AI system has achieved the goal of intelligence, AI pioneer Alan Turing in 1950 proposed the following test, which later became famous as the Turing test. The test involves two candidates (one being a computer and the other a human) and a tester (who is human). The tester can ask any questions to the candidates and needs to determine, based on their answers, which of the candidates is the human and which is the computer. To avoid any clues from the style of communication, all communication between tester and both candidates takes place through a keyboard. While the Turing test has been widely adopted, it has also received a lot of criticism. For example, philosopher John Searle in 1980 presented the Chinese Room Argument,[6] which is based on the following thought experiment. Assuming that there is a computer program that passes the Turing test in Chinese, Searle could also pass the Turing test in Chinese by manually executing that computer program step by step. However, Searle, who does not speak Chinese, would only apply syntactic rules and manipulate symbolic strings; he would have no understanding of the meaning or semantics of Chinese. In conclusion, a computer program that passes the Turing test may simply simulate human intelligence, without actually possessing intelligence and consciousness. The thought experiment above clearly supports this view because, while foundation models such as GPT-4 can converse with humans using a human language, they only imitate human speech without any understanding and therefore they cannot be considered "conscious."

## *The Metaverse*

An increasingly important aspect of AI is its potential to be integrated with other technologies in an embedded system. This can be seen with autonomous vehicles (an integration of AI, robotics, and sensing devices such as LIDAR and cameras), Unitree's Go2 robotic dog (an integration of autonomous vehicle technology with GPT-4, resulting in a robot dog that can respond to spoken commands), autonomous surgical robots for dental implants (an integration

---

5. Raymond Tallis, "Bewitched by Language," in *Aping Mankind* (London: Routledge, 2014), 183–208.

6. John Searle, "Minds, Brains and Programs," *Behavioral and Brain Sciences* 3, no. 3 (1980): 417–57.

of AI, precision robotics, and augmented reality), and – especially – in the metaverse (an integration of AI with realistic simulation, the script-writing capability of computer-game technology, artificial-life technology, and virtual reality/augmented reality).

"Metaverse," a term coined by Neal Stephenson in a 1992 science fiction novel called *Snow Crash*, combines two words: "meta" and "universe." As the term is now used, "the metaverse is a collection of multiple advanced virtual worlds that are interconnected with each other and the physical world through specialized hardware and biological interfaces and software technologies, services, and data."[7] This concept, though introduced in 1992, is only now beginning to be implementable with the tremendous advances in many technological areas, including artificial intelligence. The metaverse is an open-ended technology that aims to provide a service platform to enable individual users to conduct their daily work and home lives in an extended-reality world; to form online communities; to monitor their own health; to engage in e-commerce; to be entertained and educated through attendance at cultural events, concerts, and courses; to engage in playing interactive computer games; to provide remote health care; and so on.

The technologies used in the metaverse include natural language processing (NLP, which involves language modeling, word prediction, text-to-speech processing, and semantic labeling), machine vision (object detection and segmentation, image restoration and enhancement, pose estimation, and action recognition); VR/AR (virtual reality, augmented reality, and mixed reality); blockchain (data collection and sharing, data storage and management, and data security); networking (ultrareliable and low-latency communications, multi-access edge computing, and intelligent spectrum utilization); digital twin (data-driven modeling, physical-digital view integration, and analysis-monitoring-prediction-simulation); and neural interfaces (brain-computer interfaces, invasive and noninvasive signals, and mental-state analysis). Machine learning and artificial intelligence play a crucial role in these technologies. The vision of the metaverse is currently being pursued by large companies such as Meta/Facebook, Microsoft, Baidu, and Tencent.

While the technology is being advanced by corporate interests, philosophers ponder the implications of the metaverse and what might be the meaning of reality in the future. In the metaverse, one might be seeing a simulated or real

---

7. Melodena Stephens, *Metaverse and Its Governance*, IEEE Global Initiative on Ethics of Extended Reality (XR) Report (New York: Institute of Electrical and Electronics Engineers, 2022), 7.

world in virtual reality, or in augmented reality. The context which a person sees in a simulated world combined with senses through augmented reality could convince a person of events which might not have occurred in the real world.

Such a possibility of altering one's experience could be viewed positively as enhancing one's experience and improving one's life. For example, there are already some works that use such a simulated environment for Parkinson's disease sufferers: when a freezing of gait is about to occur, an electric pulse is administered to the appropriate spot in the brain to stop the freezing of gait from occurring or to reduce it. On the other hand, if such a machine falls into the hands of a totalitarian regime, it might be used to "bend" the mind of a person through prolonged usage. One might be able to create a parallel universe in one's mind with a "reality" different from the real world. It can readily be seen that such possibilities raise significant questions in diverse areas, which should not be brushed aside.

On a technical level, the implementation of the metaverse raises great engineering challenges to ensure data security, privacy, integrity, authentication, and authorization, in a governance structure.

From a mental-health point of view, the prolonged exposure of a person to an extended-reality environment, either alone or in a community, raises a variety of questions. These include consideration of how we relate to each other, how we relate to the world around us, how we relate to ourselves, and how changes in these modes of relating impact our mental health.

From a philosophical point of view, issues of identity and reality come to the fore. For example, in a metaverse virtual objects can be created with realistic appearance, which may lead us to re-evaluate what is real. According to David Chalmers, a computer simulation *is* real, as it provides the experience of the object being real to one's mind, through tactile and visual senses.[8] With the integration of communication networks as core infrastructure, a metaverse can help humans to overcome the limitations of physical distance. With its data storage, and its simulation possibilities, it might eventually also allow humans to overcome the limitations of time, as the metaverse can record a human's emotions, activities, and geographical location, reconstruct the emotional state and the events which took place in history, and forecast future events based on the recorded history.

From the point of view of religious experience, as a metaverse platform could be used by a religious community, this would raise the questions of what

---

8. David Chalmers, *Reality+: Virtual Worlds and the Problems of Philosophy* (New York: W. W. Norton and Co., 2022).

reality is, what transcendence and immanence are, and what a worship-service experience might mean to the participants.

While some of the above scenarios might sound far-fetched, powerful North American and Chinese companies alike are driving the development of the metaverse, and are racing to release the first metaverse platform which may dominate the market. Governments see the potential of the metaverse to better control their citizens and are also investing a lot of resources into its development. Healthy metaverse platforms will require strong regulations and rules and a clear governance structure to deliver their services in a trustworthy, reliable, and robust manner, and to provide accountability, responsibility, security, and privacy.

## The Perspective on AI from Three Continents: Europe, America, and Asia

So far, we have outlined what AI is, the notions of weak and strong AI, and their relationships to machine learning, Big Data, and the metaverse. These considerations have raised both ethical and philosophical issues, which are both of academic interest and of pressing significance for practical applications.

The main players in AI research and technology are from three large geographical areas: Europe, America, and Asia. Although AI is more than *just* technology, it is *at least* technology. The cultural outlook on AI of these geographical regions is therefore colored by their cultural outlook on technology. In this section, we consider the different responses of these broad regions to the potentials and risks of AI, and its deployment in society.

### *Europe*

Europe has historically been a society in which Christianity – Protestant or Catholic – has been the state religion. However, since the Enlightenment, the influence of religion has gradually weakened and has been replaced by humanism. So, broadly speaking, Europe is now considered a post-Christian region, dominated by a humanistic view of human nature. The general view of technology is to exploit technology for the benefit of humankind, with regulatory oversight to curb excesses.

Of the three regions considered, Europe has adopted the most critical approach to AI. While industry has invested heavily into research and development in AI, and governments have funded various research-and-development programs and centers, Europeans tend to be concerned about the potential negative impacts of AI, in particular breaches of sensitive private data and black-box decisions on important matters such as hiring, medical insurance, or clinical therapeutic applications. The European Union is currently preparing the worldwide-first legal framework for regulating AI, the AI Act, with the goal of mitigating negative impacts, and fostering trustworthy AI. The upcoming law distinguishes applications and systems that create an unacceptable risk, such as a government-run social-credit scoring system; high-risk applications, such as a CV-scanning tool that ranks job applicants; and other applications deemed low-risk. Systems of unacceptable risk will be banned. High-risk applications will be subject to specific legal requirements. They will be assessed by oversight bodies that have the power to order the withdrawal of a commercial AI system or require that an AI model be retrained. Low-risk applications will be largely left unregulated.

In summary, Europe has focused on weak AI, and has adopted a more critical view out of concern for privacy preservation and explainability.

## North America

North America is a continent that, in the formation of its present nation states, was settled by mainly European migrants who were fleeing religious persecution or poverty at home, or were pursuing colonial ambitions. This has led to an outlook on technology which is distinct from that found in Europe. Broadly speaking, fueled by the capitalist drive emerging in the 1800s and early 1900s, North America wishes to exploit technology for a major return in terms of wealth. In other words, it has generally less concern for the human side of technology, in favor of a concern for its economic benefits.

Consequently, North America has embraced AI more enthusiastically than Europe. America boasts many of the leading AI universities and companies, including Google, Microsoft, and Meta/Facebook, and the US government is aiming to maintain American leadership in AI research and development. The National AI Initiative Act of 2020 coordinates the initiatives of the federal government to accelerate AI research and application with the goal of driving economic prosperity and national security. High-impact AI applications include autonomous vehicles, precision medicine, and military drones and weapons. The National AI Initiative acknowledges the risks of AI and aims to ensure trustworthy AI that is not biased against minorities. With such caveats, it aims to prepare the US workforce for the integration of AI systems across all sectors of the economy and society. While most efforts adopt the more pragmatic view of weak AI, many American scientists believe in strong AI.

For example, Google's Ray Kurzweil is a long-time advocate of the possible capabilities of AI. He has said that "machine intelligence will surpass human intelligence, leading to the merger of biological and non-biological intelligence, and immortal software-based humans."[9]

Despite strong advocacy of the metaverse by firms such as Meta/Facebook and Microsoft, the US government is yet to seriously consider oversight and a regulatory framework for its development. Although the US government is being strongly urged to pay attention to AI's development, it is generally taking a "wait and see" approach concerning the introduction of regulation at some time in the future. Only with the recent strong worldwide interest in GPT technology, such as ChatGPT/GPT-4 (as discussed in the case study below), has the US government started to take more seriously the challenges of balancing the economic gains and the risks posed by such systems.

In conclusion, America has taken a more optimistic approach to AI than Europe. It is not only a leader in harnessing the potential of weak AI, but is actively advancing the agenda of strong AI.

## *Asia*

The major force in Asia with respect to AI is China. Another Asian giant in information technology, Japan, a democratic Buddhist country, appears not to have embraced AI much. This is possibly due to its almost stagnant economic growth, its population demographics, and low investment in information and communication infrastructure. South Korea, another big IT country, a Confucian/Buddhist/Daoist society, appears to be catching up with the AI development in Europe and North America, but its scale and ambition are comparatively smaller than those expressed by China. For this section, we therefore focus the Asian perspective on China.

Unlike North America, China has a large homogeneous population and, until about a century ago, was minimally influenced by developments in the West (i.e. Europe and North America). Even then it took a cautious view of Western developments. Its indigenous religious outlook is a pluralistic one, aiming to merge Confucianism, Daoism, Chinese Buddhism, and popular religion with a Marxist socialist state machinery. Thus, its AI initiatives are coordinated through a whole-of-government approach, and the roadmaps are published. In general, it can be said that China wishes to exploit technology,

---

9. Ray Kurzweil, "The Law of Accelerating Returns," in *Alan Turing: Life and Legacy of a Great Thinker*, ed. Christof Teuscher (Berlin: Springer, 2004), 381.

while harmonizing it with the will of heaven/the state, with one's immediate social circles, and with the rest of the society.

Coming from such a viewpoint, China has embraced AI enthusiastically, seeing it as one of the major future technologies which will propel the nation into becoming a leading technology provider in the world. China's fourteenth Five-Year Plan for National Economic and Social Development (2021–25) includes the objective of increasing R&D spending to 7 percent of GDP per annum, to grow the digital economy to 10 percent of GDP, and to build a comprehensive information infrastructure. This is an intergovernmental portfolio initiative, emphasizing fundamental research which promises to bring benefits to the citizens in the long run. At the precompetitive level, research among leading universities, top research institutes, and big tech companies is coordinated by the Beijing Academy of Artificial Intelligence (BAAI), a research collaboration hub. Its aim is to foster long-term research on the fundamentals of AI technology, and it occasionally releases open-source programs. The short-term and medium-term research and development in the area of AI is carried out by commercial firms, such as Huawei, Tencent, and Alibaba, overseen by the state policies. For example, Baidu, ByteDance, and Tencent are competing with the top US technology companies, such as Meta/Facebook, on a metaverse. Theirs is intended to be one with Chinese characteristics, including stronger security and identity authentication.

A document which presents a technology-development roadmap to the year 2035 and regulation oversight mechanisms of the state outlines China's objectives, the planned policy initiatives to achieve the objectives, and the oversight mechanisms which will ensure that AI technology will benefit citizens and not just the major corporations in China or abroad.[10] In other words, the Chinese government is well aware of the potential of technologies such as AI and the metaverse in pursuing its ambition of being the leading technology provider in the world. The Chinese government is using the state machinery to provide oversight, funding for basic research, and incentives for translating basic research results to industries. It fosters the early adoption of AI technology among its large population at home, and uses trade relationships and foreign aid to promote and deploy its AI systems abroad.

---

10. Jeffrey Ding, *Deciphering China's AI Dream: The Context, Components, Capabilities, and Consequences of China's Strategy to Lead the World in AI* (Centre for the Governance of AI, Future of Humanity Institute, University of Oxford, March 2018).

## A Christian Perspective on AI

Having discussed the different views of AI across the continents, we will now discuss the Christian perspective on AI, highlighting both similarities with the secular perspective, and aspects where the Christian perspective is distinctive.

When we speak of "the" Christian view, we must note the manner in which there is diversity, as well as commonality, across Christian perspectives. Christians across different denominations and cultures agree on primary issues, such as the nature of humans and the nature of God, in particular the triune relationship between God the Father, God the Son, and God the Holy Spirit, as espoused in the Nicene Creed. This is accepted by Roman Catholics, mainstream Protestant Christian denominations, and Orthodox Christian denominations. There exist, however, a range of views on secondary issues, such as traditions, interpretations of certain passages of Scripture, policies, practices, and the assessment of technology.

The Christian view presented here is based on the biblical claim that humans were created by God in his image (Gen 1:27) – that is, in God's likeness and for relationship with him – and given the responsibility to govern and care for God's creation (Gen 1:26–28). Within this responsibility, humans are given the freedom and the intellect to explore nature, to understand its wonders, and to use technology in easing their living conditions. Equally important is the biblical teaching that humans failed to live up to their calling when they chose to eat from the tree of knowledge in order to be like God. In doing this, they abandoned their dependence on, and responsibility to, God (Gen 3). For the issues at hand, a big question is how humans can exercise the freedom provided in creation to explore and dominate AI responsibly, in a manner honoring God and serving his creation in a fallen world.

Christians generally appreciate the positive impact of AI systems for more accurate medical diagnoses, or systems that automate dangerous or repetitive operations. AI systems that support the discovery and design of new drugs or enable precision farming, which promises to produce more food with a smaller environmental footprint, are also viewed positively. Such systems are powerful tools that can assist humans in fulfilling their calling to care for creation. Interestingly, such a view also finds consonance with a Confucian/Daoist worldview, and with secular worldviews.

Christian and secular views start to diverge when it comes to the use of AI systems for public safety. While everybody appreciates the safety benefits AI systems can provide, many Christians would argue that some systems, for example the Chinese social-credit system, or the Indian identity system, compromise too much individual privacy for the sake of safety. Such a view is at odds with the Confucian/Daoist view, for which the main concern is that a technology needs to contribute to the aim of harmonizing with the will of heaven/the state and with one's immediate social circle. As such, Confucian/Daoist positions are less concerned with privacy issues than with the benefits which AI might bring to the objectives of the state to bring benefits to its citizens.

Christians tend to be more critical of the storage and exploitation of personal information if such information is used for financial gain. They require some safeguards as to the use of such information – for example, use of only an anonymous version of the information, without any possibility of an individual being identified. Christians in general would also have some difficulties with the more grandiose objectives of the metaverse, such as the creation of a digital twin of a person, brain control of physical objects, or worship services on a metaverse platform. In fact, the scope of collection of personal information and its central role played in a metaverse platform, for example the digital twin, would be unsettling for a Christian, due to its great potential for being misused.

On the matter of responsibility for an AI system, Christians generally agree that humans need to supervise the work of an AI system or that, when a black-box AI system is operating outside a preset safety limit, it should automatically revert back to operate with a known, well-tested method. In the Christian worldview, it is clear that humans remain responsible for the actions and decisions of a machine, which is what an AI system is. Humans are the only players that will, at the end of the day, be judged by God. However, it is becoming increasingly difficult to pinpoint the actual human who is to be held responsible: Is it the CEO of the company that has developed and sold the AI system, the official of a government agency or company that has bought and runs the system, or even the programmer of the AI system who best understands its function? The fallen nature of humans suggests that humans ultimately prioritize their own interests over those of others, and are prone to exploit the great potential of AI to gain more power or wealth at the expense of others. Examples of this include wealthy individuals who can extend their lives through expensive methods of precision medicine not available to ordinary people, or governments and companies that use AI to tighten their control of their citizens or increase the revenue from their customers. Humans, therefore, need to be held accountable, suitable oversight and regulatory frameworks have to be in place, and suitable laws need to be passed and enforced.

Christians live in a society governed by human institutions which are run by fallen human beings. Nevertheless, the Bible makes it clear that Christians are called to obey their God-given governments (Rom 13:1–7). The only exception is if the government wants Christians to disobey God; in that case the principle of "fearing God more than human beings" applies (see Acts 4:19). In any case, Christians are called to pray for their governments (1 Tim 2:1–2) and to stand up for the freedom of conscience and speech, and for justice for the weak. We note that any curtailment of freedom will not be the result of the use of Big Data or AI technology, but these powerful tools certainly make it easier for governments to curtail freedom.

Believers in strong AI claim that they will be able to create systems with consciousness and ultimately even create superhumans, if necessary through the implantation of chips to enhance bodily functions. This belief is based on the worldview of physicalism, which holds that everything which exists is nothing but physics, that is, matter. In such a worldview, it is not unreasonable to assume that consciousness emerges as systems become more and more complex and capable until a "singular point" is reached where consciousness occurs. This worldview is not inconsistent with a Confucian/Daoist worldview. In Confucianism, there is no formal concept of a soul, in the sense it is used in the West, while a Daoist would consider such "AI upgrades" as one way of achieving immortality. The amazing recent successes of AI – from playing Go, to driving cars, to creating art – may give the impression that current AI systems have already reached the level of human intelligence. Indeed, they may appear indistinguishable from humans in a Turing-test setting, and so be called "intelligent" by that measure. However, as demonstrated by the Chinese Room Experiment, a computer passing the Turing test merely has to simulate the function of a human; it does not need to understand humans or be conscious. This is consistent with the Christian worldview which holds that consciousness is an attribute of a soul.

The *Encyclopedia Britannica* defines the soul as "the immaterial aspect or essence of a human being."[11] The influential Christian theologian and philosopher Augustine defined the soul as "a special substance, endowed with reason, adapted to rule the body."[12]

While some Christians view humans as having a body (*soma*), soul (*psyche*), and spirit (*pneuma*), most modern Bible scholars argue that the concepts of "spirit" and "soul" are used interchangeably in the Bible and view humans as having a body and a soul. Either way, Christians agree on the existence and

---

11. "Soul," *Encyclopaedia Britannica* (2022), https://www.britannica.com/topic/soul-religion-and-philosophy.

12. Augustine of Hippo, *De quantitate animae* 13.12.

importance of the soul as a nonmaterial aspect of humans. The soul makes a human a "living being," an "image of God," able to relate to God and fulfill the human calling to be stewards of his creation. The soul is given by the Creator God and transcends the mortal body. The soul is the consciousness that connects the life and the afterlife of a person. As a gift of God, it cannot be created by human beings. In fact, from a Christian perspective, the attempt to create superhumans seems to be another human attempt to be like God.

Based on this view of human nature, most Christians believe that even future AI systems will not achieve consciousness and are not likely to rebel against humans to take over the world. They consider the risk of humanity's extinction by AI, highlighted in a recent open letter from numerous AI experts, as unrealistic.[13] However, Christians realize that more and more advanced AI systems will be extremely powerful tools that can be used both for doing good and for doing harm. Given the fallen nature of humanity, the risk of AI being misused by "bad actors" is real and needs to be safeguarded against.

## Case Study: ChatGPT and GPT Technology

As a case study, we discuss the recent development of ChatGPT, and related generative AI technology. In November 2022, OpenAI released ChatGPT, an internet-based conversational assistant, for anyone in the general public to evaluate. ChatGPT can seemingly answer any question a human inquirer may pose in English. Earlier versions of ChatGPT – GPT (Generative Pre-Trained Transformer), GPT-2, and GPT-3 – could display bias and sometimes give inappropriate responses. However, these problems have to a large extent been corrected using reinforcement learning human feedback (RLHF), which has been incorporated in a later version of ChatGPT, GPT-4, released in March 2023.

Generative AI is based on an advanced neural-network architecture, called a transformer, which is essentially a sequence-to-sequence model, where the input is a sequence of words and the output is another sequence of words. We note that the vocabulary of a transformer, that is, the set of words that it can use in its output, is fixed after it has been trained. ChatGPT was pretrained on a very large corpus of texts, which was available on the internet as of mid 2021,

---

13. Centre for AI Safety, "Statement on AI Risk" (2023), https://www.safe.ai/statement-on-ai-risk. See also Dan Hendrycks, Mantas Mazeika, and Thomas Woodside, "An Overview of Catastrophic AI Risks," *arXiv* 2306.12001 (2023).

and fine-tuned on some target text datasets, so that the output sequence in response to a prompt by the human user would appear as if written by a human.

As the GPT model is trained on information available on the internet which includes information which might be harmful, not helpful to the human inquirer, or might not be true, a further step of training based on human feedback, using reinforcement learning (RLHF), was performed. RLHF used a carefully curated smaller dataset, which consisted of pairs of responses, one preferred and the other nonpreferred. RLHF used the nonpreferred responses to discourage the model from outputting harmful, unhelpful, or untrustworthy responses. Here in the customization step using human feedback in the form of sample responses lies the risk of misuse. For example, it is relatively simple to reverse the roles of the preferred responses and nonpreferred responses and produce a model which would give harmful, unhelpful, and untrustworthy responses to the human inquirer. In other words, it is the creators of the human feedback who control how such a GPT model will respond to human inquiries. Thus, a generative AI system is vulnerable to misuse or abuse by malevolent elements of society.

The amazing ability of ChatGPT to converse with humans in English on any topic one cares to raise, as well as its ability to exhibit step-by-step reasoning, fascinates the public. It has hundreds of millions of users per day around the world, and it is estimated that revenue through a monthly subscription model will hit one billion US dollars by the end of 2024. This phenomenon raises the hope among entrepreneurs, futurists, and engineers to speculate that we might be seeing some "sparks" of artificial general intelligence (AGI). However, it also causes concern among many scientists and engineers that an AI apocalypse might be approaching. Twenty-two eminent scientists, technologists, engineers, entrepreneurs, and futurists were polled for their views on two questions: (1) "Is the success of GPT-4 and today's other large language models a sign that an AGI is likely?" and (2) "Is an AGI likely to cause civilizational disaster if we do nothing?"[14] Most scientists/engineers answered both questions in the negative, while most entrepreneurs/futurists and some engineers answered question 1, question 2, or both, in the positive. One of those polled, Yoshua

---

14. Eliza Strickland and Glenn Zorpette, "The AI Apocalypse: A Scorecard," IEEE Spectrum, 21 June 2023, https://spectrum.ieee.org/artificial-general-intelligence.

Bengio, followed up with an invited essay in *The Economist* to air his concerns on the rapid development of generative AI.[15]

Recently, President Joe Biden gathered representatives of Amazon, Anthropic, Google, Inflection, Meta, Microsoft, and OpenAI – seven of the leading big tech companies in the US who are the driving force in the development of generative AI – to announce that these seven companies will adhere to a voluntary code of conduct: to produce safe, secure, and trustworthy products. Moreover, President Biden indicated that there will be an Executive Order which will regulate the development of AI, without stifling its positive potential for humankind. Europe has long espoused a regulatory framework for AI systems, categorizing them according to their risk if released to the general public. It classifies generative AI in the category of high risk and demands that such products be designed so as to prevent them from generating illegal content. It is likely that this AI Law will be adopted by the EU by the end of 2023.[16]

This burst of political activity shows that, in both America and Europe, governments are concerned about the rapid growth of generative AI and are considering how best to protect their citizens, by having safe, secure, and trustworthy products. America, true to its capitalist perspective, would consider introducing a regulatory framework, without jeopardizing its positive potentials in benefiting humankind. Europeans, on the other hand, are more concerned to protect their citizens from the risks which are posed by generative AI. Asians, especially the Chinese, would tend to explore and exploit the generative AI technology, in harmony with the will of heaven/the state.

From a Christian perspective, humans were created good, and it was only after the fall that evil entered the world. Humans are entrusted with the care of God's creation, and technology can serve as a powerful tool to fulfill this mandate. We seek to customize GPT models using well-intended RLHF datasets to produce helpful, harmless, and trustworthy responses, as a way of expressing our Christian love for our fellow human beings and of exercising our duty of care for nature. However, since the fall there exist malevolent elements in humankind. These malevolent elements, with sufficient computational resources and technical expertise, could make use of the same technology

---

15. Yoshua Bengio, "One of the 'Godfathers of AI' Airs His Concerns," *The Economist*, 22 July 2023, https://www.economist.com/by-invitation/2023/07/21/one-of-the-godfathers-of-ai-airs-his-concerns.

16. See the postscript at the end of this chapter for discussion of the Chinese, USA, and EU frameworks and their passage into law.

to harm, to be unhelpful, or to disseminate disinformation, as most of the technology, including the RLHF datasets, has been open sourced. This is almost unavoidable as any technology can be used for the glory of God and to benefit humankind, or misused for a person or group's own interests.

Governments have the God-given duty to care for their citizens. Therefore, it is the responsibility of governments to oversee, regulate, and safeguard the use of AI technology by its citizens. Governments and parliaments should set the laws and regulations governing AI products and leave the policing of compliance to the justice system. This will hopefully minimize the risk of AI being misused as a tool by malevolent elements in society. As for dealing with sovereign states which might use AI technologies to further their ideologies, throughout recent history there are examples of a two-pronged approach: moral persuasion through international collaboration, and economic sanction when human dignity is violated. Over time, one hopes that evil will be kept in check, until the return of our Lord in glory.

## Conclusion

In this chapter, we have discussed the different perspectives on AI from three different continents: Europe, North America, and Asia. We have seen that Europe has adopted the most critical approach to AI and is already in the process of enacting laws to restrict the application of AI, governed by concerns over privacy preservation and explainability. North America has embraced AI more enthusiastically, driven largely by its leading AI universities and companies. However, some of these leading companies recently agreed to voluntary safeguards, including testing the security of AI and making the results of those tests public. The US government is taking steps to encourage big tech companies to self-regulate, and indicates that an Executive Order will provide a regulatory framework to regulate AI technologies. China has pursued AI applications most aggressively, without apparent restrictions, aiming to become a world leader in this technology, as well as using it to control its citizens more effectively.

We have also attempted to sketch a Christian perspective on AI. Some aspects are shared with the secular perspectives across the continents, such as appreciation of the potential positive impact in medicine, and the assessment that current AI systems have not yet attained consciousness. Other aspects are unique to a Christian perspective. Based on the belief that humans have been created in God's image, most Christians believe that it will not be possible to create conscious AI systems. Based on their understanding of the fallen human nature, they are aware of the great risks of misusing AI and the need to engage in initiatives to minimize these risks.

This chapter has touched upon a broad range of topics from various disciplines. Below we provide a list of suggestions for further reading. The field of AI has been advancing at an amazing speed, and much more discussion is needed. We hope that this chapter will inspire a constructive dialogue about the nature and the impact of AI, as well as ways to manage it, bringing together Christians and non-Christians as well as those from the different continents and cultures.

## Postscript: Developments After the Completion of this Chapter

Artificial Intelligence is a fast-moving field, and there have been four important developments, one technical and three political, between completing this chapter and the book going to press. We briefly note them here.

The technical development relates to the known difficulties in the fine-tuning step of Large Language Models (LLMs), of which GPT is its most famous example. The fine-tuning using RLHF (Reinforcement Learning Human Feedback) is well known to require a large amount of manually labelled fine-tuning samples, moreover, it is difficult to train. In December 2023, a new method called Direct Preference Optimization (DPO)[17] has largely eliminated these issues. The method can be implemented on a low-cost commodity graphics processing unit (GPU) and makes the fine-tuning of LLMs accessible to people with a much smaller financial budget than those available to big tech companies. This "democratization" of LLMs could be positive or negative, depending on one's viewpoint. The availability of LLMs to people with smaller budgets would further accelerate the development of LLMs, so that it can be applied to practical problems with small datasets. On the other hand, malevolent segments of society would be able to use LLMs for their own purposes more readily.

This technical breakthrough came during a time when China, the USA, and Europe enacted into law their respective regulatory frameworks for safe, trustworthy, and secure generative AI systems. In August 2023, a regulatory framework called *Measures for the Administration of Generative Artificial Intelligence Services* became effective in China. In October 2023, President Biden

---

17. Rafael Rafailov, Archit Sharma, Eric Mitchell, Stefano Ermon, Christopher D. Manning, and Chelsea Finn, "Direct Preference Optimization: Your Language Model is Secretly a Reward Model," *37th Conference on Neural Information Processing Systems (NeurIPS 2023)*.

signed an *Executive Order on the Safe, Secure, and Trustworthy Development and Use of Artificial Intelligence*. And in March 2024, the long-awaited EU *AI Act* passed through the European Union Parliament.

While this is not the place to analyze these three initiatives in detail, it is fair to say that they are influenced by their respective cultural heritage. Both China and the USA do not wish to stifle the developments of services provided by generative AI systems for their respective citizens, and they both put guardrails around such services, so that it is safe, secure and trustworthy for their respective citizens to benefit from such services. However, Article 4 of the Chinese *Measures* re-iterates the importance for such services to respect socialist values. These include refraining from generating content which incites subversion of state authority, overthrowing of the socialist system, endangering national security and interests, and tarnishing the national image. This complies with the Confucian/Daoist values, of harmonizing with those in the society and the will of heaven/will of the party. The USA's *Executive Order*, on the other hand, requires companies to share their test data pertaining to the safety of their services with the government, institute standards, tools to evaluate the safety of these services, and the need to protect privacy of the individual. This accords with the founding principles of equality, privacy, safety, and freedom of the individual. Finally, the EU *AI Act* groups AI services into four categories – from unacceptable risk to limited risk – and prescribes for each category the associated risk mitigation measures. This Act aims to protect people's safety, to ensure that such services are secure, and the services can be trusted. In other words, the safety and freedom of their citizens need to be guaranteed. It is highly likely as more and more generative AI system services are introduced, these laws will be tested, refined, and extended.

These three initiatives came at a good time, as LLMs become more accessible to people with smaller financial budgets. Similar regulatory frameworks for LLMs are afoot in other developed and developing economies.

## References

Augustine of Hippo. *De quantitate animae*.
Bengio, Yoshua. "One of the 'Godfathers of AI' Airs His Concerns." *The Economist*, 22 July 2023. https://www.economist.com/by-invitation/2023/07/21/one-of-the-godfathers-of-ai-airs-his-concerns.
Centre for AI Safety. "Statement on AI Risk." 2023. https://www.safe.ai/statement-on-ai-risk.

Ding, Jeffrey. *Deciphering China's AI Dream: The Context, Components, Capabilities, and Consequences of China's Strategy to Lead the World in AI*. Centre for the Governance of AI, Future of Humanity Institute, University of Oxford, March 2018.

*Encyclopaedia Britannica*. "Soul." 2022. https://www.britannica.com/topic/soul-religion-and-philosophy.

Esmaeilzadeh, Hadi, and Reza Vaezi. "Conscious Empathic AI in Service." *Journal of Service Research* 25, no. 4 (June 2022): 549–64. DOI: 10.1177/10946705221103531.

Hendrycks, Dan, Mantas Mazeika, and Thomas Woodside. "An Overview of Catastrophic AI Risks." *arXiv* 2306.12001 (2023).

Huang, Ming-Hui, and Roland Rust. "Artificial Intelligence in Service." *Journal of Service Research* 2, no. 2 (2018): 155–72.

Kurzweil, Ray. "The Law of Accelerating Returns." In *Alan Turing: Life and Legacy of a Great Thinker*, edited by Christof Teuscher, 381–416. Berlin: Springer, 2004.

Moor, James. "The Dartmouth College Artificial Intelligence Conference: The Next Fifty Years." *AI Magazine* 27, no. 4 (2006): 87–91.

Rafailov, Rafael, Archit Sharma, Eric Mitchell, Stefano Ermon, Christopher D. Manning, and Chelsea Finn. "Direct Preference Optimization: Your Language Model is Secretly a Reward Model." *37th Conference on Neural Information Processing Systems (NeurIPS 2023)*.

Searle, John. "Minds, Brains and Programs." *Behavioral and Brain Sciences* 3, no. 3 (1980): 417–57.

Stephens, Melodena. *Metaverse and Its Governance, IEEE Global Initiative on Ethics of Extended Reality (XR) Report*. New York: Institute of Electrical and Electronics Engineers, 2022.

Strickland, Eliza, and Glenn Zorpette. "The AI Apocalypse: A Scorecard." *IEEE Spectrum*. 21 June 2023. https://spectrum.ieee.org/artificial-general-intelligence.

Tallis, Raymond. "Bewitched by Language." In *Aping Mankind*, 183–208. London: Routledge, 2014.

## Further Reading

Introduction to the principles and practice of artificial intelligence:

Russell, Stuart, and Peter Norvig. *Artificial Intelligence: A Modern Approach*. Harlow: Pearson, 2021.

Considerations regarding strong AI:

Awret, Uziel, ed. *The Singularity: Could Artificial Intelligence Really Out-Think Us (And Would We Want It To)?* Exeter: Imprint Academic, 2016.

Bostrom, Nick. *Superintelligence: Paths, Dangers, Strategies*. Oxford: Oxford University Press, 2014.

Kurzweil, Ray. *How to Create a Mind: The Secret of Human Thought Revealed.* New York: Penguin, 2012.

Introduction to the metaverse:
Hackl, Cathy, Dirk Lueth, Tommaso Di Bartolo, and John Arkontaky, eds. *Navigating the Metaverse: A Guide to Limitless Possibilities in a Web 3.0 World.* Hoboken: Wiley, 2022.

Regional views of technology – from European, North American, and Asian perspectives:
Kerikmäe, Tanel, ed. *Regulating eTechnologies in the European Union: Normative Realities and Trends.* Berlin: Springer, 2014.
Kim, Dongwoo. *Artificial Intelligence Policies in East Asia: An Overview from the Canadian Perspective.* Vancouver: Asia Pacific Foundation of Canada, 2019.
Verkerk, Maarten J., Jan Hoogland, Jan van der Stoep, and Marc J. de Vries. *Philosophy of Technology: An Introduction for Technology and Business Students.* Translated by M. Nelson. London: Routledge, 2016.
Wong, Pak-Hong, and Tom Xiaowei Wang, eds. *Harmonious Technology: A Confucian Ethics of Technology.* London: Routledge, 2021. Especially ch. 5: Pak-Hong Wong, "Artificial Intelligence, Personal Decisions, Consent, and the Confucian Idea of Oneness," 66–78.
Yates, Joshua, and James Davison Hunter, eds. *Thrift and Thriving in American Capitalism and Moral Order from the Puritans to the Present.* Oxford: Oxford University Press, 2011.

Analyses of the massive AI-based technosocial interventions in India and China:
Chowdhry, Bhagwan, Amit Goyal, and Syed Anas Ahmed. "Digital Identity in India." In *The Palgrave Handbook of Technological Finance*, edited by Raghavendra Rau, Robert Wardrop, and Luigi Zingales, 837–53. London: Palgrave Macmillan, 2021.
Sithigh, Daithi, and Mathias Siems. "The Chinese Social Credit System: A Model for Other Countries." *The Modern Law Review* 82, no. 6 (2019): 1034–71.

Philosophical engagement with what AI and related technologies do to humanity:
Chalmers, David. *Reality+: Virtual Worlds and the Problems of Philosophy.* New York: W. W. Norton and Co., 2022.
Verbeek, Peter Paul. *What Things Do: Philosophical Reflections on Technology, Agency, and Design.* Translated by Robert P. Crease. University Park: Pennsylvania State University Press, 2005.

Explicitly Christian responses to questions of AI and related technologies:

Hawkins, David J. *Christ and Modernity: Christian Self-Understanding in a Technological Age*. Waterloo: Wilfrid Laurier University Press, 1985.

Lennox, John, *2084: Artificial Intelligence and the Future of Humanity*. Grand Rapids: Zondervan, 2020.

van der Leest, Steve, and Derek Schuurman. "A Christian Perspective on Artificial Intelligence: How Should Christians Think about Thinking Machines?" *Proceedings of the 2015 Christian Engineering Conference* (2015): 91–107.

Wyatt, John, and Stephen Williams, eds. *The Robot Will See You Now: Artificial Intelligence and the Christian Faith*. London: SPCK, 2021.

# 10

# Engaging the Church and Wider Christian Community in Science-Faith Dialogue

Ruth M. Bancewicz, The Faraday Institute for Science and Religion, UK

## Abstract

The engagement of science and religion is often viewed through the lens of individual people: individual Christians and individual scientists. But Christians do not live isolated lives as individuals; they live as part of communities, not least of which is the community of believers: the church.

This chapter sets out some key ideas about how the church can engage with science-and-religion discourse; how it can engage with scientists, Christians, and the wider community. Given such a framework, the chapter then considers how this can be worked out on a practical level, drawing on experiences of how this has been done within the Faraday Institute as well as by other individuals or organizations.

The main aims here are threefold: first, to demonstrate to church leaders both why this topic is important and how they can engage with it without diverting resources from existing activities; second, to show scientists that they can reach out in their own and other churches, providing some ideas for doing that well; and finally, to encourage ordinary nonscientist church members that they have something to contribute to the conversation.

## Introduction

The church is the global community of Christ's followers. A local church is a community of people who gather regularly, taking part in worship, sacrament, fellowship, and learning. It is also the center from which Christians go out to serve in the world. While, in many countries, the term "Church" has come to be conflated with the buildings in which Christians meet, this chapter considers the church as the community of people.

It follows that, in a book about global perspectives on science and Christianity, the influence of the church will be felt, if not always stated explicitly, in every chapter. These influences include the global network of believers which enables scientists and theologians to get in touch with each other, whether across continents or within the same institution. They also include strands of theological thinking within denominations or local church settings that affect how people process questions of science and Christianity. Another very important influence is the way in which the church affects the scientist's day-to-day work, for example in attitudes to scholarship and experimental investigation, and the shaping of Christlike lives that serve the wider scientific community and beyond.

The influence of the church with which this chapter is primarily concerned is the juxtaposition of people from different demographics. Members of first-century churches found themselves worshipping in a situation where Jews and Gentiles, men and women, slaves and free were radically "all one in Christ Jesus" (Gal 3:28). Today, this biblical principle is reflected in the fact that many (hopefully most) churches are diverse, encompassing people with advanced qualifications and those who left education quite early in their lives, people with different ethnicities and national identities, young and old, waged and unwaged, and with a broad range of daily occupations. The guiding principle of unity in the church (Eph 4:1–6) is both a gift and a challenge, and also provides an excellent setting for conversations about science and religion.

The location for the action in this chapter will be the engagement with science that happens when the church gathers together in its regular meetings and activities, and in special events organized by local churches for their surrounding communities. The church's engagement with science over the past few centuries has been wide-ranging but patchy: creative, faith-enhancing, and influencing many great developments in the world, but at times heartbreakingly unhelpful and destructive – with a good deal of what has taken place lying in somewhat ambiguous ground in between these poles. To give an example of this ambiguity, the European passion for natural theology (essentially, evidence for God from nature) that was supported by so many in the Anglican Church was the lens through which many ordained clergy viewed their discoveries in science (or in natural philosophy, as it was then called), including the great geologists Adam Sedgwick and James Hutton. This influence was in many cases very positive, as it drove the rational investigation of the mechanisms by which God created and sustains the natural world. On the other hand, some of the great claims made by these natural-theology enthusiasts about evidence for God from design have been rightly criticized. Natural theology has also had a rather more negative influence on people's understandings of biological origins.[1]

Other chapters in this book deal with the science and theology of origins, as well as creation care, advances in medicine, and uses of technology. The question of how we can move forward as a church on these issues and many others, recovering and repairing but also building on great work done in the past, is also covered in many other publications besides this one. The focus of this chapter is to look at some ways in which the church can engage with science, drawing everyone into the discussion, using examples from the work of the Faraday Institute, and of some of our collaborators and colleagues. Unfortunately, there is not space to mention all the fantastic work in this field that is taking place around the world. There will also be many initiatives that we are unaware of or have unwittingly overlooked. We would love to hear, and learn, from them.

It is also worth clarifying that this chapter is about ministry with adults. Children and young people are an incredibly important part of the church, and deserve high-quality input on scientific topics in this context. Some exciting work is being done with children and young people, and the adults who serve them, by groups such as the Faraday Youth and Schools Team, God and the Big Bang, Learning About Science and Religion, and the Ian Ramsey Centre, to name several thriving UK-based groups. On the other hand, we find that pastors are often tempted to restrict action on scientific topics to these age groups, as if people have nothing to do with science once they leave their teenage years (or possibly young adulthood) behind. One aim of this chapter, therefore, is to highlight that adults need and can take part in activities on these topics too. This is not just because adults often teach, support, and encourage children and young people, but because they, too, interact with science every day, and also deserve to be part of the conversation about science and Christianity.

---

1. John Hedley Brooke, *Science and Religion: Some Historical Perspectives* (Cambridge: Cambridge University Press, 1991), 192–225.

Our hope is to encourage those who feel uncertain or afraid about whether to initiate such conversations, to give some ideas for getting new initiatives off the ground, and to inspire those whose first efforts didn't go as well as they had hoped that they can try again. Whether you are a church leader or a member, a scientist or not, there is something here for you. First, we will lay out some principles for engagement, before sharing some ideas and examples of practical action.

## Barriers to Engaging with Science in the UK Church

The discussion on science and Christianity has been affected by many of the same biases and power imbalances that have shaped so many other areas of human discourse. Data from a 2021 survey of over five thousand UK adults demonstrate some of these influences. Fifty-seven percent of respondents thought that science and religion are incompatible, but when asked to drill down into specific areas of science many were more positive, indicating that this is a "conflict of image rather than substance." Men were more likely to voice their opinion on the relationship between science and Christianity, and to see the relationship as one of conflict. White respondents were also more likely to be negative about the relationship.[2] This persistent conflict narrative has led many church leaders, who are often themselves largely positive about the relationship between science and religion in general, to shy away from addressing scientific topics in a church context.[3]

This section does not aim to explain why we have arrived at this place in the conversation about science and religion in the UK, but to point out some potential barriers to participation that may prevent helpful conversations from occurring in a church context. Although these trends are already being mitigated by a number of innovative programs, which will be explored in the following sections, there is still much to do to reach wider audiences and include new contributors in the discussion.

---

2. Nick Spencer and Hannah Waite, *Science and Religion: Moving Away from the Shallow End*, report (London: Theos, 2022).

3. Lydia Reid and David Wilkinson, "Building Enthusiasm and Overcoming Fear: Engaging with Christian Leaders in an Age of Science," *Zygon* 56, no. 4 (December 2021): 1087–109.

## University-Oriented Activities

Much of the discussion of science and Christianity in the past, both positive and negative, has been driven by those with tertiary-level (or higher) education. Science-and-religion activities have often centered around academic societies, conferences, lectures, and the writing of books and papers. Dissemination of specialist academic ideas in the field of science and religion has often been through membership-based organizations, conferences, lectures, papers, and books targeted for the nonspecialist, although still relatively academically oriented, audience.

Scholarly engagement is of course vital for many reasons, not least because it draws on a large body of thoughtful research and publications, but also because it can often move the discussion forward in helpful directions. On the other hand, if a high degree of involvement in academic activities is the only route for scientists, church leaders, or interested Christians to have a voice, or gain access to translatable knowledge on science and religion, many will be excluded. The science-and-religion world will in that case lose the insights of those who are not taking part, and the church will miss the opportunity to discover that the discussion about science and faith can be far more nuanced and interesting than we might otherwise think.

On a practical level, even for those with tertiary education, taking part in discussions on a topic outside one's specialist field requires a significant input of time, energy, and money, and a high level of both confidence and motivation. This naturally narrows the field to those with the resources, opportunities, confidence, and encouragement to be involved. Taking part will often involve sacrificing other aspects of life to a significant level in order to acquire knowledge and maintain outputs in a second academic field. Although some people will continue in this direction, there is a great need for conscious development of alternative routes into the science-and-religion discussion that are realistic for those – both academically qualified individuals and those with different skill sets – who do not have the resources, the opportunity, or the inclination to take this path.

## Content and Presentation

If a particular demographic dominates the science-and-religion discussion, it is inevitable that the content of the conversation will be pitched in ways that appeal to that demographic. For example, in the UK we have often seen high-flying older white male role models on the platform, talk titles that use the language of conflict, and debates or other adversarial formats.

Topics are, at times, defined by their specialist terms such as "divine action," "*imago Dei*," or "theistic evolution," and the content can on occasions be dry or divorced from practical applications. None of these things are necessarily wrong in themselves, and it is often difficult to predict which activities will appeal to certain audiences. It is hopefully an obvious point, however, that the topic and the way in which it is presented will affect who is inclined to take part in the conversation. In order to attract a broad audience within the church and its surrounding communities, it is important that we think creatively and empathetically about content and presentation, consulting with potential audience members in order to find out what they might find helpful and interesting.

Many of the well-known science-and-religion experts, or "boundary pioneers" as sociologist Elaine Howard Ecklund has called them,[4] in the UK over the last few decades have been white men such as Michael Polanyi, Charles Coulson, John Polkinghorne, and Alister McGrath, often in the later stages of their careers. This has, at least in part, reflected the predominance of this demographic in the upper echelons of academia, and the fact that it takes time to acquire knowledge and gain confidence and experience in a second academic field (for example, if a scientist is acquiring theological knowledge). These contributions are important, and we must continue to hear from them, but it is all too easy to miss the voices of those outside established science-and-religion circles, academia, and the higher echelons of church hierarchies. It is well worth putting in the extra work of looking outside networks of colleagues and friends in order to identify younger academics and those outside the predominant demographic, nurturing new speakers and giving them appropriate opportunities. Thankfully, in the last few decades this dynamic has begun to change, going beyond tokenism to serious engagement with new voices that deserve to be heard.[5]

Another issue in the science-and-religion discussion is that at times scholars, who have either earned or been given a platform, can use the opportunity to make pronouncements that are not based on solid research and intellectual activity. This dynamic can be hard to avoid because high-achieving scientists, who are often the most respected intellectuals, can at times be asked to pronounce on topics on which they have no, or very little,

---

4. Elaine Howard Ecklund, *Science vs. Religion: What Scientists Really Think* (Oxford: Oxford University Press, 2010), 45–47.

5. For example, Bethany N. Sollereder and Alister E. McGrath, eds., *Emerging Voices in Science and Theology: Contributions by Young Women* (London: Routledge, 2022).

expertise. Unfortunately, engagement like this can cause church leaders and their congregations to recoil from the conversation about science and faith, or react in ways that are understandable, such as rejecting mainstream science. A potential solution is to focus on giving the platform, wherever possible, to people who are able to put forward well-considered and up-to-date arguments. One way of doing this would be to support and equip senior scientists in the development of their ideas, encouraging collaboration with theologians, philosophers, historians, and other scholars in the field, so that they can make accurate statements.

## *Nonscientists*

Even within the demographic to which the science-and-religion discussion often appeals, many people tend to write themselves off as "not scientific enough," or others do that for them. An education system in the UK that encourages specialization in the humanities or sciences from the age of sixteen is a huge contributing factor. Many church leaders are therefore not confident to raise questions of science themselves (even in situations where they are not expected to provide all the answers), as they feel they are not expert enough on the topic.[6] The reluctance of trusted leaders to address scientific issues may be reflected in the fact that a 2018 survey of over two thousand people found that 30 percent of nonreligious people and about 10 percent of Christians thought that the church is "not compatible with science."[7] This tension is far more intensely felt in Pentecostal and independent evangelical churches than in Anglican, Catholic, or Methodist churches.[8] The challenge, then, is to engage those who have written themselves off from the conversation about science and Christianity because they found science intimidating or uninviting in the past.

---

6. Reid and Wilkinson, "Building Enthusiasm and Overcoming Fear: Engaging with Christian Leaders in an Age of Science."

7. Barna Group, *The UK Church in Action: Perceptions of Social Justice and Mission in a Changing World* (Barna Group, 2018).

8. Amy Unsworth and David Voas, "Attitudes to Evolution among Christians, Muslims and the Non-Religious in Britain: Differential Effects of Religious and Educational Factors," *Public Understanding of Science* 27, no. 1 (2013): 76–93; Andrew Village and Sylvia Baker, "Reasons Given by UK Churchgoers for Their Stance on Evolution," *Journal of Beliefs and Values* 34, no. 2 (2013): 165–77.

### *Assumed Oversensitivity*

Some people, churches, or denominations are left out of the conversation about science and Christian faith because they are perceived as being very sensitive on topics such as evolution or the Big Bang. The author has known scientists who kept quiet about their research or views on science in a church context because they were worried about how people would react. Some pastors have specifically requested that a certain topic be avoided by a visiting speaker because they know that it will create difficult conversations with certain church members. Some event organizers have assumed that people from certain denominations will not be open to the conversation about science and faith, or that leaders from those denominations will be against mainstream science.

At times, these worries are well founded, and some sensitive topics need to be avoided. There is a time and a place for dealing with controversial issues, and that is not always at the first meeting on this topic, or in public events. But we do need to make space for people to discuss these issues, hear from trusted voices, and develop their own informed views. At other times, people who were assumed to be sensitive regarding mainstream science, or even who were assumed to utterly reject it, hold a completely different or more nuanced view from what was expected. If we exclude these people from the conversation, we will be the poorer for it.

### *Audience Receptivity*

A final barrier to helpful engagement with science lies with the audience and what they are used to hearing and responding to on this topic. If the perception is that science and Christian faith are always at odds, then any event advertising that suggests otherwise might be treated with suspicion. If a particular demographic appreciates hearing messages along the lines of "You say science trumps God, but I say God trumps science," then events and resources that put forward this narrative will probably win the competition for their time and attention. The difficult question here is, how can we help everyone in the church to engage, without perpetuating the basic myth that science and faith are fundamentally at odds?

## Principles for Engagement with Science in the Church

There are many opportunities to engage with science in a church context, if one looks carefully enough. Relevant topics come to light because of new scientific discoveries, changes in government legislation, or human interactions with creation. There are also new aspects of biblical interpretation to address in every generation. The issue for many is not the opportunity to engage with science, so much as the difficulties outlined in the previous pages. In this section a series of principles will be outlined that can help pastors, scientists, and other members of the congregation to engage well with science. Some brief examples are given in this section, with the next section providing a deeper exploration of the practical outworkings of these principles.

## *Everyone Can Be Involved*

Everyone has something to receive from, and contribute to, the discussion about science and religion. Every adult has already formed some views on this topic, whether consciously or subconsciously, and these can be diverse. For example, in India, while most scientists would say that science and religion are separate, in practice religion is as present in scientific institutions as it is in any other aspect of life in that country.[9] At the opposite extreme, as we have discussed above, in the UK there is often an assumption of conflict between science and religion, even without any real evidence for it. There is, as a result of these types of dynamics, a high level of felt need by many around the world to address questions of science in a Christian context, as we and other organizations can tell by continued attendance at events, book sales, or viewing statistics for online resources. Other needs come to the fore when certain opportunities or challenges are presented to committed church members, such as the risks surrounding stem-cell research or nanotechnology.

Not everyone enjoyed science at school, for a whole host of reasons. These include limitations on teachers or curricula, student and parent attitudes, and the place each pupil might be at in his or her developmental journey. Nor does everyone engage with science in stereotypical ways today, such as through scientific careers or popular science books and documentaries. On the other hand, everyone in the church draws on scientific knowledge at some level. For example, most people in the world have received medical interventions of some kind, such as vaccinations, or learned about nutrition and hygiene. We cook, grow plants, learn how to look after farm animals or pets, build and maintain homes, and engage in a host of other activities where we benefit from scientific knowledge of one kind or another. All these activities are prospective bridges into the science-and-religion discussion.

---

9. Elaine Howard Ecklund, ed., *Secularity and Science: What Scientists around the World Really Think about Religion* (New York: Oxford University Press, 2019), 145–68.

On the faith side of things, many of those in the wider community a church seeks to serve who do not identify themselves as "religious" may well consider themselves to be "spiritual." This category may include around 10 percent of the scientists in the local area, as shown in a recent survey of biologists and physicists in universities around the world.[10] Even those who are not interested in either religion or spirituality will have opinions, ideas, or worries about the sorts of big questions that the science-and-religion discourse seeks to address, such as Who am I? What is my purpose? What is a person worth? What ought we to do?

We are called *Homo sapiens*, which in English means "wise man," for a reason. Societies may especially value or reward some types of intelligence more highly than others, or honor certain ways of displaying intelligence, but the science-and-religion discourse is richer when everyone has a voice. For example, the Faraday Institute short courses bring together people from all walks of life. Most have studied at university level, but not all in the sciences, and not all very recently. We sometimes find in the discussion times after lectures that someone who is not from a typical academic or scientific background will preface a comment with "This is probably a stupid question . . ." before asking an incredibly penetrating or important question that the speaker is only too delighted to engage with. The fact that these people think their comments are rather obvious, or might be ones they have wrestled with for a long time, shows that they possess minds that are well suited to the science-and-religion discourse, and we would be intellectually poorer if we did not hear from them. (It may be noted that many children have not yet learned to put themselves down in this way, and therefore feel much freer to ask questions or contribute to discussions. In events that are for mixed age groups, the adults can benefit from this lack of inhibition, and hear answers to the questions that they were too embarrassed to ask.)

The Equipping Christian Leadership in an Age of Science (ECLAS) project has developed a model of bringing together secular scientists and senior Christian leaders to discuss issues which affect us all, such as artificial intelligence or genetics. The insights from these meetings transcend the ability of either theologians or scientists to address the questions on their own. The church is also a place where we can come into relationship with people who can help us to move forward our thinking about science and Christianity and put it to use. For example, our church children's worker recently helped me

---

10. Elaine Howard Ecklund et al., *Secularity and Science: What Scientists around the World Really Think about Religion* (Oxford: Oxford University Press, 2019), 210.

to see that the best way to communicate how science and faith fit together in a short talk is to cut out the theory and get on with demonstrating how science can fuel our worship. Or one could take the times when I ask adult church members, from all walks of life, to describe how something they recently learned or noticed about the created order fueled their worship. In response I usually receive a series of powerful devotional vignettes rooted in everyday realities. These juxtapositions of different people, each with their own knowledge and experience of the world, can be incredibly creative. When we engage the wider membership of the church in the discussion about science and religion, everyone can grow in understanding as each member of "the body of Christ" plays its part (cf. 1 Cor 12:12–31).

## *Leadership and Market Research*

One of the most effective ways to reach new audiences can be to invite individuals representative of those demographics into positions of leadership over the activities in question. For example, my own work is informed by a small and very diverse informal advisory group of pastors from across the UK. I find that this community of people who sacrifice an hour or two of their time twice a year is a very valuable and challenging source of insight into my current and future activities. Online meetings are not always preferable, but they make it possible for a wide range of leaders to participate. Another formative experience along these lines some time ago was seeing a number of younger scientists come onto the committee of Christians in Science, and watching the impact on the age profile of our membership.

Market research is, of course, also worthwhile, and needn't be complicated. A brief survey of church leaders has been helpful on two separate occasions in my own work, informing major projects and providing an impetus for fresh funding bids.

As an illustration for both of these points, the US-based ministry Science for the Church has a program called "The Standard Model" which includes stages of building a team, surveying the congregation, and examining the church's priorities before trying a new activity.

## *A Little Creativity Can Go a Long Way*

With creativity, ingenuity, and hard work on the part of the organizers, some of the practical barriers to participation in the science-and-religion discussion can also be overcome. The standard method of widening engagement with science and Christianity in the UK has been to hold a public lecture. This type of event can draw in a large crowd if the topic is interesting, the speaker is well known or respected, the time and location are right, and the event is well publicized. Many more may listen or watch online in their own time if a recording can be made available. As mentioned above, however, in-person or online lectures are not always attractive or realistic for everyone. The alternatives, such as plays, comedy, exhibitions, or hands-on science days, are usually harder work to organize and put on, as well as being more expensive, but can draw in whole new audiences.

For example, some of the UK-based Christian festivals prefer to host discussion panels or hands-on science, rather than seminars. The "Wonder Day" family hands-on science events organized by Dr. Gavin Merrifield have helped churches to reach hundreds of people of all ages from their surrounding communities. I organized an exhibition of scientific images in my own church, with written explanations by those who produced them saying how their science and faith worked hand in hand. Everyone who came into the building had the opportunity to engage with these images, even if just for a few minutes. These activities varied in the level of commitment required to put them on, but all of them reached people who might not have attended a lecture or listened online.

## *Things Are Not Always as Sensitive as Expected*

Of course, we do need to be very gentle and loving in the way we discuss questions of science and faith in any context, not least in the church. We must be wise and gracious, trying to be aware of potential sore points, differences of opinion, or clashing agendas. But we mustn't let oversensitivity make us avoid conversations about science altogether – particularly in contexts where there is a high degree of mistrust or misunderstanding about science where that content is most needed. For example, I remember one scientist who was terribly worried about raising the question of science and faith in his own US-based conservative evangelical church. But when the event he helped organize took place, he was pleasantly surprised to find that the expected storm of controversy never arrived. He had spent so long with his own unexpressed worries, he had lost touch with where people in his church were at in their thinking on this subject.

The discussion about science and faith in the last several decades has moved on in a number of denominations and their seminaries, and there are many opportunities today to have more nuanced discussions than might have been possible in the past. For example, the ECLAS UK-based Science for Seminaries programme awarded grants to a broad range of institutions, including Regents Theological College (the main training school for the Elim Pentecostal Church) and the London School of Theology (an evangelical, interdenominational college). We find that leaders of churches or denominations are often very willing, indeed interested and grateful, to have opportunities to discuss the science-and-religion issues that affect them – especially the controversial ones. Even those who choose to hold a view that the earth is young may have a positive overall view of science. For example, the majority of people taking a young-earth view in a UK survey believed that the benefits of science outweigh the risks, even on some quite controversial topics such as stem-cell research and genetically modified crops.[11] The door is often opened much wider than expected to the discussion of science and Christian faith, if approached sensitively and appropriately.

## Strategies for Engaging with Science in the Church and Its Wider Communities

Within the ethos outlined in the previous section, a number of strategies are often successful in helping the church and its wider communities to engage well with science.

### *Making Life Easier for Hard-Pressed Church Leaders*

Church leaders have always been busy, but the COVID-19 pandemic put extra pressure on them in recent years as they sought to find ways to stay in touch with and serve their congregations in restricted and traumatic circumstances. The economic impact of COVID, as well as war and the effects of climate change, will continue to put pressure on churches around the world, and their leaders, in the years to come. In light of these circumstances, how can we support church leaders as they seek to engage with science? The answer, first of all, is gently! A "little and often" approach may be best for most situations. Effective engagement could, for example, happen two or three times a year, taking the form of promoting an event or resource, showing a short video, or interviewing a scientist. It can be difficult for church leaders to prioritize or plan activities such as these, and this is where scientists can assist. If church leaders have good relationships with one or more scientists in their congregations,

---

11. Spencer and Waite, *Science and Religion*, 41–44.

and know that they will be reminded every few months that "perhaps it's time for some science engagement, and here is one way we could do it which fits in with the overall ethos of the church," then they will almost always be extremely grateful.

There are certain things that church leaders always need to support, such as Sunday services, adult small groups, or activities for certain demographics, such as elderly people's groups or men's breakfasts. Rather than diverting time or resources from existing activities, we can actively help with them, or relieve some of the burden of them, by providing appropriate ready-made resources for a science-focused activity.

Tailoring resources that already exist for a new situation can also be a relatively straightforward way to help existing groups. For example, I have recently worked with a denomination that posts teaching resources on their website in a certain format. An existing study was repurposed (with permission) for their use without too much effort on either side. I have also worked with colleagues in other countries who have translated and adapted material from my projects to suit their own particular circumstances.

Finally, providing funding can be an effective way to help new initiatives to get off the ground. For example, the Scientists in Congregations programs in the US and UK have awarded small grants to teams of church leaders and scientists who came up with creative ways of helping their congregations and local communities to engage with science.

## *Giving a Platform to Scientists Who Are Christians*

One of the most effective ways to demonstrate that science and Christian faith can work well together is to invite a Christian who is a scientist to tell his or her story. A number of books, websites, video projects, and countless events have also drawn on this principle, giving a voice to many "boundary pioneers" who can represent incarnationally the harmony between science and faith. The effects of these activities can ripple out for decades.

Often, scientists need a little encouragement to get started. In *Test of Faith: Spiritual Journeys with Scientists*, the eminent neuroscientist Bill Newsome describes how he was invited to give a talk about science and faith on his own campus.[12] He was reluctant at first, because he "did not want that level of complexity to enter into [his] relationships with [his] academic colleagues."

---

12. Bill Newsome, "Life in the Lab," in *Test of Faith: Spiritual Journeys with Scientists*, ed. Ruth Bancewicz (Eugene: Wipf & Stock, 2010), 47–56.

In the end, he said yes, and was grateful for the opportunities it afforded for colleagues to open up with him about their own beliefs.

This pattern of a step of faith followed by a positive reaction (in at least some quarters) is repeated in the lives of many scientists I meet. I can think of one UK-based science lecturer, Dr. Ruth Hogg of Queen's University Belfast, who contributed her story of integrating faith and science to my book *God in the Lab*.[13] When some postgraduate students on the same campus read the book they approached her, asking if she could support them in forming a Christian postgraduate student group. Another scientist I know decided, on taking up her first university lectureship, to make her faith public right from the start and has never regretted that decision.

Telling one's own story is an excellent route into the conversation about science and Christian faith for scientists who do not have the time or the inclination to enter the academic science-and-religion arena. Of course, not everyone has a well-worked-out story to tell, or is capable of sharing it in a way that is accessible to nonscientists. This is where training can be helpful. At the Faraday Institute, we have run a number of courses to equip scientists and others involved in the discussion about science and faith to communicate their ideas clearly and engagingly in talks, radio interviews, and written articles. These courses are especially well received by younger (and more diverse) generations of communicators, who can be identified and equipped through these training programs before being given suitable platforms to contribute to the discussion.

Another way to involve scientists in the conversation is to invite them to respond to relevant news stories. For example, we all saw the beautiful images coming from the James Webb Space Telescope in the summer of 2022. Mentioning a story that will already be familiar to many in the congregation, then asking a scientist to comment on how this ties in with his or her faith, can be a very natural way of introducing engagement with science into a church activity.

It is worth noting that many people with science-oriented careers might not see themselves as scientists, or scientific, because they are not academic researchers. In your church, these could include people involved in health care, agriculture, engineering, teaching, or industry. It is well worth drawing into the conversation people from any sector that uses scientific knowledge, and helping them to think about how their faith and the science they use at work fit together.

---

13. Ruth Bancewicz, *God in the Lab: How Science Enhances Faith* (Oxford: Monarch, 2015), 59–89.

## *Engaging the Whole Person*

In its regular ministry and mission, the church engages with the whole person through a wide range of activities that includes telling stories, singing and making music, prayer, silence, movement and different postures such as kneeling, dancing, or making the sign of the cross, and visual aids such as paintings or sculptures. Bread and wine, water, candles, and incense also stimulate our senses and our minds in so many ways.

Our engagement with science can be similarly multidimensional. As described above, a living person provides possibly the best illustration for the integration of science and faith, especially if the group is small enough to allow for meaningful interactions with the speaker.

Hands-on science demonstrations can enable nonscientists (and scientists from a different field) to experience firsthand what science is, as well as the wonder and fascination of scientific exploration and discovery, the aesthetics of different experimental systems, and some of the challenges of life in the lab. The process of sourcing, packing, transporting, setting up, and clearing up experiments can add a significant amount of work to an event, but is nearly always worth the extra effort. Experiencing hands-on science can at times be very moving for those who have not had the opportunity to do so during their education. It is also possible to source more simple demonstrations that cut down some of the work, such as USB microscopes, fossils, or optical illusions. More ambitious endeavors might include taking part in citizen science, organizing a field trip, or a visit to a working laboratory.

The performing arts also provide us with new and creative ways to get our message across. Plays, comedy, dance, and song are all highly effective ways to get a message across on multiple levels. For example, the one-man show *Fire from Heaven* about Michael Faraday held my attention for seventy-five minutes in a way that a lecture of the same length could never have done.[14] A comedy such as *The God Particle* not only draws in a completely different audience, but can get across its points in a far gentler way than a straight lecture can often achieve.[15]

Video is a potentially powerful way to share (relatively) immersive experiences with those who cannot attend in-person events. This format also allows for relatively easy translatability for other countries or language groups. The initial budget for a professionally produced film can be intimidating, but

---

14. Written and produced by Murray Watts and performed by Andrew Harrison.

15. A "rom-com sci-fi play about science, faith, and the importance of keeping an open mind" by James Carey.

with good distribution the impact is shared among a far greater audience. For example, the *Test of Faith* documentary, produced by the Faraday Institute, reached an estimated 5.5 million viewers in the first few years after its release.

Busy workers often listen to podcasts as they do chores or exercise, and flick through social media or online articles as they wait in line or commute. These are relatively easy formats to work with, and can reach huge numbers of people if they are available in well-used channels such as the church or denominational social media feed, podcast, or newsletter. When people are maxed out with family life, studies, or demanding jobs, these low-hanging fruit are often – with the possible exception of Sunday services – the only ways to reach them.

In short, creativity and some lateral thinking can open up untapped audiences. To give one final and quite unusual example, I had a conversation with a trainee church leader who said there was no way his sending church would engage with science. I encouraged him that I could work with whatever activities were already happening. This resulted in my visiting the parent and toddler group to lead a brief interactive session with the children, and to engage in conversation with the parents as they supervised a science-related craft activity. I found that most of the adults present – whether religious or not – were very keen to think about science and Christianity, and were full of questions. Some were taking time off from science-related careers, and were glad to open up about their own experiences. If I had taken a traditional approach, such as by giving a formal lecture, I would have ignored this potential for new conversations to take place.

## *Building Relationships of Trust*

Every church, denomination, or parachurch organization has its trusted figures. If these "opinion formers" value the science-faith discussion and are willing to say so publicly, then this can go a very long way in promoting helpful conversations. If these leaders have their own helpful stories to tell, that has an even greater impact. For example, some years ago, Alister McGrath was better known for historical and systematic theology than for his engagement on science and theology. It was very helpful to be able to point out to more conservative Christian audiences, who saw him as a trusted figure, that he was also a scientist who happened to think evolutionary biology is compatible with Christian theology.

These relationships of trust also include particular media outlets, such as Christian radio shows and magazines. For example, Premier Christian Radio's

*Unbelievable?* apologetics debate show, which Justin Brierley hosted for many years, has given a platform to many excellent voices on this topic. Relationships of trust are also of key importance in the other direction, when suggesting content to channels like these. Radio presenters and journalists are constantly bombarded with unsolicited content, so building a good rapport with them is a key priority. This can take time, but ultimately opens many doors.

## *Finding Common Ground*

When there are known sensitivities about science and religion it is essential to find common ground where a positive conversation can take place before opening up any sensitive issues. For example, my first engagement with many churches is usually an interactive talk that shares what science is, the positive contribution of Christian theology to the development of science, a theology of science, the stories of a number of scientists who are also Christians, and some scientific stories that evoke a sense of wonder and awe. A theology that enables congregations to fuel their worship with some beautiful scientific images, for example, is an excellent first step to deeper conversations about more detailed doctrinal issues such as the fall or human origins.

Intentionally teaching the basics of the doctrine of creation from time to time can be a helpful way of demonstrating (by implication, even if not directly mentioned) that many of the controversial issues – such as details about who were Adam and Eve, or what exactly was the impact of the fall – are secondary to the core gospel truths. This approach can free people up to explore any origins-related issues that concern them without worrying they will lose their faith in the process. For those who continue to find mainstream science a problem, this type of teaching can reassure them – or challenge them – that others are free to take a different view.

## *Giving Science Space on the Most Respected Platforms*

Although church leaders may slightly overestimate the impact of their own teaching and influence on their congregations,[16] the Sunday service and other forums where key teaching is usually delivered are excellent places to start engaging with science. The advantage of these existing platforms, as well as the authority they lend to the message, is that they have a "captive audience" of

---

16. Peter Lynas, *Changing Church: Autumn Survey – Discipleship, Evangelism and Community Transformation*, report (London: Evangelical Alliance, 2021), 3–4.

people who will come and listen or take part in whatever is offered. Separate, specialist events are good, but those who feel "not scientific" or are otherwise not inclined or not able to come will be absent from those events.

## Collaboration

Another route into the science-and-religion conversation for busy scientists, besides the academic path and telling one's own story, is to collaborate. The Faraday Institute recently played host to a seminar by a philosopher-theologian and a scientist. Together they were able to address different strands of the discussion in a way that served the audience more fully. I have also mentioned the approach ECLAS takes in its conferences, bringing together scientists and theologians for a discussion. In an increasingly competitive and damaged world, this may well be the way forward, rather than expecting each person to acquire large bodies of knowledge from outside his or her principal field in order to take part in the conversation. Can we take this principle further in developing yet more partnerships between scientists and theologians, where they can produce collaborative talks, articles, and other resources, or events that draw on their diverse areas of expertise?

## Conclusions

I conclude with a challenge and an encouragement. The challenge is that this is not an issue the church can afford to ignore. If we allow any of the barriers mentioned above to force us to abandon the science-and-religion discussion in some contexts, we unwittingly open the door to allow others to inform our congregations. In a recent survey, the UK Evangelical Alliance found that church leaders tended to overestimate the impact of Sunday services, small groups, and spiritual mentoring on their congregations' spiritual formation, and underestimate the impact of books, Christian radio, podcasts, and webinars.[17] In other words, unless we recommend resources for our church members on topics and in a format they appreciate, they will find content themselves. Of course, independent learning is a good thing, but part of the role of shepherding a congregation is to lead people to good sources of information. Pastors also have the opportunity to ensure that the congregations' browsing is informed by a solid foundation of theology, including a theology of science.

---

17. Peter Lynas, *Changing Church: Autumn Survey – Discipleship, Evangelism and Community Transformation*, report (London: Evangelical Alliance, 2021), 3–4.

An anonymous US-based contributor summed up this dynamic very well in a comment on an online article of mine some years ago:

> I've ... noticed a surprising amount of silence over science-faith issues, even in contexts where outsiders might expect there should be lively discussion.... But that apparent lack of visible engagement should not be mistaken for a total absence of the "intuitive cognitions" rumbling underneath the surface of the laity.... I suspect that in an age where we're already feeling fractured from neighbor, parishioner, and classmate in our political lives, we are loath to initiate conversations that we think (often rightly!) will just foment even more division. So we let the sleeping dogs lie. But ... those dogs are not really asleep, and their quiet labors continue under the surface directing our cultural thought habits into the deepening ruts of conflict theses that continue to threaten and cause shipwreck to the faith of many.

It is true that church leaders are bombarded with issues and need to make difficult choices about what activities they spend time on. But in an increasingly scientific society, I believe that a healthy engagement with science is, and can easily be, an integral part of our ministry and mission.

The encouragement I have to give is that church leaders are usually respected voices in their church communities and beyond, so a little engagement on this topic can go a long way. If the Christian message is contextualized for a scientific society, in the same way that the gospel writers contextualized their messages for different audiences, this can have a huge impact. Scientists can be motivated in their day-to-day work, and also be strengthened to share their experience of science and Christian faith working hand in hand. Young people can be inspired to study science and pursue scientific careers. People of all ages can be encouraged that we don't have to choose between science and religion. The church can have a voice in society, as it negotiates how to support scientific research and use new technologies. The conversation about science and faith can broaden and deepen as more and more voices take part. The opportunities are there; the resources are there; let's make the most of them!

## References

Barna Group. *The UK Church in Action: Perceptions of Social Justice and Mission in a Changing World*. Barna Group, 2018.
Brooke, John Hedley. *Science and Religion: Some Historical Perspectives*. Cambridge: Cambridge University Press, 1991.
Ecklund, Elaine Howard. *Science vs. Religion: What Scientists Really Think*. Oxford: Oxford University Press, 2010.
Ecklund, Elaine Howard, et al. *Secularity and Science: What Scientists around the World Really Think about Religion*. Oxford: Oxford University Press, 2019.
Lynas, Peter. *Changing Church: Autumn Survey – Discipleship, Evangelism and Community Transformation*. Report. London: Evangelical Alliance, 2021.
Newsome, Bill. "Life in the Lab." In *Test of Faith: Spiritual Journeys with Scientists*, edited by Ruth Bancewicz, 47–56. Eugene: Wipf & Stock, 2010.
Sollereder, Bethany N., and Alister E. McGrath, eds. *Emerging Voices in Science and Theology: Contributions by Young Women*. London: Routledge, 2022.
Spencer, Nick, and Hannah Waite. *Science and Religion: Moving Away from the Shallow End*. Report. London: Theos, 2022.
Unsworth, Amy, and David Voas. "Attitudes to Evolution among Christians, Muslims and the Non-Religious in Britain: Differential Effects of Religious and Educational Factors." *Public Understanding of Science* 27, no. 1 (2013): 76–93.
Village, Andrew, and Sylvia Baker. "Reasons Given by UK Churchgoers for Their Stance on Evolution," *Journal of Beliefs and Values* 34, no. 2 (2013): 165–77.

## Further Reading

Helps nonscientists and others to appreciate the connections between science and Christian faith by addressing curiosity, imagination, beauty, wonder, and awe, plus a chapter on life in the lab.
Bancewicz, Ruth M. *God in the Lab: How Science Enhances Faith*. Oxford: Monarch, 2015.

Fully illustrated with drawings and photographs, this book demonstrates some of the principles outlined in *God in the Lab*.
Bancewicz, Ruth M. *Wonders of the Living World: Curiosity, Awe, and the Meaning of Life*. Oxford: Lion, 2021.

This short book is a great example of accessible storytelling, as well as sharing why science and Christian faith can work together.
Hutchings, David, and Tom McLeish. *Let There Be Science: Why God Loves Science and Science Needs God*. Oxford: Lion, 2017.

Provides empirical data on how church leaders in the UK view science, and outlines ways of fostering fruitful engagement.

Reid, Lydia, and David Wilkinson. "Building Enthusiasm and Overcoming Fear: Engaging with Christian Leaders in an Age of Science." *Zygon* 56, no. 4 (2021): 1087–109.

Unpacks the sensitivities of relating to science in a more conservative Christian environment, suggesting ways forward into more helpful engagement.

Ecklund, Elaine Howard. *Why Science and Faith Need Each Other: Eight Shared Values That Move Us beyond Fear.* Grand Rapids: Brazos, 2020.

Gets to the heart of where the science-and-Christianity conversation is at for young adults.

Cootsona, Greg. *Mere Science and Christian Faith: Bridging the Divide with Emerging Adults.* Downers Grove: IVP, 2018.

Written by possibly the most famous "boundary pioneer," this very readable story tells how he came to faith and how science and Christian faith can work together. It does not shy away from controversy, but shares a way of relating the two that does justice to genuine Christian faith and the scientific endeavor.

Collins, Francis S. *The Language of God: A Scientist Presents Evidence for Belief.* New York: Free Press, 2006.

An example of science being used as fuel for worship. This is the most scientifically well-informed of Giglio's publications, with a foreword from astronomer Dr. Jennifer Wiseman.

Giglio, Louie, and Matt Redman. *Indescribable: Encountering the Glory of God in the Beauty of the Universe.* Colorado Springs: David C. Cook, 2011.

Outlines some principles for engaging with science, as well as some sample sermons.

Hoezee, Scott E. *Proclaim the Wonder: Engaging Science on Sunday.* Grand Rapids: Baker, 2019.

Examples of science-based ideas for Bible-based "Messy Church" activities.

Gregory, David, ed. *Messy Church Does Science.* Abingdon: BRF, 2017.

# Conclusion

# Local Perspectives of Global Significance

Mike Brownnutt, University of Hong Kong

## Abstract

The works collected together in this book have illustrated the rich, interlinked, multifaceted nature of the contributions to be made by the varied perspectives on science and Christianity which exist around the world. In concluding, we step back from the details of each case to consider a number of common threads which recur across the varied contexts. Given the diverse local examples of science and Christianity from around the world, this chapter considers what insights might be gained about science and Christianity globally.

## Introduction

This volume set out to showcase insights from global perspectives on science and Christianity. If the world were simply homogeneous, the insights of people from Brazil or Kenya would be identical to the insights of people elsewhere, and therefore add nothing new globally. If the world were simply fragmented, the insights from Brazil or Kenya would be alien to people from elsewhere, and therefore add nothing helpful globally. In a globalized world, however, the insights from Brazil and Kenya would be different enough to be interesting, and similar enough to be relevant. We hope that the perspectives presented have, indeed, been global.

In selecting subjects for this volume, we set out to engage with a diversity of topics. This active attempt at variety makes it all the more significant when certain themes nonetheless surface repeatedly. The unexpectedly recurrent themes suggest that something interesting is going on below the surface. In this chapter we highlight some of these recurrent themes and trace them through the book.

## The Many Facets of Biological Origins

Several chapters mention Darwin, evolution, creationism, or intelligent design. The topic arose in both chapters which originated from the UK (chs. 2 and 10). In chapter 2, it arises as a historic struggle, stretching back a full century to the start of the CiS story, and continuing to some extent into the present. In chapter 10, it arises in the present as a topic with which some people are nervous to engage, lest they stir up controversy. And yet it is a topic which, in Dr. Bancewicz's experience, is often less divisive than people fear, and can be discussed with nuance and grace.

In the Greek Orthodox context recounted in chapter 5, Darwinism and the critique thereof were co-opted to a wide variety of causes. These included struggles over the influence of Western materialism; shibboleths for what constituted the essence of Greekness; defense of, or opposition to, Marxist ideology; the Greek Civil War; and political struggles within the Orthodox Church itself. This, if nothing else, suggests that responses which engage with the struggles of people in the UK are likely to utterly miss the concerns of people in Greece.

We should therefore not anticipate finding a one-size-fits-all magic bullet to resolving any tensions between Christianity and evolutionary theory.

That much being said, chapter 4 (from Brazil) and chapter 7 (from New Zealand) both point fingers in similar directions when discussing the cause of the increased tensions they see around evolution: secularism. When the academy and the public sphere provide spaces for considered engagement of faith and theology with scientific thought, the tensions can be defused. By contrast, when religious thought is excluded from discussions within the academy and the public sphere, religious communities – cut off from the moderating influences that such discussions would have provided – can move toward more fringe ideas. To the extent that this dynamic applies elsewhere, countries which hope that sound science can be safeguarded by the exclusion of religion from the classroom – by a wall of separation between church and state – may note the experiences of Brazil and New Zealand as cautionary tales.

Local Perspectives of Global Significance 225

## The Inseparability of Science and Religion

The difficulty of separating (or even differentiating) science from religion was explicitly addressed in chapter 3 (from Hong Kong) and chapter 6 (from Kenya). Lest this be seen as a quirk of science and religion beyond the West, the same dynamic arises implicitly, but clearly, in chapter 8 (from Canada).

Hopes and dreams and passions; a clear vision of what is worth doing, and how it is worth being done: these qualities are not out of place in science. Indeed, they provide the necessary framework on which are hung the more mundane scientific tasks of measuring chemical concentrations or counting whales. In like manner, getting out into the world and doing something; understanding what effect a given intervention will have, and making appropriate interventions in light of that understanding: these are not inappropriate to religion. Indeed, they constitute a natural expression of religious life. Chapter 8 demonstrates that, even in the "enlightened" modern West, things which – at first glance – might get neatly filed under one or other label of "religion" or "science," in fact necessarily suffuse and flow seamlessly back and forth between the ways of faith and the study of nature.

## Incarnation

Just as science cannot be separated from religion, so the spiritual cannot be divorced from the physical. The significance of incarnation formed another recurrent theme.

The insights of chapter 4 (from Brazil) hinged on the incarnational nature of the communities involved. They are literal, physical, material instantiations, consisting of real relationships between real people. We cannot abstract science, or religion, or the interactions between them to some purely intellectual immaterial plane. If "dwelling among us" was not below God himself, as Word incarnate, far be it from us to undervalue the significance of dwelling together. When different groups speak of themselves, the word they choose for their group can be telling: a political *organization*, a student *body*, a legal *profession*. Of all the options available, it is surely no coincidence that we speak both of a scientific *community* and a religious *community*.

Chapter 8 (from Canada) highlighted the incarnational significance of all creation. Living in community, the vision of "dwelling among" here is not limited to living with people, but to living with the land; coming to personally know and love the trees, the rivers, and the soil for which they are caring.

Zooming back, then, to the individual level, chapter 10 (from the UK) notes the power and incarnational significance of a single person. Scientists who are Christians incarnate, in a single body, the possibility of relating science and Christianity. All the books carefully explaining how science and religion can be reconciled in principle do not compare to the explanatory power of a Christian who is a scientist. A person who has reconciled science and Christianity within him- or herself stands as the literal embodiment of that possibility.

## Money

Money and finance, in its various forms, provides a recurrent if strongly ambivalent theme. Chapter 4 (from Brazil) provides a helpful framework for understanding science, religion, money, and their diverse interactions. The porosity between the fields of financial capital, technological capital, scientific capital, moral capital, and social capital means that they can never be independent: a change made in one field will necessarily have implications for the others. And yet the distinctions between the fields mean that what is optimal for one field will rarely be optimal for others.

Several other chapters provide practical illustrations of the tensions that arise, and which, to a greater or lesser extent, may be mitigated. Chapter 2 (from the UK) provides an open and frank account of the perennial difficulties of finding funding faced by all organizations relating science and religion. Chapter 9 (from Canada and Macau) highlights the moneymaking prospects of AI, while also noting the moral hazards that these prospects introduce. Chapter 8 (from Canada) shows how a Conservative politician aligned, in his own thinking, conservation and conservatism: viewing living within one's means ecologically as a logical extension of living within one's means fiscally.

## Politics

Possibly the single most prominent and most recurrent theme is the connection of science and religion to politics. Chapter 4 (from Brazil) flows seamlessly between, sociology of science, and philosophy of religion without breaking step. The political engagement in chapter 5 (from Greece) takes diverse forms: from opposition to foreign powers, to forging of a national self-image, or internal domestic rivalries. But whatever its form, there is no point at which one can distill out some "pure" vision of Greek engagement with Darwin which is not interpreted through politics. Chapter 6 (from Kenya) underscores the manner in which any understanding of science, or religion, or their engagement, is necessarily embedded in a cultural matrix, and that no sense can be made of this without understanding the political dimension. This political dimension is both local and regional, historic and present. Chapter 7 (from New Zealand) highlights the significance of the political decision to exclude religion from the public sphere, and the political decision to make exceptions to this rule for Māoritanga. Chapter 8 (from Canada) places a politician, Preston Manning, and his politics front and center as one of the key actors in the narrative. Finally, chapter 9 (from Canada and Macau) hums with the nation-building efforts of world governments, as the scientific narrative of each continent is shaped by their respective political narratives.

Being able to separate the messy world of politics from the (already complicated enough) interactions of science and religion can make life simple, and even safe. Consider the oft-busted myth of Galileo: "No, no!" we insist; "the Galileo affair was not a dispute between science and religion. It was driven by politics." Myth debunked, job done. The bracketing out of politics allows us to downplay the conflict between science and religion. It allows us to fob all the disagreements off onto the political bits, and keep the science and the religion clean.

Prompted by the contributions of this volume, however, we may have unearthed a new question: How is it that sixteenth-century Italy is possibly unique in all of history – a singular time and place in which science and religion can be meaningfully disentangled from political considerations? Or, if that question does not take our fancy, we can instead ask: What happens to the account of Galileo if we take seriously the political nature of both science and religion?

## Other Religions

Discussions dominated by Western narratives have historically had the luxury of being able to broadly neglect the diversity of religions which coexist in most cultures. In Europe, one may see mention of Protestantism and Catholicism. In North America, one may see a contrast drawn between the views of evangelicals and those of Pentecostals. But one will rarely find serious consideration of how Islam, Buddhism, or Vodou play into the discussion. In the West, the situation is rapidly changing. The need for both Christian and secular institutions to consider the engagement of other (i.e. non-Christian) religions with science is becoming ever more pressing. Beyond the West, the need to engage with diverse religious viewpoints is generally the status quo.

Chapter 3 (from Hong Kong) and chapter 6 (from Kenya) each argued that discussions of science and Christianity (in Asia and Africa respectively) need to come to terms with cultural practices which (by some categorizations) are religious, and which (by some categorizations) are unchristian. It is not sufficient to attempt to settle the questions of whether such cultural views and practices are (or are not) religious, or whether they are (or are not) Christian. Regardless of how these questions are answered, the discussion of science and Christianity still needs to understand these views and practices, and work through their implications.

Chapter 9 (from Canada and Macau) showed how the direction of AI research is shaped by the cultural river in which societies find themselves, and that engagement with research policy requires an understanding of such. Christians working on AI in Asia do not need to accept Confucianism, but they do need to understand it. At the very least, they need to understand that appeals to personal privacy and human rights will carry much less weight in China than appeals to societal stability.

Finally, chapter 7 (from New Zealand) provides examples of the opportunities afforded by working together with different religious groups. While Christianity on its own is excluded from much of public life in New Zealand, Islam and Māori spirituality may provide conversation partners which can open the door to Christian voices being heard.

While we deliberately selected varied topics, and explicitly asked the authors to present their own local perspectives, the recurrence of these major themes suggests that there are deeper issues of global applicability being raised. The handful of recurrent themes noted in this chapter are not exhaustive of the deeper global themes raised within these chapters, much less exhaustive of the important themes that become apparent when considering the global discourse at large. We hope, however, that they will serve as inspiration or provocation for people both to speak out about their own perspectives on science and Christianity in a global context, and to listen carefully to the perspectives of others.

# Authors

All authors are writing here in personal capacities. The opinions they express in this volume should not be taken as representing any official stance of their respective organizations.

## Ruth M. Bancewicz (UK)

Ruth Bancewicz is church engagement director at the Faraday Institute for Science and Religion, where her remit is to equip and encourage UK churches to include engagement with science as part of their regular ministry and mission. She studied genetics at the University of Aberdeen and the University of Edinburgh.. Her first professional foray into the world of science and faith was a part-time post as the development officer for Christians in Science, at the same time as working as a postdoctoral research fellow at the University of Edinburgh. She moved to Cambridge to join the Faraday Institute when it was founded in 2006, to develop resources for churches. Ruth was appointed as the Faraday Church Engagement Director in 2018. She remains a member of Christians in Science, and is an elected fellow of their US counterpart, the American Scientific Affiliation. She is a member of City Church Cambridge, and is currently studying theology, ministry, and mission at Ridley Hall, UK.

## Edward Berkelaar (Canada)

Edward Berkelaar is professor of chemistry and environmental science at Redeemer University Canada. Edward grew up on a farm in Nova Scotia. He studied biology and chemistry at Acadia University before moving to Ontario to complete his MSc and PhD in environmental toxicology at the University of Guelph. Upon completion of his studies, he and his wife, Dawn, worked at Educational Concerns for Hunger Organization (ECH ), an organization based in North Fort Myers, Florida, USA, that is dedicated to supporting people doing agricultural development work overseas. Edward has been at Redeemer since 2003, where he teaches a variety of chemistry and environmental studies courses and serves as associate dean of natural sciences and mathematics. He has carried out research on trace-element accumulation by plants and, more recently, been involved in a long-term water monitoring project of urban watersheds in Hamilton.

### Prof. Bernard Boyo (Kenya)

Bernard Boyo has a PhD from Fuller Theological Seminary, USA, looking at the role of the church in the social and political issues affecting the Kenyan context. He currently serves as director of the School of Mission and Theology at Daystar University. His research interests include public theology, economic, and sociopolitical impacts on suffering communities, and religion's role in and response to these. He has been involved in research projects at the intersection of science and religion, including consideration of Christianity at the intersection of faith, traditional, and biomedical healing.

### Dr. Henry Brouwer (Canada)

Henry Brouwer is emeritus professor of chemistry and environmental science at Redeemer University, Canada. After completing his PhD in physical organic chemistry at the University of Western Ontario, Henry taught high school for fifteen years before joining the faculty of Redeemer as professor of chemistry. There he started the chemistry program, and later the environmental studies program. He carried out research jointly with Dr. Tom Murphy at the Canadian Centre for Inland Waters on remediation of contaminated sediments. He also taught environmental chemistry at the Au Sable Institute of Environmental Studies, a field station for North American Christian college and university students located in northern Michigan, USA. Since retiring, he has served as one of the leaders of the Climate Witness Project, a group within the Christian Reformed Church tasked with creating greater awareness of climate change in local church communities.

### Dr. Mike Brownnutt (Hong Kong SAR)

Mike Brownnutt obtained his first master's degree (MSc in physics) and his PhD (in experimental quantum mechanics) from Imperial College London, UK. He then worked at the University of Innsbruck for eight years, writing his habilitation on his research there, which developed scalable architectures for trapped-ion quantum computers. He completed a second master's degree (MA in theology) from the University of Chester, UK, considering how faith is understood by various parties in the discourse on the relationship between

Christianity and science. He spent seven years at the University of Hong Kong, serving as associate director of the Faith and Science Collaborative Research Forum, and researching framings for science and religion which do not presuppose modernist assumptions. He now serves as Course Director of the Faraday Institute for Science and Religion in the UK. In his spare time, he is working on a PhD with the University of Birmingham, UK, on nonmodern philosophy of science and religion.

## Rev. Guilherme de Carvalho (Brazil)

Guilherme de Carvalho is a Brazilian Baptist theologian and pastor based in Belo Horizonte, Brazil. He studied theology at Mackenzie Presbyterian University in São Paulo, obtaining a master's in theology at the Faculdade Teológica Batista de São Paulo (focusing on New Testament exegesis) and another master's in science of religion at São Paulo Methodist University (focusing on philosophical theology). He taught theology in Belo Horizonte for some years and started the Associação Kuyper para Estudos Transdisciplinares. After a time at L'Abri branches in Europe, he and his wife founded L'Abri Fellowship Brazil, and planted Esperança Church, both in Belo Horizonte (Minas Gerais). He and Dr. Roberto Covolan gathered a group of academics to found the Associação Brasileira de Cristãos na Ciência (ABC²), with the support of Templeton World Charity Foundation, Inc. He is currently serving as the president of ABC².

## Prof. David Clements (Canada)

David Clements is professor of biology and assistant dean (research) in the Faculty of Natural and Applied Sciences at Trinity Western University (TWU). Having completed a BSc at Western University and a PhD at Queen's University, David carried out postdoctoral research at the University of Guelph. At TWU, David teaches botany and ecology, including field courses on Salt Spring Island and Hawaii. He manages TWU's field research sites: the main campus Ecosystem Study Area, the Blaauw Eco Forest nearby, and the Crow's Nest Ecological Research Area on Salt Spring Island. His research on invasive species ecology takes place in British Columbia, China, Australia, and beyond. Climate change in relation to invasive species is another major focus. He was a founding board member of the Christian environmental organization A Rocha Canada, serving on the board for fifteen years, and still serves on the science advisory committee. He is also actively involved in local stewardship groups and writes the Green Beat column for the *Langley Advance Times* newspaper.

## Prof. Martin Ester (Canada)

Martin Ester obtained a master's degree from the University of Dortmund, Germany, and a PhD from ETH Zurich, Switzerland, both in computer science. Having worked at Swissair, Zurich, and the University of Munich, Germany, he moved to Canada in 2001 and became a professor at Simon Fraser University (SFU). From 2005 to 2010, he served as the director of SFU's School of Computing Science. His research interests are in the areas of data mining and machine learning, with a current focus on causal inference, transfer learning, and explainable machine learning. Many of the applications driving his research are in precision medicine. In 2014, he received the Test of Time Award of the Association of Computing Machinery Special Interest Group of Knowledge Discovery and Data Mining for his work on density-based clustering, and in 2019 he was elected as a fellow of the Royal Society of Canada. For almost ten years, Martin has, together with three SFU colleagues, been offering a public lecture series "God and Reason," exploring questions at the nexus of science and Christian faith.

## Prof. Paul Ewart (UK)

Paul Ewart obtained a BSc and PhD in physics from Queen's University Belfast, Northern Ireland, and was then an (SERC) advanced fellow at the Blackett Laboratory, Imperial College of Science and Technology, London, UK. In 1979 he moved to the University of Oxford as a tutor and fellow of Worcester College, and as lecturer in the physics department, later serving as head of the Department of Atomic and Laser Physics. He has been visiting professor at the Joint Institute for Laboratory Astrophysics, Colorado, USA, the École Normale Supérieure, France, and the University of Otago, New Zealand. His research has included fundamental physics of quantum and nonlinear optics, lasers, and development of novel laser-based techniques with applications in chemistry and engineering science. He is convener of the Oxford Forum for Science and Religion, and is a former chairman of Christians in Science.

## Prof. Keith R. Fox (UK)

Keith R. Fox is emeritus professor of biochemistry at the University of Southampton, UK, and former director of the Faraday Institute for Science and Religion in Cambridge. He studied natural sciences at the University of Cambridge, specializing in biochemistry, where he completed a PhD in the Department of Pharmacology in 1980. He stayed in Cambridge for postdoctoral work and was a research fellow at Emmanuel College. He moved to Southampton in 1987 as a lecturer in biochemistry and pharmacology, and became professor of biochemistry in 2000. His research interests concern DNA structure and its recognition, and his scientific work has been published in over two hundred papers and articles. He was senior executive editor of *Nucleic Acids Research*, fellow of the Royal Society of Chemistry, and editor of *Science & Christian Belief*. He is a former chairman and trustee of Christians in Science. He has special interests in bioethics, creation/evolution, and genome modification. He is ordained in the Church of England.

## Prof. Andrew Halestrap (UK)

Andrew Halestrap is emeritus professor of biochemistry and senior research fellow at the University of Bristol. He obtained his first degree in natural sciences at the University of Cambridge in 1970 before moving to Bristol to study for his PhD, and subsequently joined the academic staff. In that capacity, he ran a large research group and several teaching programs. He has published more than two hundred original research papers and was elected a fellow of the Academy of Medical Sciences in 2008. In 2010 he was awarded the Keilin Memorial Lecture and Medal of the Biochemical Society. Andrew has served in various leadership and teaching roles in the church and academia, including being a past chair of the British Heart Foundation Project Grants Committee and the Bristol Heart Institute. His research interests include how lactic acid crosses cell membranes, and the role of mitochondria in the healthy and diseased heart. He is passionate about helping people to see how science is a friend and not an enemy of the Christian faith. Until recently he was the national chair of Christians in Science.

## Dr. Nicola Hoggard Creegan (New Zealand)

Nicola Hoggard Creegan is a theologian based in Auckland, and is codirector of New Zealand Christians in Science. Her research specializes in the interface between evolutionary theory and systematic theology, with broad interests also in all issues of public and contextual theology and ecology. She is the author of *Animal Suffering and the Problem of Evil* (Oxford University Press, 2013) and with Andrew Shepherd, has coedited *Creation and Hope* (Pickwick Publications, 2018) and *Taking Rational Trouble over the Mysteries* (Pickwick Publications, 2013). She was a part of the Human Nature Project at the Center for Theological Enquiry in Princeton, USA (2012–13), and the Human Distinctiveness Project at Notre Dame, USA (2015–16).

## Dr. Samuel M. Karenga (Kenya)

Samuel M. Karenga graduated with a PhD in chemistry from Oklahoma State University, USA. His research was in the development and characterization of polymeric ligands for electrochromatography. He was a postdoctoral fellow at Lawrence Berkeley National Laboratory, a US Department of Energy science laboratory managed by the University of California, Berkeley. He taught chemistry at San Francisco State University and now lectures at Mount Kenya University, where he also serves as the director of graduate studies. His research interests are in separation science and phytochemistry. As a Christian, he is a believer in science as a God-given gift for the benefit of humanity. He has therefore participated in projects touching on science and the Christian faith.

## Dr. Peter G. Kirira (Kenya)

Peter G. Kirira obtained his master's degree in chemistry from Kenyatta University, Kenya. He then moved to Nagasaki University, Japan, where he undertook his PhD in pharmaceutical chemistry. He proceeded to Kyoto University's Department of Chemistry for a postdoctoral program under Prof. Keiji Maruoka. Peter then returned to work as a senior scientist at the Kenya Medical Research Institute before relocating to academia as a senior lecturer and deputy director of research at Mount Kenya University. He is currently serving as ddeputy vice-chancellor, Administration, Planning, and Institutional Advancement at Mount Kenya University. His research interests are in drug research, and he has published articles on drugs from nature as well as novel processes for synthesis of antimalarial and anticancer drugs. He has also championed implementation of projects on entrepreneurship, graduate employability, and community engagement as part of student academic life. He was part of the team that established the Christian and Scientific Association of Kenya, a platform that allows discourse on the intersection of science and religion in the African context.

## Dr. Efthymios Nicolaidis (Greece)

Efthymios Nicolaidis is director of research and head of the History, Philosophy, and Didactics of Science and Technology Research Program of the Institute of Historical Research at the National Hellenic Research Foundation, Greece. He is also the coordinator of the Science and Orthodoxy Around the World project, as well as other projects on the history of science. Born in Athens in 1954, he studied physics and the history of science in France. His research predominantly considers the relations between science and religion, the history of astronomy, the history of science in Byzantium and the Ottoman Empire, and the spread of modern European science. His publications include the overview *Science and Eastern Orthodoxy* (Johns Hopkins University Press, 2011; rev. ed. in French: Garnier, 2018). Efthymios was president of the International Union of the History and Philosophy of Science (2013–17), and is currently permanent secretary of the International Academy of the History of Science (since 2017).

## Dr. Kostas Tampakis (Greece)

Kostas Tampakis is associate researcher of history of science and technology at the Institute of Historical Research of the National Hellenic Research Foundation, Greece. He holds a diploma in physics, an MSc in science education, and a PhD in the history of science, all from the University of Athens. He has been a research associate at Darwin College, University of Cambridge, and a visiting scholar at the history and philosophy of science department, University of Cambridge, UK. He was also the Ted and Elaine Athanassiades postdoctoral research associate with the Program in Hellenic Studies, Princeton University, USA. His research interests include the history of the relations of science and Orthodox Christianity, science and literature, as well as the history of science in Greece and the Greek-speaking regions (eighteenth–twentieth century). His work has been published in peer-reviewed journals such as *Isis*, *British Journal for the History of Science*, *History of Science*, and *Zygon*.

## Prof. Ah Chung Tsoi (China)

Ah Chung Tsoi obtained his master's and PhD in control engineering at the University of Salford, UK. He subsequently held positions at several universities across New Zealand and Australia, and served as the executive director of the Mathematics, Information and Communication Sciences Inter-disciplinary

Cluster of the Australian Research Council (2003–5). He has served as the director of Monash eResearch Center, Monash University, Australia (2005–7), vice president (research and institutional advancement) of Hong Kong Baptist University (2007–10), and dean of the Faculty of Information Technology at Macau University of Science and Technology (2010–16). Since his retirement, he served as a technical consultant to the office of vice rector (administration), University of Macau, and he retired completely in 2019 in Brisbane, Australia, serving as an emeritus professor, University of Wollongong. His current research interests include neural networks, artificial intelligence, information retrieval, image and video classifications, and web spam detection. He has received a BD degree from the University of Otago, New Zealand, and has research interests in science and faith issues, particularly from an Asian perspective.

## Dr. John Wood (Canada)

John R. Wood is emeritus professor of biology and environmental studies at The King's University, Alberta, Canada, and executive director (interim) of the American Scientific Affiliation. John completed his MSc in biology at Central Washington University, USA, and earned his PhD from the University of California, Berkeley, in stream ecology and insect behavior. His current research includes the North American response to edible insects, and the ecological and theological understanding of physical death. He and psychologist Dr. Heather Looy have explored global food security in relation to the West's cultural blind spot regarding accepting food insects. Before moving to Canada in 1989, John taught at Simpson College in California. His professional work includes the development of undergraduate environmental science programs. He was a reviewer for the ECO Canada national accreditation process for environmental science and environmental studies programs. John is also the former academic dean of the Au Sable Institute of Environmental Studies.

# Appendix 1

# Organizations and Institutions

There is an extensive web of organizations involved in activities related to the topics discussed in this book. Some limit their activities to specific cities, or specific countries, while others have a wider geographical remit. Some are directly affiliated with specific universities, or specific denominations, while others are independent of these. Some focus on specific disciplines within science, some engage with science more generally, and others have an even broader remit of which science is only one part. This complex interconnected web is not static, with new organizations being founded or spun out, and existing organizations being renamed, merged, or wound up; some involve major institutions planning for the long haul, while others are small projects lasting only as long as their current grant funding. This dynamic situation means that any list will be both incomplete, and out of date as soon as it is published. Nonetheless, we provide here some examples of organizations working in the science-and-Christianity space, grouped loosely by geographical region.[1] This list may act as a starting point for people wishing to dig deeper.[2]

The first and most obvious benefit of knowing about these organizations is being able to draw directly on what they do. You can look up their websites, watch their videos, read their papers, buy their books, join their membership, and attend their conferences.

Another benefit is the ability to draw on their insights regarding how to do what they do and how they do it. None of the groups featured in this volume simply started on its own. They all started by talking to people: emails,

---

1. When looking up your country of interest, remember to also check the final section, "Transnational Organizations." A Rocha, for example, works in twenty countries on six continents. The Anglican Communion Science Commission covers 165 countries! Rather than list each separately, these have been put in a separate transnational list at the end. Conversely, do remember that many of these organizations, while being nominally based in one country, are only an email away from you on the other side of the world.

2. Inclusion in this list does not imply any relationship between us and the organizations listed. Inclusion here does not constitute our endorsement of the organizations or the positions they hold, nor does it suggest that they endorse or agree with us.

phone calls, coffee, pizza. If you want to set up a group looking at science and Christianity in Zimbabwe, there are people on this list who would love to hear about it, and who would love to help.

Finally, at a basic pragmatic level, this list can provide leverage. Maybe you want to do a research project that connects science to Christianity, but your secular university is not sure that it is appropriate. "That's fine," you say. "The University of Oxford does it. But if you don't want to be like Oxford, you do your own thing." Or maybe you want your theology lectures to lean into some of the scientific implications of the material, but your Catholic seminary is hesitant. "That's fine," you say. "The Vatican does it. But if you would rather not follow their lead on this one . . ." Be gracious about it. But it's amazing what doors can be opened when people realize who else is doing it.

## Africa

### The Centre for Religion, the Environment, Science and Development (CRESAD), Ghana

https://www.aci.edu.gh/research/centres/cresad

A research center at the Akrofi-Christaller Institute of Theology, Mission & Culture in Akropong-Akuapem. It carries out research into African religious approaches to studying ecological science.

### Christians in Science Ghana, Ghana

A nonprofit organization, founded in 2013, which seeks to support Christians in Ghana to bring their Christian faith to bear on the pursuit of science.

### Christian & Scientific Association of Kenya (CSAK), Kenya

Based at Mount Kenya University, but with activities across Kenya. Members are predominantly professional scientists, but they welcome anyone with an interest in science and religion. Their aim is for Christians who are interested in science to explore how the interaction between Christianity and science in the African context can best synergize each other. (See also chapter 6.)

## Asia

### Christian Association for the Psychology of Religion, Hong Kong SAR

https://www.psy-religion.com/

Based in Hong Kong. Engages with academic research and discussions on psychology of religion as it pertains to the region.

**Faith and Science Collaborative Research Forum (FaSCoRe), Hong Kong SAR**
https://faithandscience.hku.hk/
Based at the University of Hong Kong, FaSCoRe carries out research into the interrelationships between science and religion in Asian contexts, and works to equip university faculty to engage with the issues raised. It is part of the wider Faith and Global Engagement research cluster at HKU. (See also chapters 3, 9.)

**Christian Scholars' Fellowship (CSF), Japan**
http://shigakukai.org/
The purpose of the Christian Scholars' Fellowship (*Shigakukai*) is to encourage and support young scholars and graduate students professing a Christian faith who aspire to become academics or equivalent professionals, by providing opportunities for fellowship and research grants.

## Australasia

**Institute for the Study of Christianity in an Age of Science and Technology (ISCAST), Australia**
https://iscast.org/about/
ISCAST is a network of people, from students to distinguished academics, exploring the interface of science, technology, and Christian faith.

**New Zealand Christians in Science (NZCIS), New Zealand**
www.nzcis.org/
New Zealand Christians in Science connects scientists who are active Christians, and resources the church, students, and the wider community on faith and science. (See also chapter 7.)

## Europe

**Center for Science and Faith (CVT), Denmark**
https://teol.ku.dk/afd/center-for-videnskab-og-tro/
Center for Videnskab og Tro is a collaboration between the Faculty of Health Sciences and the Faculty of Theology at the University of Copenhagen, committed to researching, teaching, and disseminating the connection between science and faith as it pertains across academic disciplines.

**The Blaise Pascal Network (Sciences, Cultures and Faith), France**
https://sciences-foi-rbp.org/

Réseau Blaise Pascal (Sciences, Cultures et Foi) comprises around thirty French-speaking Christian groups who work on questions relating to sciences, cultures, and faith. These draw on diverse disciplines including science, philosophy, and theology.

### Chair of Science and Religion, Lyon, France
https://www.ucly.fr/l-ucly/nos-ecoles/chaire-science-et-religion/
Chaire Science et Religion, at the Catholic University of Lyon, develops a teaching and research program on the relationship between science and religion, providing mediation and dialogue through an interdisciplinary and philosophical approach.

### Interdisciplinary University of Paris (UIP), France
http://www.uip.edu/
Université Interdisciplinaire de Paris aims to disseminate and bring together different visions of the world based on the study of contemporary scientific paradigms and philosophies of the spirit, bringing together scientists, philosophers, religious leaders, and economists.

The UIP organizes international seminars and conferences attended by well-known scientists, philosophers, and internationally renowned figures (Seminars and Speakers) in collaboration with other bodies (Partners).

### Science and Christian Faith Association, France
https://scienceetfoi.com/
L'association Science et Foi Chrétienne operates with the encouragement of the BioLogos Foundation to provide the French-speaking world with answers to frequently asked questions about the Christian faith, science, and the origins of the world and life.

### Evangelical Scientists' Network, France and Switzerland
http://rescev.free.fr/
Réseau des scientifiques évangéliques brings together professionals and students from scientific fields, as well as others with professional interest in the field, to discuss and develop a Christian vision of the nature of scientific practice, and its engagement with religious practice.

**Institute for Faith and Science (IGUW), Germany**
https://www.iguw.de/
The Institut für Glaube und Wissenschaft was established to promote the dialog between believing and thinking, and to equip people to join in with such dialogue.

**Karl Heim Society, Germany**
https://www.karl-heim-gesellschaft.de
In the spirit of theologian Karl Heim, the Karl-Heim-Gesellschaft seeks a thorough investigation of basic scientific and theological questions, and their effects on society. They have various publications and host an annual conference.

**Science & Orthodoxy around the World (SOW), Greece and beyond**
www.project-sow.org/
Based at the National Hellenic Research Foundation in Athens, SOW aims to chart the various positions on the relations between science and religion across the entire Orthodox Christian world, setting the foundation for an organized and advanced dialogue between science and Orthodoxy. (See also chapter 5.)

**Interdisciplinary Documentation of Science and Faith (DISF), Italy**
https://www.pusc.it/centri/disf
The Centro di Documentazione Interdisciplinare di Scienza e Fede is a research and training center at the Pontifical University of the Holy Cross in Rome. Its initiatives, including the DISF Portal, are intended to encourage a more mature synthesis between faith and reason among those in academic and pastoral professions.

**Science, Theology, and the Ontological Quest (STOQ), Italy**
https://en.pusc.it/fil/progetti-di-ricerca/stoq
An interdisciplinary, multi-institution project coordinated by the Pontifical Council for Culture and based at the Faculty of Philosophy at the Pontifical University of the Holy Cross. It promotes study and research in the field of relationships between Science and Faith.

**Vatican Observatory, Italy**
https://www.vaticanobservatory.org/
The Vatican Observatory is one of the oldest astronomical institutes in the world, tracing its roots to Pope Gregory XIII in 1582. Now headquartered just outside Rome, this official work of the Vatican City supports a dozen priests and brothers from four continents who study the universe utilizing modern scientific methods.

### Copernicus Center for Interdisciplinary Studies, Poland
https://www.copernicuscenter.edu.pl/en/
Based at the Jagiellonian University in Krakow, the center carries out research into science and religion, among other topics. It offers its own master's degree course in philosophy in science, and a specialization course in science and religion, as well as postgraduate research opportunities.

### Religious Hypotheses and the Study of Human Nature, Romania
https://religioushypotheses.com/
Coordinated locally by the Agora Christi Foundation, working with the University of Oxford and the Romanian Academy, this project aims at answering the question of how religious claims – from tradition or from sacred scriptures – can contribute to the study of human nature when they are tested as hypotheses.

### Sciences of the Origin, Serbia
https://sciorigin.weebly.com/
Hosted at the University of Belgrade, in collaboration with the Ian Ramsey Centre for Science and Religion at the University of Oxford. The project considers commonalities across cosmology, biology, and archeology regarding our search to understand the origin of the universe, the origin of life, and the origin of mind.

### Hana and Francisco José Ayala Chair of Science, Technology, and Religion (CTR), Spain
https://www.comillas.edu/catedra-hana-francisco-jose-ayala-ctr
Cátedra Hana y Francisco José Ayala de Ciencia, Tecnología y Religión, based at Comillas Pontificial University, Madrid, is a space for research, teaching, and dissemination. It promotes multidisciplinary reflection on the dialogue between science, technology, and religion within the Catholic Church and beyond, including with nonreligious people and institutions, particularly in Spain and Portugal.

### Science, Reason, and Faith Group (CRYF), Spain
https://www.unav.edu/web/ciencia-razon-y-fe
Grupo Ciencia, Razon y Fe, at the University of Navarra, carries out interdisciplinary work on issues in which science, philosophy, and religion are related. To this end they engage in research, teaching, and dissemination.

## Anscombe Bioethics Centre, UK
https://www.bioethics.org.uk/
The Anscombe Bioethics Centre is an Oxford-based research institute serving the Catholic Church in the United Kingdom and Ireland. The Centre promotes the study of Catholic bioethics in service of the common good.

## Christians in Science (CiS), UK
https://www.cis.org.uk/
CiS is a network of people encompassing research scientists, engineers, theologians, and philosophers, as well as students, school teachers, administrators, and anyone interested in science-and-faith issues. (See also chapters 2, 10.)

## Developing a Christian Mind (DCM), UK
https://dcmoxford.org/
Based in Oxford, DCM provides space for postgraduate students, postdocs, and faculty to consider how they integrate their Christian faith and their academic life. They cover a wide variety of disciplines and include science-specific tracks.

## Equipping Christian Leadership in an Age of Science (ECLAS), UK
https://www.eclasproject.org/
Based in the UK, ECLAS aims to help church leaders to connect with world-class science and scientists, to develop well-informed, theologically grounded, practical knowledge about the world and our place in it. (Mentioned in chapter 10.)

## The Faraday Institute for Science and Religion, UK
https://www.faraday.cam.ac.uk/
Based in Cambridge, but with national and increasingly international reach, the Faraday Institute is an interdisciplinary research institute working to improve public understanding of religious beliefs in relation to the sciences. (See also chapter 10. Mentioned in chapters 2, 4.)

## Grasping the Nettle, Scotland, UK
https://www.graspingthenettle.org/
Grasping the Nettle is an interdenominational movement formed by church leaders in Scotland to promote dialogue within the church and society at large about belief in God, especially in relation to science. Its activities include public talks, lectures, and conferences, as well as other events involving music, drama, and film.

**Ian Ramsey Centre for Science and Religion, UK**
https://www.ianramseycentre.ox.ac.uk/
Based at the University of Oxford, the Ian Ramsey Centre for Science and Religion conducts research into religious beliefs and theological concepts in relation to the sciences. (Mentioned in chapter 10.)

**New Visions in Theological Anthropology (NViTA), UK**
https://set.wp.st-andrews.ac.uk/
Based at St Andrews University, New Visions in Theological Anthropology is a project designed to get theologians thinking carefully about theological anthropology on those questions that involve evolutionary biology, developmental psychology, and cognitive science. This project is intended as an exercise in science-engaged theology.

**Scholarship & Christianity in Oxford (SCIO), UK**
https://www.scio-uk.org/
SCIO is committed to the integration of Christian vocation and scholarship. It works with undergraduates, graduates, and faculty from member campuses in North American and International Affiliates. They engage with a wide variety of disciplines and have specific activities for science and STEMM.

**Science and Religion Forum (SRF), UK**
https://www.srforum.org/
The SRF provides a community exploring the interaction of science and religion in the twenty-first century. It hosts public lectures and an annual conference.

**Science, Knowledge and Belief in Society, UK**
https://www.birmingham.ac.uk/research/skbsrg/
Based at the University of Birmingham, the Science, Knowledge and Belief in Society Research Group is a multidisciplinary team of researchers based in the School of Philosophy, Theology and Religion that conducts social scientific and humanities-based research.

**Society, Religion and Technology Project (SRT), UK**
https://www.churchofscotland.org.uk/about-us/our-views/science-and-technology
Society, Religion and Technology (SRT) was set up by the Church of Scotland fifty years ago to examine the ethical and social implications of new technology. Through its reports, it advises the Church on policy regarding some of the biggest issues facing us today.

### Pontifical Academy for Life, Vatican City
https://www.academyforlife.va/content/pav/it.html
The pontifical Academy for Life focuses on the study, information, and formation of the principal problems of biomedicine and of law. It currently has five projects: artificial intelligence; robo-ethics; global bioethics; consciousness, neuroscience, and ethics; and human genome editing.

### Pontifical Academy of Sciences, Vatican City
https://www.pas.va/
The Pontifical Academy of Sciences is international in scope, multiracial in composition, and nonsectarian in its choice of members. The work of the Academy comprises six major areas: fundamental science; science and technology of global problems; science for the problems of the Majority World; scientific policy; bioethics; and epistemology.

### Pontifical Academy of Social Sciences, Vatican City
https://www.pass.va/en.html
The Pontifical Academy of Social Sciences has the aim of promoting the study and progress of the social, economic, political, and juridical sciences, offering the church the elements which it can use in the study and development of its social doctrine. The Academy also reflects on the application of that doctrine in contemporary society.

## North America

### Canadian Scientific & Christian Affiliation (CSCA), Canada
https://www.csca.ca/
CSCA is a fellowship of scientists and those interested in science who want to understand how science should best interact with the life-giving Christian tradition. CSCA members come to these challenges as researchers in academia and industry, as professors, theologians, philosophers, administrators, and as students just getting started. (See also chapters 8 and 9.)

### Centre for Studies in Religion and Society (CSRS), Canada
https://www.uvic.ca/research/centres/csrs/
CSRS hosts a community of interdisciplinary scholars, researchers, students, artists, and community members to research religion in relation to aspects of society including science, politics, law, history, and the arts.

### Center for Studies in Science and Religion (CECIR), Mexico
https://investigacion.upaep.mx/index.php/centro-de-estudios-en-ciencia-y-religion

Centro de Estudios en Ciencia y Religión (CECIR) is an academic and research organization at the Universidad Popular Autónoma del Estado de Puebla (UPAEP). It has the objective of promoting constructive intellectual and human dialogue between the world of science and religion, through research, teaching, and dissemination, particularly in Latin America.

### American Scientific Affiliation (ASA), US
https://network.asa3.org/

ASA's mission is to integrate, communicate, and facilitate properly researched science and theology in service to the church and the scientific community. (Mentioned in chapters 2 and 7.)

### Association of Christians in the Mathematical Sciences (ACMS), US
https://acmsonline.org/

Based in the US, though open to a broader membership. In addition to engaging with Christianity and mathematics, they have a computer science subgroup, for Christians who are interested in the relationship between faith and computer science.

### Au Sable Institute of Environmental Studies, US
https://www.ausable.org/

Au Sable Institute offers environmental science programs for students and adults of all ages: primary and secondary school, college, and graduate school. The college academic program offers field-based, university-level classes with academic credit offered by more than fifty colleges and universities. (Mentioned in chapter 8.)

### BioLogos, US
https://biologos.org/

BioLogos seeks to meet the need for virtual and actual meeting places to ask questions, discuss issues, and learn from the top Christian minds in the sciences and theology. (Mentioned in chapter 7.)

## Center for Advanced Study in Religion and Science (CASIRAS), US
https://www.casiras.org
Founded in 1972, CASIRAS is an independent society of scholars and scientists from various fields who pursue critical, interdisciplinary studies of possibilities for constructively relating religion and science.

## Center for Theology and the Natural Sciences (CTNS), US
https://www.gtu.edu/centers/ctns
CTNS is a center within the Graduate Theological Union (GTU), Berkeley. It promotes the creative mutual interaction between theology and the natural sciences through research, teaching, and public service. (Mentioned in chapter 7.)

## Christian Engineering Society (CES), US
https://www.christianengineering.org/
CES members are interested in applying biblical principles to the design of technology. This includes consideration of God's special concern for the poor and disadvantaged, and their stewardship and unfolding of the creation. They look for opportunities to use their skills as engineers in ways that build God's kingdom.

## Counterbalance Foundation, US
https://counterbalance.org/
A nonprofit educational organization working to promote the public understanding of science, and how the sciences relate to wider society, including questions relating to religion. It seeks to provide integrated responses to complex questions.

## Dialogue on Science, Ethics, and Religion (DoSER), US
https://www.aaas.org/programs/dialogue-science-ethics-and-religion
DoSER is a program of the American Association for the Advancement of Science (AAAS), established to facilitate communication between scientific and religious communities. It is committed to relating scientific knowledge and technological development to the purposes and concerns of society at large.

### Educational Concerns for Hunger Organization (ECHO), US
https://echonet.org/
ECHO equips and empowers hungry families with knowledge and the life-giving grace of God. Practicing environmental restoration or agricultural development rooted within a Christian worldview, they teach small-scale sustainable farming methods so families can provide for themselves and their communities.

### Evangelical Environmental Network (EEN), US
https://creationcare.org/
EEN is a ministry that educates, inspires, and mobilizes Christians to be faithful stewards of God's provision, to get involved in local action, and to advocate for actions and policies that honor God and protect the environment.

### Institute for Cross-Disciplinary Engagement at Dartmouth (ICE), US
https://www.ice.dartmouth.edu/
Based at Dartmouth College, New Hampshire, ICE addresses contemporary questions of science and religion. It organizes public events and online courses, and functions as an incubator of new academic work through the ICE Fellows Program.

### Institute for Theological Encounter with Science and Theology (ITEST), US
https://faithscience.org/
An association of theologians, scientists, and others committed to a Catholic worldview in which faith and science collaborate in exploring the truth. ITEST fosters and disseminates the Catholic position that science and faith in God are complementary paths to human fulfillment.

### Institute on Religion in an Age of Science (IRAS), US
https://www.iras.org/
IRAS cultivates a community of informed and respectful inquiry and dialogue at the intersections of science with religion, spirituality, and philosophy in service of global, societal, and personal well-being.

### John J. Reilly Center for Science, Technology, and Values, US
https://reilly.nd.edu/
The John J. Reilly Center at the University of Notre Dame, Indiana, offers graduate and undergraduate programs and fosters scholarly conversation at the intersections between the humanities, social sciences, and medicine.

### Samford University Center for Science & Religion, US
https://www.samford.edu/science-and-religion/
The Center for Science & Religion seeks to stimulate critical thinking and promote dialogue on key issues central to science and religion. It supports interdisciplinary research and publication, supervises an undergraduate major in science and religion, and sponsors educational events on and off campus.

### Science for the Church, US
https://scienceforthechurch.org/
Science for the Church exists to change the posture of the church, pastors, and individual Christians as they relate to science and scientists, in the hope that they will come to embrace science as a means for spiritual growth. (Mentioned in chapter 10.)

### Science, Theology, and Religion (STAR), US
https://sparks.fuller.edu/star/
An independent department within Fuller Theological Seminary, California, STAR develops projects with scholars and experts which highlight the places where the sciences and theologizing can cooperate for mutual benefit.

### Vatican Observatory Research Group (VORG), US
https://www.vaticanobservatory.va/
In 1981, the Vatican Observatory in Rome founded the Vatican Observatory Research Group (VORG) in Tucson, Arizona. In 1993 construction of the Vatican Advanced Technology Telescope (VATT) was completed on Mt. Graham. With this optical-infrared telescope the Observatory contributes to long-term research programs.

### Yale Forum on Religion and Ecology, US
https://fore.yale.edu/
Based at Yale University, the Yale Forum on Religion and Ecology is an international multireligious project contributing to a new academic field and an engaged moral force of religious environmentalism.

### Yale Program for Medicine, Spirituality, & Religion
https://medicine.yale.edu/intmed/genmed/education/medspirel/
Based at Yale University, the program seeks to understand the implications of religious practice, communal support, and intrinsic belief for health and wellness. It hosts speakers, sponsors a fellowship program, and offers graduate courses.

**Zygon Center for Religion and Science, US**
https://www.lstc.edu/academics/zygon
The Zygon Center is located at the Lutheran School of Theology at Chicago (LSTC). It brings together scientists, theologians, and other scholars dedicated to relating religious traditions and the best scientific knowledge to gain insight into the origins, nature, and destiny of humans and their environment.

## South America

**Foundation for Dialogue between Science and Religion (DeCyR), Argentina**
http://www.fundaciondecyr.org/
Fundación Diálogo entre Ciencia y Religión (DeCyR) organizes study activities on interdisciplinary topics of common interest to science and religion. These include organizing research groups, studies, workshops, conferences, publications, and reading circles.

**Institute of Philosophy, Austral University, Argentina**
https://www.austral.edu.ar/filosofia/
The Instituto de Filosofía, at Universidad Austral, Buenos Aires, aims to generate Christian humanist thought that philosophically supports the teaching and research disciplines at the university. It also publishes the *Diccionario Interdisciplinar Austral* (Interdisciplinary Dictionary in Science, Philosophy, and Theology).

**Other Worlds, Earth, Humanity, and Remote Space (OTHER), Argentina**
https://blog.ucc.edu.ar/other/
Otros Mundos, Tierra, Humanidad y Espacio Remoto (Proyecto OTHER) is based at Universidad Católica de Córdoba. It provides a multidisciplinary approach to the search for other inhabited worlds, engaging with the scientific, philosophical, and religious challenges that arise.

**Brazilian Association of Christians in Science (ABC²), Brazil**
https://www.cristaosnaciencia.org.br/
Associação Brasileira de Cristãos na Ciência aims to construct a bridge between the scientific milieu and the Christian community in Brazil through networking, engagement, and creation of relevant materials. (See also chapter 4.)

**Brazilian Association for Philosophy of Religion (ABFR), Brazil**
https://abfr.org/
Associação Brasileira de Filosofia da Religião (ABFR) was founded in 2010 by researchers and graduate students with the goal of unifying the local initiatives and fomenting the study of this philosophical area in Brazil.

**Brazilian Society of Catholic Scientists (SBCC), Brazil**
https://catolicosnaciencia.org.br/
SBCC (Sociedade Brasileira de Cientistas Católicos) brings together professors, researchers, and graduate students who wish to serve the mission of the church from their profession and contribute to Brazilian science by promoting dialogue between faith and reason.

**Center for Research in Spirituality and Health (NUPES), Brazil**
https://www2.ufjf.br/ppgsaude/curso/linhas-de-pesquisa/nupes-nucleo-de-pesquisas-em-espiritualidade-e-saude/
Núcleo de Pesquisas em Espiritualidade e Saúde (NUPES) is based at the Juiz de Fora Federal University and carries out interdisciplinary research into the relationships between spirituality and health.

## Transnational Organizations

**Anglican Communion Science Commission (ACSC)**
https://www.anglicancommunion.org/community/commissions.aspx
The ACSC Commissioners include scientists, theologians, and church leaders from around the world, including bishops from each of the forty-one churches that make up the Anglican Communion globally. The Commission aims to equip the church to provide contextualized leadership in the engagement of science and faith.

**A Rocha**
https://arocha.org/
A Rocha is a global family of Christian organizations which engages in scientific research, environmental education, and community-based conservation projects in more than twenty countries and across six continents, with around half being in the Global South. (Mentioned in chapters 7 and 8.)

**Christian Astronomers**
https://sites.google.com/site/chrastronomer/
A mailing list to connect, encourage, and equip professional astronomers who are Christians.

**European Society for the Study of Science and Theology (ESSSAT)**
https://www.esssat.net/
ESSSAT is a scholarly organization which aims to promote the study of relationships between the natural sciences and theological views. It has members from almost every European country as well as from other continents, drawn from diverse confessional backgrounds, including nonbelievers.

**International Society for Science & Religion (ISSR)**
https://www.issr.org.uk/
ISSR is an international organization with a commitment that religion and science each proceed best when they are pursued in dialogue with each other. Among its members are scientists, theologians, historians, philosophers, and others, drawn from a variety of religious convictions.

**Society of Catholic Scientists**
https://catholicscientists.org/
An international organization with members in over fifty countries. It seeks to foster fellowship among Catholic scientists and to witness to the harmony of faith and reason. It hosts international and regional conferences, college chapters, lectures, and other activities.

**Society for Science and Religion in Asia (SSRA)**
https://ssrasia.blogspot.com/
SSRA is an independent academic organization formed by a group of academics across Asia who share an extensive background in studying the relationship between science and religion. It was established for the purposes of developing academic research, promoting education of the public, and developing new talent.

## Organisations for Christian Scholars

The following groups are not primarily oriented to science and religion, but rather constitute extensive networks of scholars who relate Christianity with a variety of academic disciplines, including sciences.

## European Leadership Forum (ELF)
https://euroleadership.org/
The European Leadership Forum is a coalition of evangelical Christian groups which seeks to provide a bridge between God's global resources and local leaders from all over Europe and beyond. Its various interconnected disciplinary networks include tracks for scientists, theologians, and academics.

## Global Faculty Initiative (GFI)
https://globalfacultyinitiative.net/
GFI seeks to promote the integration of Christian faith and academic disciplines by bringing theologians into conversation with scholars across the spectrum of faculties in research universities worldwide.

## Global Scholars
https://global-scholars.org/
Global Scholars connects, equips, and resources Christian professors to have a redemptive influence in their institutions and disciplines. They currently work with academics in sixty nations.

## Society of Christian Scholars
https://scshub.net/
The Society of Christian Scholars is a global community of, by, and for missional Christian scholars. It seeks to equip Christian academics to have a missional and redemptive influence for Christ among their students, colleagues, institutions, and academic disciplines.

# Appendix 2

# Journals

There exists a variety of journals in which writings about the interactions of science and religion can find a home. The list here is not exhaustive, but gives an indication of the range of journals available to read and/or publish in.[1]

## General Journals Relating Science and Religion

*Christian Perspectives on Science and Technology* (*CPOSAT*)
is the journal of the Institute for the Study of Christianity in an Age of Science and Technology (ISCAST). Relaunched in 2022, it is an online, open-access resource, publishing book reviews and double-blind peer-reviewed articles which discuss the nexus of science, technology, faith, ethics, and spirituality.

*Connaître*
is the journal of Association Foi et Culture Scientifique (Association of Faith and Scientific Culture). The articles reflect the questions and proposals of Christian scientists who seek to articulate objective knowledge with the expression and content of their faith. Articles are in French.

*European Journal of Science and Theology*
explores interconnections between science and theology. It aims to offer the theological community digestible yet fully competent accounts of the latest scientific research while inviting further exploration of the ethical, religious, social, and philosophical aspects of these scientific discoveries.

---

1. Inclusion in this list does not constitute an endorsement of the journals or their contents. Regardless of the criteria by which we include or exclude publications, we leave ourselves open to cries of "How could they think that?" We refer, then, back to the comments in chapter 1, and ask for grace as we seek to indicate the diverse range of publications in the science-and-religion space.

*Evangelium und Wissenschaft*
is the journal of the Karl Heim Society. In the spirit of theologian Karl Heim, the society seeks a thorough investigation of basic scientific and theological questions, and their effects on society. These are discussed in a fashion rooted in Christianity, in cooperative dialogue with a pluralistic world. Articles are in German.

*Faith & Thought*
is the journal of Faith and Thought (the Victoria Institute). It seeks to convey to nonspecialists the pastoral and ethical implications of advances in science. The full back catalog of articles (going back to volume 1 of *Transactions of the Victoria Institute* in 1857) are available open access online.

*Icoana Credintei: International Journal of Interdisciplinary Scientific Research*
is published by Ideas Forum International Academic and Scientific Association with the Faculty of Orthodox Theology and Education Sciences, Valahia University of Târgoviște, Romania. It publishes papers on the intersection of Christianity with a wide variety of societal issues including science.

*International Multidisciplinary Scientific Conference on the Dialogue between Sciences & Arts, Religion & Education (MCDSARE)*
is a journal published by the Ideas Forum International Academic and Scientific Association. It publishes the proceedings of the eponymous annual conference in Romania, addressing interconnections between natural and social sciences, humanities, and religion.

*Issues in Science and Theology*
is a publication of the European Society for the Study of Science and Theology. Each volume reflects the theme of a recent ESSSAT conference, and contains a collection of scholarly essays exploring current scholarly thinking on the interaction between science and theology.

*Perspectives on Science and Christian Faith*
is the journal of the American Scientific Affiliation. It publishes original articles, communications, and book reviews that interact with science and Christian faith in a manner consistent with scientific and theological integrity. It seeks to serve the aims of the ASA by promoting the study of the relationship between science and Scripture, and disseminating the results of such study.

*Philosophy, Theology and the Sciences*
provides a platform for constructive and critical interactions between the natural sciences in all their variety and the fields of contemporary philosophy and theology. It invites scholars, religious or nonreligious, to examine together the truth claims found in theology, philosophy, and the sciences, as well as the methods found in each discipline and the meanings derived from them.

*Quaerentibus: Teología y ciencia*
is an academic publication that seeks to encourage a well-founded debate between the natural sciences, the human sciences, and theology, using the philosophy of science to critically mediate such dialogue. Articles are in Spanish.

*Reviews in Science and Religion*
is the journal of the Science and Religion Forum. It includes reviews of books in the field of science and religion, news about the Forum, and selections from the Proceedings of the Forum's Annual Conference.

*Reviews in Science, Religion & Theology*
is a joint publication of the European Society for the Study of Science and Theology and the International Society for Science and Religion. It includes scholarly articles, book reviews, and announcements of symposia, conferences, prizes, and other initiatives by organizations in the field of science and religion.

*Science & Christian Belief*
is published by Christians in Science and Faith and Thought (the Victoria Institute). It is concerned with the interactions of science and religion, with particular reference to Christianity, and publishes original research articles, book reviews, and correspondences.

*Scientia et Fides*
is an open-access online journal promoted by the Faculty of Theology of Nicolaus Copernicus University in Torun, Poland, in collaboration with the Science, Reason, and Faith group (CRYF) at the University of Navarra, Spain. It aims to present rigorous research regarding different aspects of the relationship between science and religion, and accepts articles written in English, Spanish, Polish, French, Italian, and German.

*Studies in Science and Theology*
is a publication of the European Society for the Study of Science and Theology and provides a companion series to *Issues in Science and Theology*. It contains

original essays on the interaction between science and religion which stem from the European Conference on Science and Theology.

*Theology and Science*
is the journal of the Center for Theology and the Natural Sciences. It engages scientific discourse in dialogue with both Christian and multireligious perspectives. It provides a critical and wide-ranging collection of articles and reviews that promote the creative mutual interaction between the natural sciences and theology.

*Unus Mundus: explorando interfaces entre ciência, filosofia e teologia*
is the online publication of Associação Brasileira de Cristãos na Ciência (ABC$^2$). It includes columns, articles, essays, book reviews, and podcasts on a range of topics relating to science and religion. Content is in Portuguese.

*Zygon: Journal of Religion and Science*
aims to bring together the best thinking from the physical, biological, and social sciences with ideas from philosophy, theology, and religious studies. It seeks to consider the whole range of the sciences, and is open to religious and nonreligious perspectives, from the West and around the globe, including religious naturalism, secular humanism, and atheism.

## Religion and Physical Sciences

*Journal of Holistic Mathematics Education*
is an open-access online journal hosted by Universitas Pelita Harapan in Tangerang, Indonesia. It publishes articles about research, teaching, philosophy, and curriculum development which show holistic approaches in mathematics and Christian education. Abstracts are in English, though the articles need not be.

## Religion and Environmental Sciences

*Journal for the Study of Religion, Nature and Culture*
is the journal of the International Society for the Study of Religion, Nature and Culture. It explores, through the social and natural sciences, the complex relationships among human beings, their diverse "religions," and the earth's living systems, while providing a venue for analysis and debate over what constitutes an ethically appropriate relationship between our own species and the environments we inhabit.

*Philosophy Activism Nature*
publishes articles, essays, and poetry exploring the philosophical underpinnings of environmental thought. The journal seeks in particular to explore the interface between ecology and environmental philosophy, on the one hand, and religion, mythology, and Indigenous thought, on the other. Dialogue between modern science and ancient or more traditional understandings of reality is also encouraged.

*Worldviews: Global Religions, Culture, and Ecology*
studies the relationships between religion, culture, and ecology worldwide. It addresses how cultural and ecological developments influence the world's major religions, giving rise to new forms of religious expression, and how in turn religious belief and cultural background can influence people's attitudes toward ecology.

## Religion and Medical Sciences / Social Sciences

*Journal of Religion and Health*
was founded by the Blanton-Peale Institute. It publishes original articles that deal with mental and physical health in relation to religion and spirituality of all kinds, placing particular emphasis on their relevance to current medical and psychological research.

*Journal of Religion, Spirituality & Aging*
is an interdisciplinary, interfaith professional journal bridging theory and practice. It informs secular professionals in health and social care, as well as providing a resource for religious professionals who work with aging people and their families.

*Journal of Spirituality in Mental Health*
is given to the scholarly study of spirituality as a resource for counseling and psychotherapeutic disciplines. It crosses the disciplines of psychology, spirituality, theology, sociology, and cultural analysis, as it seeks to enhance the understanding of spirituality as a core component of human well-being in individual, relational, and communal life.

## Scientific Study of Religion

*Implicit Religion*
is the journal of the Centre for the Study of Implicit Religion and Contemporary Spirituality. It offers a platform for scholarship that challenges the traditional boundary between religion and nonreligion and the tacit assumptions underlying this distinction.

*International Journal for the Psychology of Religion*
is devoted to psychological studies of religious processes and phenomena in all religious traditions. It publishes research reports, commentaries on relevant topical issues, book reviews, and statements addressing previously published articles. It may also publish articles on the psychology of religion in a specific country.

*Journal of Empirical Theology*
publishes articles on comparative research, both quantitative and qualitative, in religion on the macrolevel of society, the mesolevel of institutions, and the microlevel of patterns and processes of identity formation and group formation. It offers an international forum for scholars from different religions and contexts.

*Journal for the Scientific Study of Religion*
is the journal for the Society for the Scientific Study of Religion. It publishes articles, research notes, and book reviews on the social-scientific study of religion. Substantive areas include both microlevel analysis of individuals' experience with religion and macrolevel analysis of religious organizations, institutions, and social change.

*Psychology of Religion and Spirituality*
is published by the American Psychological Association. It publishes original articles related to the psychological aspects of religion and spirituality. Articles considered include full-length research reports, brief reports, and literature reviews.

*Social Compass*
is the journal of the International Society for the Sociology of Religion. It publishes original research and review articles which reflect the wide variety of research being carried out by sociologists of religion in all countries. Articles are in either English or French.

*Sociology of Religion*
is the journal of the Association for the Sociology of Religion. It aims to advance scholarship in the sociological study of religion. It publishes original-research articles, agenda-setting essays, comments on previously published works, and critical reflections on the research act.

## Philosophy of Religion

Many journals which count philosophy of religion as their core remit will regularly and explicitly draw connections with science, and particularly with the philosophy of science. While not dealing exclusively with science and religion, these journals are at least worth keeping on the radar.

*African Journal of Religion, Philosophy and Culture*
approaches its subjects of religion, philosophy, and culture in a holistic manner. It is not limited to traditional disciplines, but will also include emerging areas that contribute new vistas in our understanding of religion as a broad discipline with a bearing on Africa and beyond.

*American Catholic Philosophical Quarterly*
is produced by the American Catholic Philosophical Association. Each issue features scholarly articles, topical discussions, and reviews dealing with all philosophical areas and approaches.

*Faith and Philosophy*
is the journal of the Society of Christian Philosophers. It seeks to contribute to the continuing effort of the Christian community to articulate its faith in a way that will withstand critical examination, and to explore the implications of that faith for all aspects of human life.

*Forum Philosophicum*
is published through the Jesuit University Ignatianum in Krakow, Poland. It is open to inquiries into subjects traditionally of interest to Christian philosophy, to philosophy shaped by Jewish and Islamic religious concerns, to problems explored in contemporary theistic positions and in the philosophy of religion, and to new insights into the evolving borderlines and conflicts between the rational and the irrational.

*International Journal for Philosophy of Religion*
provides a medium for the exposition, development, and criticism of philosophical insights and theories relevant to religion in any of its varied forms. It represents no single institution or sectarian school, philosophical or religious.

*Philosophia Christi*
is the journal of the Evangelical Philosophical Society, published with the support of Biola University in La Mirada, US. It seeks to foster the scholarly discussion of philosophy and philosophical issues in the fields of apologetics, ethics, theology, and religion.

*Revista Brasileira de Filosofia da Religião*
publishes philosophy texts – written either in systematic form or based on the history of ideas – about the religious phenomenon or the issues related to the concept and reality of God. Articles are in Portuguese.

## Science and Religion Shading into Other Disciplines

It is hopefully clear from what has been written in this volume that there is no neat boundary to be drawn around science-and-religion beyond which science-and-religion does not go. Science-and-religion suffuses, and is suffused by, discussions of politics, and history, and technology, and philosophy, and education . . . Once one starts pulling on this thread, one starts to notice that papers on science-and-religion can and do turn up in all sorts of places, well beyond journals for science-and-religion simpliciter. Without wishing to chart the web of connections into eternity, we note in closing that many of the chapters of this volume drew on journals that fit squarely in such fields. Thus, even though journals like the *American Political Science Review*, or the *Bulletin of Science & Technology Studies*, or *Isis* would not be considered science-and-religion journals, it can be worth remaining aware of, and open to, the insights they can offer on the subject.

# Subject and Author Index

**A**
ABC² 61–65, 231, 250, 258
ABFR 251
abortion 56, 142
academics 10–11, 67, 83
acculturation 123–125
ACMS 246
ACSC 251
acupuncture 37–38, 43–45, 48, 50–55
Adam and Eve 59, 218
*African Journal of Religion, Philosophy and Culture* 261
African names for the supreme being 115
African political history 125
African thought 113, 120, 124–26
Agassiz, Louis 96
age of the earth 19
age profile 33, 211
agriculture 139, 215
AI. *See* artificial intelligence
*Aktines* 101
Alexa 176
Alexander, Denis 20, 23, 62
AlphaFold 176
AlphaGo 176–77
Althusius, Johannes 81
*American Catholic Philosophical Quarterly* 261
American Scientific Affiliation. *See* ASA
Analytic intelligence 179
Anaplassis 97
angels 40, 46
Anglican Communion Science Commission. *See* ACSC
animal testing 56
Anscombe Bioethics Centre 243
anthropic principle 20
antidifferentiationism 76
anti-evolutionists 16
anti-intellectualism 144
Aotearoa 132, 135, 146–47, 149
Aquinas 81
A Rocha 148, 156–60, 166–67, 170, 173, 237, 251
A Rocha Canada 155, 157–61, 163, 166–68, 170, 232
artificial intelligence 4, 11, 20, 197, 210, 226
  apocalypse 193, 198
  research 175–77, 185–86, 228
  Safety 192, 197
  strong 180, 185–87, 191, 198
  weak 179, 181, 186–87
ASA 20, 135, 246, 256
Assi, Gustavo 62
Association of Christians in the Mathematical Sciences. *See* ACMS
atheism 97, 99, 101, 104
atmospheric physics 7
ATMOS Research 162
Atwood, Margaret 156, 158, 160–61, 171–72
Auckland University 133, 135, 138, 140–41
augmented reality 183–84
Augustine 19, 80, 82, 84, 86, 88, 191, 197
Au Sable 164–67, 169, 230, 236, 246
Au Sable Institute of Environmental Studies. *See* Au Sable
autonomous vehicles 176, 182, 186
autonomy 69, 75–76, 79, 81, 86
autonomy of science 75–77
awe and wonder 152

**B**
Baidu 183, 188

Ballantine, Bill 139–40, 148
Bancewicz, Ruth 11, 22, 62, 201, 214–15, 221, 229
Barbour, Ian 38, 58
Barclay, Oliver 17–18
Barrett, David 120
barriers 204
Barton, Ruth 141
basic research 188
basis of faith 26
Beams, Jesse 78
*Being a Christian in . . .* 27, 30
Bellah, Robert 143
Berkelaar, Edward 11, 151, 229
Berry, Christine 137
Berry, Sam 20
Berry, Wendell 155, 158
Bible 19, 21, 45, 105, 126, 136, 142
 authority of 15–16, 19, 143
Bible studies 147
biblical Christian views 16, 22
biblical interpretation 19, 209
biblical scholarship 29
Big Bang 9, 140, 149, 203, 208
Big Data 176, 185, 191
Big Questions 131
biochemistry 11
biodiversity loss 153–54
bioethics 26
biological origins 203, 224
BioLogos 135, 240, 246
biology 11, 27, 52, 63, 100, 103–4
biomedicine 119, 122, 245
Bischoff, Theodor 96
Blaise Pascal Network 239
blockchain 183
blood transfusion 125
bonesetting 116
Borges, Jorge 92, 107
boundaries 37, 56–59, 64, 78, 171
Bourdieu, Pierre 69–70, 77, 89
Bowen, Deborah 161
Boyd, Robert 18
Boyo, Bernard 10, 111, 126, 230

Brazilian Association for Philosophy of Religion. *See* ABFR
Brazilian Association of Christians in Science. *See* ABC²
Brazilian Society of Catholic Scientists. *See* SBCC
bridge building 61, 65, 75, 87
bridge community 63–64, 86
Brierley, Justin 218
Briggs, Andrew 62
brokenness in creation 154
Broom, Neil 141
Brouwer, Darren 169
Brouwer, Henry 11, 151, 230
Brownnutt, Mike 1, 10, 37, 223, 230
Bryant, John 21–22, 25
Büchner, Ludwig 98, 107
Buddhism 55, 187, 227
bursaries 27–28
Butler, Samuel 136
ByteDance 188

C
Cabral, Marcelo 63, 65
CASIRAS 247
Canadian Perspectives 151
Canadian Scientific & Christian Affiliation. *See* CSCA
capital 64, 70, 77
 moral 85, 226
 scientific 70, 77
 temporal 77
career development 29
Catholic Church of Kenya 117
CECIR 246
Center for Advanced Study in Religion and Science. *See* CASIRAS
Center for Research in Spirituality and Health, Brazil. *See* NUPES
Center for Science and Faith. *See* CVT
Center for Studies in Science and Religion. *See* CECIR
Center for Theology and the Natural Sciences. *See* CTNS

Centre for Religion, the Environment, Science and Development. *See* CRESAD
Centre for Studies in Religion and Society, Canada. *See* CSRS
CES 247
Chalmers, David 184
chance 101, 107
chaplaincy 29, 135
character formation 8
charismatic 19, 24, 67, 97
ChatGPT 187, 192–93
chemistry 11, 27, 52, 63, 95, 141, 165, 169, 234
children and young people 203
Christ against culture 143
Christian and Scientific Association of Kenya. *See* CSAK
Christian Association for the Psychology of Religion 238
Christian Astronomers 252
Christian community 34, 87
Christian Engineering Society. *See* CES
Christian festivals 212
Christian Graduate 19–20, 35
Christianity in society 137
*Christian Perspectives on Science and Technology. See* CPOSAT
Christian Scholars' Fellowship 239
Christians in Engineering 21
Christians in Science. *See* CiS
Christians in Science Ghana 238
Christian student groups 26, 134
Christian Union of Scientists. *See* CUS
Christian Unions 16–17, 29, 31
Christian universities 153
Church 2, 11, 24, 27, 32, 34–35, 67–68, 79, 97, 99, 103–5, 115, 140, 142, 201–2, 206–8, 210, 213, 218–19
  Anglican Church 65, 143, 202
  attendance 134
  community 24
  Greek Orthodox 10, 94, 97, 103, 108, 224
  Eastern Orthodox 103

engagement 201
evangelical 26, 133, 138, 207, 212
evangelical mission 67
history 142
influence 202
leaders 11, 26–27, 34, 201, 204–5, 207, 211, 213–14, 217–20, 222
liberal sectors 140
local 16, 26–27, 32, 202, 230
members 201, 208–9, 211, 219
of Greece 94, 99
politics 94
Roman Catholic 143
and state 8, 10, 69, 224
student groups 29
CiS 8–10, 15–17, 19–35, 211, 224, 229, 232–33, 243, 257
  affiliated churches 32
  aims 22, 32
  membership 21, 27–28, 31, 33–34
City of God 80, 88
civil society 82
Clements, David 11, 151, 231
climate change 7, 153–54, 156, 158, 161–63, 170, 213
climate communicator 162
Coakley, Sarah 135
cognitive psychology 141
Collins, Francis 135
commerce 2, 6, 8, 176, 183
common good 82, 85–87
common sense 19, 126
communal well-being 111
communal worship 123
communication 30, 71, 164, 166, 179, 182, 187
  cross-cultural communication 12
communication networks 184
community 10, 61, 63–65, 68, 86–87, 111–12, 140, 167, 184, 225
  of believers 201
  of creation 160
  religious 184, 225
  science 162

scientific 22, 24, 76, 80, 84–85, 202, 225, 246
spiritual 87
community ethos 151
community farming 159
complex equality 73
computer vision 177
conferences 18, 20, 26–27, 29–30, 33–34, 133, 166, 205, 219
conflict 23, 38, 123, 128, 133, 204
Confucianism 4, 55, 187, 189–91, 197, 199, 228
Connaître 255
Connect Conference 30, 33
connection to the land 147
consciousness 73, 83, 158, 175–77, 179–82, 191–92, 195
conservation 102, 155, 168, 226
conservative students 96
conspiracy theories 2
Constantinidis, George 99
consumption 153
Copernicus Center for Interdisciplinary Studies, Poland 242
Coulson, Charles 206
Counterbalance Foundation 247
COVID 13, 32–33, 103, 117–18, 144, 177, 213
COVID vaccine 13
Covolan, Roberto 62, 65, 231
CPOSAT 255
creation 16, 19–20, 26, 101–6, 168–69, 189, 194, 225
creation care 11, 151–52, 155, 158–61, 164–67, 189, 203
creationism 17, 23–24, 35, 67, 91, 103, 105, 107–8, 131–34, 136–37, 148, 213, 224
CRESAD 238
critical realism 76
critical theory 144
critical thinking 99
CRYF 242, 257
CSAK 118, 238
CSRS 245

CSCA 9, 34
CTNS 247
CTR 242
cultural alienation 124
cultural diversity 125
cultural history 127
cultural practices 85, 111, 124, 126, 228
cultural practices of healing 122
culture 2, 5, 8, 11, 17, 19, 67, 71, 73, 83, 111, 114, 119, 128, 145
  African 113–15, 124, 126
  Canadian 151
  Western 115, 123
CUS 101–2
CVT 239

D
DALL.E 176
Daoism 37, 55, 57, 59, 187, 189–91, 197
Darwin, Charles 10, 91–92, 94–95, 98, 100–102, 105–9, 136, 141, 149, 224, 226
  Church acceptance 137
Darwinism 9, 16, 91–92, 95, 98, 100, 107, 136–37, 224
  in Greece 91, 95–96, 98, 105, 109
  in New Zealand 136, 149
data storage and security 183–84
Davison Hunter, James 62, 68, 86, 199
"day" in Genesis 1, meaning 4
DCM 243
Deane-Drummond, Celia 135
declaration of faith 29
DeCyR 250
deductive reasoning 116, 176
deep-learning 179
Deep Sight Trust 139
Delmouzos, Alexandros 99–100
demon possession 44
demons 46, 50, 52–53, 55
denomination 143
Descartes, René 47
design 107, 189

## Subject and Author Index

Developing a Christian Mind, UK. *See* DCM
development officer 22–23, 25, 28, 31, 34, 229
DeWitt, Calvin 164–65, 171–72
dialogue 38, 61, 64, 67–68, 70–71, 78–79, 86–87, 126, 131, 135, 140, 144–45, 148, 180, 196
Dialogue on Science, Ethics, and Religion. *See* DoSER
dichotomies 39, 41, 44–45, 57
differentiationism 76
digital platforms 33
digital twin 183, 190
Direct Preference Optimization. *See* DPO
discussion groups 26
diseases 116–19, 123, 125
DISF 241
diversity 2, 4, 12–13, 70, 72, 74, 114, 120, 170, 189, 223, 227
  of life 153
  of nature 168
divine intervention 46, 118
Dobzhansky, Theodosius 102–3
doctrine of creation 218
Dodecapolis 63
donations 32
donors 31
Dooyeweerd, Herman 69, 71, 74, 89
DoSER 247
Dosios, Leandros 95
DPO 196
dreams and visions 120
du Bois-Reymond, Emil 96

E
early-career scientists 28–31, 33
earthkeeping 166
earthkeeping missionary 166–67, 170
ECHO 229, 248
Ecklund, Elaine Howard 206, 209–210, 221–22
ECLAS 210, 213, 219
ecologists 11

economics 153
education 2, 10, 63–64, 66, 69, 73, 80, 92, 99, 103, 105, 118, 123, 164, 202
  tertiary 205
Educational Concerns for Hunger Organization. *See* ECHO
EEN 248
effectiveness 30–31, 122
Einstein, Albert 47
empathic intelligence 179
endorphins 46, 52–53
engagement 62–63
engineering 11, 27, 41, 215
Enlightenment 37–39, 185
environment 21–22, 80, 115, 126, 151, 154–55, 160
environmental crisis 154
environmental issues 153, 158, 160, 163
environmental protection 175
environmental stewardship 152, 156, 158, 165
Equipping and Supporting the Next Generation 28
Equipping Christian Leadership in an Age of Science. *See* ECLAS
Esmaeilzadeh, Hadi 180–81, 198
essay competition 27, 30–31
ESSSAT 256–57
Ester, Martin 11, 175, 232
ethics 34, 75, 82, 97, 155, 185
  medical 56
ethnic churches 132
eugenics 49, 137
*European Journal of Science and Theology* 255
European Leadership Forum. *See* ELF
European Society for the Study of Science and Theology. *See* ESSSAT
euthanasia 56, 142
evaluation 31
evangelical 17, 19–20, 24, 26, 67–68, 134–35, 160, 164, 166, 213, 253

Evangelical Alliance  21, 23, 26, 218–19, 221
evangelical belief  24
evangelical community  23–24, 26, 28
Evangelical Environmental Network. *See* EEN
Evangelical Philosophical Society  262
evangelicals  67, 227
Evangelical Scientists' Network, France and Switzerland  240
Evangelical Union  138
evangelism  65
*Evangelium und Wissenschaft*  256
evidence from design  203
evolution  16, 18, 20, 24, 26, 92, 95–96, 99–107, 133–34, 139, 143, 179, 208, 217, 224
  teaching of  102, 104
  theistic  24, 206
  theory of  106
evolution of ideas  148
Ewart, Paul  10, 15, 23, 232
excluded middle  40
executive officer  34
exegetical analysis  126
existential threat  4
explainability  175, 179, 186, 195
extended-reality  183–84
extrabiblical knowledge  19

F

Facebook  148, 183, 186–88
facts  40, 163
faith  15, 18–19, 21, 27, 35, 37, 40, 44, 68–69, 79–80, 86–87, 96, 106, 112, 131, 134, 137, 147, 211–12, 216, 240, 251
  biblical  20
  and philosophy  261
  and politics  155
  and reason  79, 241, 251–52
  and spirituality  135
  and theology  224
Faith and Science Collaborative Research Forum  9. *See* FaSCoRe

*Faith and Thought*  21, 256–57
faith-based environmental programs  164
faithful presence  62, 65, 68, 86–87
fall  138, 190, 192, 194, 218
false prophets  45
Faraday Institute  22–23, 30, 62, 201, 203, 210, 215, 217, 219, 229
Faraday Institute for Science and Religion. *See* Faraday Institute
Faraday, Michael  216
Faraday Youth and Schools  203
FaSCoRe  239
Faw, Rick  165
feminism  100, 144
festivals  26, 30, 140
Feynman diagrams  9
finances  23, 25, 30, 32
fine tuning  9
Finlay, Graeme  133, 141
Finnis, John  70, 83–84, 89
*Fire from Heaven*  216
folk knowledge  120
food preservation  116
food security  153, 162
forces of nature  115
*Forum Philosophicum*  261
Foundation for Dialogue between Science and Religion, Argentina. *See* DeCyR
Fox, Keith  10, 15, 23, 233
freedom  81, 126, 189, 197
freedom of speech  191
free will  4
Friends of CiS  32
funding  9, 15, 17, 23, 25, 28, 31, 34, 188, 211, 226

G

Gaitanou-Gianniou, Athena  100
Galen  48, 57
Galileo  227
Geering, Lloyd  139–40, 149
gender equality  143
generative AI  192–94, 197

genetic modification  125
genetics  102, 210
genuine mechanism  45–46, 48–49
geography  8
GFI  253
Gifford Lectures  35, 38
Gillett, Grant  141
Glinos, Dimitris  100
global  1, 3–4, 6, 8, 153
Global Faculty Initiative. *See* GFI
global perspectives  6, 202, 223
global significance  223
*Global Weirding*  162
God and science  138
God and the Big Bang  30
God of the Gaps  19
*God Particle*  216
God's Gardeners  158–60, 171
goods  64, 67, 69–74, 77, 80, 82–87
    human goods  61, 70, 74, 80–81, 86
    scientific goods  70, 72, 77
    social goods  73–74
Google  186, 194
gospel  29, 87, 145, 155, 171, 218
    creation-wide implications  167
GPT-3  176, 192
GPT-4  180–82, 187, 192–93
GPT technology  180, 187
Graduate Fellowship  17
grant support  25, 34
Grasping the Nettle, Scotland  243
graviton  47
gravity  46–49, 52
Greek Orthodox apologetics  91, 93
Greek politics  93
Greek professors of theology  94
Greenbelt  26
Greenman, Jeffrey  156

**H**
Haeckel, Ernst  97, 100–102, 107
Halestrap, Andrew  10, 15, 28, 233
Hana and Francisco José Ayala Chair of Science, Technology, and Religion, Spain. *See* CTR

handbook  29–30
Handmaid's Tale  156, 160, 170
Harrison, Peter  38–39, 60, 216
Hatzopoulos, Constantinos  100
healing  42, 56, 114, 116, 118–23, 125–27, 230
    African methods  118
    African traditional healing  119
    in Africa  118, 122
    practices  114, 116, 119–20, 127
    traditional  57, 119, 121, 123, 127
    Western healing  118, 127
health  51, 69, 121, 123, 125, 153
    and healing  121
    care  121, 183, 215
    human  175
    in Africa  122
Hector, James  136
Hedley Brooke, John  135, 203
herbal medicine  119, 122
heredity  49
Heribert-Nilsson, Nils  102
higher education  205
history  8, 10–11, 15, 39, 63, 93, 95, 104, 119, 227
    of science  132, 141
    of science and theology  132
Hoggard Creegan, Nicola  131, 233
holistic  10, 111–12, 115, 117, 120, 126–27, 132, 140, 144–46, 155
Hooykaas, Reijer  18, 20
Huang, Ming-Hui  179
Huawei  188
human flourishing  70, 72
humanism  185
humanities  63, 67, 131, 144, 207
human nature  185, 189, 192, 242
human origins  102, 218
human rights  228
Hutton, James  136, 203
Huxley, Thomas Henry  102
hygiene  209

**I**
Ian Ramsey Centre  203, 242, 244

Ian Ramsey Centre for Science and Religion. *See* Ian Ramsey Centre
ICE 248
Icoana Credintei 256
IDEA 26
identity 64, 72–74, 78, 86, 105, 112, 115, 184, 188, 260
identity pathologies 72
IGUW 241
ill health 118
Illouz, Eva 72–73, 88
Image of God 86, 103, 189, 192, 206
immanence 185
immunization 116–17, 125
*Implicit Religion* 260
incarnation 65, 68, 86, 225
independence 38
Indian identity system 189
indigenous knowledge 114
inductive approach 113
inoculation 116
Instagram 148
Institute for Cross-Disciplinary Engagement at Dartmouth. *See* ICE
Institute for Faith and Science. *See* IGUW
Institute for Theological Encounter with Science and Theology. *See* ITEST
Institute for the Study of Christianity in an Age of Science and Technology. *See* ISCAST
Institute of Philosophy, Austral University, Argentina 250
Institute on Religion in an Age of Science. *See* IRAS
integration 38, 76, 126
Intelligent Design 23–24, 224
Interdisciplinary Documentation of Science and Faith, Italy. *See* DISF
Interdisciplinary University of Paris 240
*International Journal for Philosophy of Religion* 262

*International Journal for the Psychology of Religion* 260
international members 16, 33
International Multidisciplinary Scientific Conference on the Dialogue between Sciences & Arts, Religion & Education. *See* MCDSARE
International Society for Science & Religion. *See* ISSR
International Society for the Sociology of Religion 260
Inter-Varsity Fellowship. *See* IVF
intuitive intelligence 179
IRAS 248
ISCAST 239, 255
Islam 120, 227–28
ISSR 252, 257
*Issues in Science and Theology* 256–57
ITEST 248
IVF 15–18, 137–38, 140

**J**
James Webb Space Telescope 215
Jeeves, Malcolm 17–18, 20
John J. Reilly Center for Science, Technology, and Values 248
John Templeton Foundation. *See* JTF
Jones, Gareth 141
*Journal for the Scientific Study of Religion* 260
*Journal for the Study of Religion, Nature and Culture* 258
*Journal of Holistic Mathematics Education* 258
*Journal of Religion and Health* 259
*Journal of Religion, Spirituality & Aging* 259
*Journal of Spirituality in Mental Health* 259
Journals 255
JTF 23–25, 27–28, 34
justice 5, 58, 69–70, 87, 153, 191, 195
justice for the poor 2

## K

kaitiakitanga 145
Kantiotis, Avgoustinos 102, 104
Karenga, Samuel 10, 111, 234
Karl Heim Society, Germany 241
Katharine Hayhoe 156, 161–163, 171–72
Kaufmann, Stuart 124
Kazantzakis, Nikos 98
Kepler, Johannes 19
Kikuyu 112–13, 116, 118–19, 121, 127
King, Carolyn 141
Kingfisher Farm 166
Kirira, Peter 10, 111, 234
knowledge 39–40, 72, 78–79, 82–87, 113, 146, 205, 219
Krimbas, Vasos 98, 102–4, 109
Kuhn, Thomas 76
Kuiper, Roel 78, 85, 89
Kurzweil, Ray 187
Kuyper, Abraham 69, 81

## L

Lamarck, Jean-Baptiste 96, 98, 100, 102, 106–7
Large Language Models 196
LASR 203
Laudato Si 7, 13
launch lunches 30
Lausanne Movement 65
law 137, 186, 194
leadership 29, 32–33, 63, 68, 186, 211, 233, 251
leadership training 63
Learning About Science and Religion. *See* LASR
lectures 10, 29, 96, 205
legacy 31
Lewis, C.S. 18
Liakopoulos, Ilias 97
liberation theology 67
liberty 82, 126
Liebig, Justus von 96
life extension 190
life force 48

Little Campbell River Watershed 160
local groups 15, 23, 26–27, 33, 63, 142
  local group leaders 28, 33
local issues 5–6
Logos 65
London School of Theology 213
love of creation 170
loving God 6

## M

Maasai 115, 126–27
machine learning 176–78, 181, 183, 185
MacKay, Donald 18, 20, 36
MaddAddam trilogy 161
Makrakis, Apostolos 97
Malcolm, Wilf 144
malevolent elements 193–95
Manning, Preston 154–57, 171–72, 227
Mann, Robert 141
Man, Science and God 138, 149
Māori 11, 132, 137, 141, 143, 145–48
Māori and Pākehā tension 145
Māori spirituality 132, 145, 147, 228
Māori ways of knowing 132, 146
Māori worldview 150
marine biology 168
market research 211
Marsden, Samuel 137
Martin, Jacob 141
Marxism 9–10, 100, 104, 187, 224
Mātauranga Māori 146
materialism 96–97, 100–101, 104–6
mathematics 58, 140
Mbiti, John 112, 120, 128
MCDSARE 256
McGrath, Alister 135, 206, 217
McKirland, Christa 141
McLeish, Tom 135, 221
mechanical intelligence 179
mechanisms 43, 45–49
medical insurance 186
medicine 11, 56–59, 63, 118, 125, 127, 137, 143, 195, 203
  African 10, 57

African engagement with Western
    medicine  122
  Chinese  10, 51, 56–57, 59
  modern  116, 123
  traditional  118–23, 126–28
  Western  39, 42, 48, 50–51, 55–57,
    119–20, 122, 127
membership  15, 21, 23, 25, 27
  retaining members  25
mental-health  184
mentoring  29–31, 148
Merrifield, Gavin  212
Merton, Robert  75–76, 88
Merton, Thomas  79
Metanexus  141
metaverse  182–85, 187–88, 190,
    198–99
Microsoft  183, 186–87, 194
military drones  186
military schools  93
miracles  4–5, 9, 26
misconceptions  96
misunderstandings  23
Mitsopoulos, Konstantinos  97
modernism  6, 39, 41, 44, 55–56

money  226
monism  97, 101
morality  55–56
Morton, John  138–41, 143, 149
Mott, John  137
mystical powers  121

N
nanotechnology  209
national identity  94, 108, 145, 176
national security  186, 197
natural disasters  26
natural history  98
naturalism  53
natural language processing  177, 183
natural resources  151
natural selection  20, 102
nature  37, 48, 65, 79, 106, 132, 146,
    189, 194, 196

nature-and-science  147
nature of God  126
networking  28, 62, 68, 183
neural interfaces  183
neural networks  178–79
neuronal pathways  46
New Atheists  23
Newsome, Bill  214
Newton  47–48, 52
Newtonian mechanics  3, 47
New Visions in Theological
    Anthropology. *See* NViTA
New Wine  26
New Zealand Christians in Science.
    *See* NZCIS
New Zealand church history  146
New Zealand science curriculum  146
next generation  16, 27, 29, 31, 165
Nicene Creed  189
Nicolaidis, Efthymios  10, 91, 94, 105,
    235
Nietsche, Friedrich  98
nonbiomedical medicine  122
nonrealist considerations  49–50
nonscientists  207
Núcleo de Pesquisas em Espiritualidade
    e Saúde. *See* NUPES
NUPES  251
nutrient runoff  153–54
nutrition  209
NViTA  244
NZCIS  9, 131, 133, 140–41, 147–48,
    233, 239

O
objective facts  44
objectives  23, 29–30, 83, 188
observation  19, 47, 54, 113, 116
occult powers  122
ocean acidification  153
O'Donovan, Oliver  80
Oladejo, Olusayo Bosun  125
Oliver Barclay Lecture  31
online lectures  33
online resources  209

ontology 52
oral history 114
Organizations and Institutions 237
Origin of Species 98, 136
origin of the universe 20
origins 5, 9, 15, 59, 140
Orr, David 164–65
Orthodox Christian apologetics 91, 108
Orthodox Christianity 94–96, 98, 101, 109
Orthodox Church 10, 91–95, 97, 99, 101–3, 105, 108–9, 189, 224, 235, 241, 256
OTHER 250
Other Worlds, Earth, Humanity, and Remote Space, Argentian. *See* OTHER
outreach 22, 24, 32
ozone depletion 153

**P**
Packer, James 19
paganism 57
pain 54
Pākehā and Māori tension 145
Palamas, Kostas 98
paleontology 102
pandemic 32–33, 118, 213
panentheism 139
pantheism 139
Papamichael, Gregorios 100
Papanastasiou, Alexandros 100
Paris Climate Accords 7
Parkinson's disease 184
particle physics 47
Partnership 28
Pascal, Blaise 74
Pasteur, Louis 96
pathologies of differentiation 71
pathologies of power 73
pawpaw 152
Peacocke, Arthur 135
Pentecostals 227
personal evangelism 16

personal relationships 17, 20
personhood 9, 20, 51, 54–56, 111–12, 119, 141, 184, 190, 192, 195, 210, 216
Perspectives on Science and Christian Faith. *See* PSCF
phenomenological questions 47
*Philosophia Christi* 262
philosophical issues 185
philosophy 11, 41, 63–64, 69, 87, 106, 119, 191
  African, of life 112
  African, of wholeness 123
  natural 203
  of religion 226
  of science 79, 86
*Philosophy, Theology and the Sciences* 135, 257
phrenology 137
physicalism 53, 191
physics 11, 27, 62–64, 67, 101
Piraeus Association of Scientists 105
Pithecanthropus 102
podcasts 217, 219
Polanyi, Michael 70, 79–84, 88–89, 206
polemics 96
polio vaccine 118
political history 11, 127
political science 161
political theory 226
politicians 11, 64, 170
politics 2, 6, 8, 10, 64, 67, 69–72, 92, 108, 137, 145, 153–54, 158, 171, 226–27
Polkinghorne, John 135, 206
pollution 153
Polytechnic School of Athens 93
polytheism 72
Pontifical Academy for Life 245
Pontifical Academy of Sciences 245
Pontifical Academy of Social Sciences 245
population growth 153
positivism 144
postgraduate students 215

poverty  91, 112, 118, 162, 186
power  72–73, 103
practical universality  78
prayer  17, 32, 46, 118, 132, 145
PréCiS  25, 27
precision medicine  186, 190
precision robotics  183
precolonial Africa  115
prejudice  137, 144
Premier Christian Radio  217
privacy  178, 18486, 189, 195, 197, 228
professional societies  29, 80
projection theories  83
*Prometheus*  97
prophesy  45
prosperity gospel  122
PSCF  256
pseudoscience  59, 87
psychology  72
*Psychology of Religion and Spirituality*  260
psychosocial beliefs  111
public knowledge  44
public lectures  26, 244
public service  137
Pythagoras  58, 106

**Q**
qi  4, 41, 45–46, 48, 52, 56
*Quaerentibus Teología y ciencia*  257
quantum mechanics  4

**R**
racial identity  145
racism  144–45
Ragouet, Pascal  77–78, 88
realism  20, 51, 54
reality  12, 45, 51, 54–55, 61, 65, 70, 74, 83–84, 112, 146, 183–85
Reformed Christianity  139
refugee migration  162
regulatory frameworks  187, 190, 194–97
Reinforcement Learning Human Feedback. *See* RLHF

relationships  17, 30, 65, 68, 72, 79, 87, 93, 117, 146, 151, 162–63, 167, 188, 213–14, 217, 225, 241, 251–52, 258–59
relativity  47
religion
　African, traditional  114
　and culture  111, 125
　and philosophy  198
　private  145
　traditional  112
religiosity  94, 121, 123
religious beliefs  22, 111–12, 117
　diversity  125
religious dogma  99
religious experience  72, 184
Renaissance  69
Research Scientists' Christian Fellowship. *See* RSCF
residential conference  27
reverence  20, 114
*Reviews in Science and Religion*  257
*Reviews in Science, Religion & Theology*  257
*Revista Brasileira de Filosofia da Religião*  262
Rhoides, Emmanuel  98
Rick Faw  172
RLHF  192–94, 196
Robinson, Peter  156
robot dog  182
robotics  177, 182
Roper, Duncan  140
RSCF  15, 17–22, 35
Ruka, Jay  146
Russell, Colin  20
Russell Group universities  25
Rust, Roland  179, 198

**S**
sacred-secular divide  124
Samford University Center for Science & Religion  249
sanctity of life  56
sangoma  57

SBCC 251
S&CB 17, 21, 23, 35, 233, 257
Scholarship & Christianity in Oxford. See SCIO
School of Theology 93-94, 135
Science and Christian Faith Association, France 240
science
  citizen 216
  climate 162
  computer 11, 63
  and culture 89
  earth 27
  environmental 236, 246
  and Scripture 16
  sociology of 76, 78, 226
  and worship 211, 222
  Western 39, 46-47
Science and Orthodoxy around the World 9
Science and Religion Forum. See SRF
*Science & Christian Belief.* See S&CB
science communication 162
science curriculum 132, 146
science education 8, 93
Science-Faith Dialogue 61, 201
Science for the Church 211, 249
Science in the Church 208
Science, Knowledge and Belief in Society 244
Science Network 29
Science & Orthodoxy around the World. See SOW
Science, Reason, and Faith Group, Spain. See CRYF
Sciences of the Origin, Serbia 242
Science, Theology, and Religion. See STAR
Science, Theology, and the Ontological Quest, Italy. STOQ
*Scientia et Fides* 257
scientific knowledge 76, 116-17, 209, 215, 247, 250
Scientists in Congregations 214
Scientists' Study Group 18

SCIO 244
SCM 137-38, 143, 149
Searle, John 182
secularism 11, 66, 68, 132, 134, 136, 140-41, 144, 224
  in New Zealand 131
secular-sacred divide 34
Sedgwick, Adam 203
self-awareness 72, 75
Seraphim of Piraeus, Metropolitan 105-8
shalom 62, 68, 85, 167
Shinn, Terry 76-78, 88
shore ecologists 140
Sibani, Clifford Meesua 123, 128
sickness 116-18, 125
Sir Halley Stewart Charitable Trust 22, 34
Siri 176
six-day creation 103
Skaltsounis, Ioannis 97
skepticism 12, 79
Skliros, George 100
social architecture 63, 69-70
social coherence 70, 96
social compass 260
social-credit system 176, 189
social life 69, 81-82, 84
social media 3, 142, 217
social responsibility 65
social sciences 64, 69
social structures 76, 81
social symbiosis 78
societal perceptions 111
society 3, 34, 40, 54, 69, 73-76, 80-82, 85, 87, 89, 100-101, 112, 149, 177, 186-87, 195, 220
Society for Science and Religion in Asia. See SSRA
Society of Catholic Scientists 67, 252
Society of Christian Scholars 253
Society, Religion and Technology Project. See SRT
sociology 69-70, 76-78, 86, 88-89
*Sociology of Religion* 261

soil health 161
solar panels 154
soul 46, 53, 106, 175, 191, 198
Soungras, Spyros 95–97, 101
Southgate, Christopher 135
SOW 241
speaking skills 30
Spencer, Herbert 96
Spencer, Nick 204, 213, 221
Spiridon Miliarakis 95
spirit-and-nature 147
spiritual devotion 16
spiritual law 82
spiritual realm 112
spiritual support 32
Spring Harvest 26
SRF 244
SRT 244
SSRA 252
Standard Model 47–48, 211
STAR 249
statement of faith 18, 21
Stavrianos, Lefteris 104–5
stem cell research 56, 209, 213
STEM subjects 143
Stenhouse, John 136–38, 141, 149
stewardship 20–21, 151, 156, 160, 164, 166, 168–69, 192
Stob Lectures 80, 88
STOQ 241
straw man 23
Streamkeepers 163–64, 170
Student Christian Movement. *See* SCM
student CiS groups 29, 31
student conferences 27, 31, 33
students 21–22, 27–30, 32, 34, 99
*Studies in Science and Theology* 257
study groups 87
superhuman intelligence 175
supernatural 40–41, 44, 46, 111, 114, 119, 123
supreme being 115, 117
sustainable agriculture 161

T

Tallis, Raymond 182
Tampakis, Kostas 10, 91, 95, 235
TANSA 140–41
Tarling, Nicholas 144, 150
Taylor, Charles 83
teaching 29, 48, 99–100, 102, 104–5, 126, 137, 215
technology 21, 34, 63, 119, 177, 181–83, 185–90, 192, 194–95, 199, 203, 239, 242, 244–45, 247, 255, 262
TED talk 162
Templeton foundations 135
Templeton Religion Trust. *See* TRT
Templeton World Charity Foundation. *See* TWCF
Tencent 183, 188
tertiary education 144
Tertiary Students Christian Fellowship. *See* TSCF
testability 40, 44–45
*Test of Faith* 62, 214, 217, 221
tetanus boycott 117
theology 4, 11, 62, 64, 66, 69, 75, 79, 87, 95, 100, 134–35
   Christian 161, 217–18
   creation care 155
   of creation 151
   environmental 135
   green 158
   mission 65
   natural 202–3
   of origins 203
   of politics 125
   of science 218–19
   science-engaged 141
   scientific 79
   students 148
   systematic 133, 141, 217, 233
*Theology and Science* 135, 258
*Theology and the Natural Sciences in Aotearoa*. *See* TANSA
theology courses 66
Theosophy 107

*Thinking about . . .*  26–27, 30
Thrassivoulos Vlissidis  100
Tongan Assemblies of God  148
Torrance, Thomas  79
training courses  29
training data  176, 178
transcendence  185
transhumanism  9
transnational organizations  237, 251
transversal regime  78
tree of knowledge  189
Trempelas, Panagiotis  100–101, 107
trephining  116
Trinity  9
TRT  27–29, 31, 34
trust  2–3, 7, 68, 131, 217
TSCF  134, 138
Tsoi, Ah Chung  11, 175, 235
Turing, Alan  182, 187, 198
Turing test  182, 191
Turner, Harold  139, 141, 149
TWCF  9, 62, 141
typhoon  6

**U**
UCCF  15, 18, 21, 27, 29–32
*Unbelievable?*  218
Universities and Colleges Christian Fellowship. *See* UCCF
*Unus Mundus*  258
Uzzah  54

**V**
vaccination  2, 12, 103, 117, 125, 209
vaccine hesitancy  2
Vaezi, Reza  180–81, 198
value for money  25, 34
value judgments  44
values  40–41, 207, 221
Vatican Observatory Research Group. *See* VORG
Verbeek, Cindy  163–65, 172
Victoria Institute  21, 256–57
Virchow, Rudolph  96
virtual assistants  176

virtual reality  183–84
vitalism  48
vocation  20, 34, 73, 244
Vogt, Carl  98, 102
Volos school trial  99
von Heldreich, Theodor  95
von Humboldt, Alexander  96
VORG  249

**W**
Waitangi Day  145
Walton, John  59
Walzer, Michael  69–70, 73
Ward, Keith  135
Ward, Kevin  142–43, 147
waste generation  153
Water Monitoring Project  169
water quality  169–70
Weber, Max  69
website  22, 25–26, 28–29, 31, 106
Western imperialism  117
Western materialism  96, 224
Western missionary enterprise  117
wetland  169
whale whisperer  168–70
White, Bob  23
Wilberforce Foundation  142, 149
Wilf, Malcolm  140
wind power  7
wisdom  126, 153, 161
witchcraft  116, 118
wonder  12, 20, 45, 153, 168, 216, 218
Wonder Day  212
Wood, John  11, 151, 236
Word Alive  26
workshops  29–30, 33
worldviews  19, 43, 49, 55–56, 146, 172, 189, 259
   African  113
worship  32, 52, 114, 117, 121, 123, 185, 190, 202, 211, 218
writing skills  30

## Y

Yale Forum on Religion and Ecology 249
Yale Program for Medicine, Spirituality, & Religion 249
yin and yang 45
young earth creationism.
    *See* creationsism
younger academics 147, 206
younger generations 142

## Z

Zohios, Ioannis 96–97
zoology 18, 138, 141
Zwamborn, Elizabeth 168–69
*Zygon* 94, 109, 135, 204, 222, 235, 258
Zygon Center for Religion and Science 250

Langham Literature and its imprints are a ministry of Langham Partnership.

Langham Partnership is a global fellowship working in pursuit of the vision God entrusted to its founder John Stott –

> *to facilitate the growth of the church in maturity and Christ-likeness through raising the standards of biblical preaching and teaching.*

**Our vision** is to see churches in the Majority World equipped for mission and growing to maturity in Christ through the ministry of pastors and leaders who believe, teach and live by the word of God.

**Our mission** is to strengthen the ministry of the word of God through:
- nurturing national movements for biblical preaching
- fostering the creation and distribution of evangelical literature
- enhancing evangelical theological education

especially in countries where churches are under-resourced.

**Our ministry**

*Langham Preaching* partners with national leaders to nurture indigenous biblical preaching movements for pastors and lay preachers all around the world. With the support of a team of trainers from many countries, a multi-level programme of seminars provides practical training, and is followed by a programme for training local facilitators. Local preachers' groups and national and regional networks ensure continuity and ongoing development, seeking to build vigorous movements committed to Bible exposition.

*Langham Literature* provides Majority World preachers, scholars and seminary libraries with evangelical books and electronic resources through publishing and distribution, grants and discounts. The programme also fosters the creation of indigenous evangelical books in many languages, through writer's grants, strengthening local evangelical publishing houses, and investment in major regional literature projects, such as one volume Bible commentaries like *The Africa Bible Commentary* and *The South Asia Bible Commentary*.

*Langham Scholars* provides financial support for evangelical doctoral students from the Majority World so that, when they return home, they may train pastors and other Christian leaders with sound, biblical and theological teaching. This programme equips those who equip others. Langham Scholars also works in partnership with Majority World seminaries in strengthening evangelical theological education. A growing number of Langham Scholars study in high quality doctoral programmes in the Majority World itself. As well as teaching the next generation of pastors, graduated Langham Scholars exercise significant influence through their writing and leadership.

To learn more about Langham Partnership and the work we do visit **langham.org**

www.ingramcontent.com/pod-product-compliance
Lightning Source LLC
Chambersburg PA
CBHW060945230426
43665CB00015B/2069